James Bowling Mozley

Eight Lectures on Miracles

James Bowling Mozley

Eight Lectures on Miracles

ISBN/EAN: 9783743350458

Manufactured in Europe, USA, Canada, Australia, Japa

Cover: Foto ©Thomas Meinert / pixelio.de

Manufactured and distributed by brebook publishing software (www.brebook.com)

James Bowling Mozley

Eight Lectures on Miracles

EIGHT

LECTURES ON MIRACLES

PREACHED BEFORE

THE UNIVERSITY OF OXFORD

IN THE YEAR M.DCCC.LXV.

ON THE FOUNDATION OF

THE LATE REV. JOHN BAMPTON, M.A.

CANON OF SALISBURY.

BY

J. B. MOZLEY, B.D.

///

VICAR OF OLD SHOREHAM.

LATE FELLOW OF MAGDALEN COLLEGE.

London,

RIVINGTONS, WATERLOO PLACE;

| HIGH STREET, | TRINITY STREET, |
| Oxford. | Cambridge. |

1865.

Dei Voluntas rerum natura est.—*St. Augustine.*

Miracles well attested do not only find credit themselves, but give it also to other truths, which need such confirmation.—*Locke.*

The miracle, by displaying phenomena out of the ordinary connexion of cause and effect, manifests the appearance of a higher power, and points out a higher connexion, in which even the chain of phenomena in the visible world must be taken up.—*Neander.*

EXTRACT

FROM THE LAST WILL AND TESTAMENT

OF THE LATE

REV. JOHN BAMPTON,

CANON OF SALISBURY.

—— " I give and bequeath my Lands and Estates to the
" Chancellor, Masters, and Scholars of the University of
" Oxford for ever, to have and to hold all and singular the
" said Lands or Estates upon trust, and to the intents and
" purposes hereinafter mentioned; that is to say, I will and
" appoint that the Vice-Chancellor of the University of Ox-
" ford for the time being shall take and receive all the rents,
" issues, and profits thereof, and (after all taxes, reparations,
" and necessary deductions made) that he pay all the re-
" mainder to the endowment of eight Divinity Lecture Ser-
" mons, to be established for ever in the said University, and
" to be performed in the manner following :

" I direct and appoint, that, upon the first Tuesday in
" Easter Term, a Lecturer be yearly chosen by the Heads
" of Colleges only, and by no others, in the room adjoining
" to the Printing-House, between the hours of ten in the
" morning and two in the afternoon, to preach eight Divinity
" Lecture Sermons, the year following, at St. Mary's in Ox-
" ford, between the commencement of the last month in Lent
" Term, and the end of the third week in Act Term.

" Also I direct and appoint, that the eight Divinity Lecture
" Sermons shall be preached upon either of the following Sub-
" jects—to confirm and establish the Christian Faith, and to
" confute all heretics and schismatics—upon the divine au-
" thority of the holy Scriptures—upon the authority of the
" writings of the primitive Fathers, as to the faith and prac-
" tice of the primitive Church—upon the Divinity of our Lord
" and Saviour Jesus Christ—upon the Divinity of the Holy
" Ghost—upon the Articles of the Christian Faith, as compre-
" hended in the Apostles' and Nicene Creeds.

" Also I direct, that thirty copies of the eight Divinity Lec-
" ture Sermons shall be always printed, within two months
" after they are preached; and one copy shall be given to the
" Chancellor of the University, and one copy to the Head of
" every College, and one copy to the Mayor of the city of
" Oxford, and one copy to be put into the Bodleian Library;
" and the expense of printing them shall be paid out of the
" revenue of the Land or Estates given for establishing the
" Divinity Lecture Sermons; and the Preacher shall not be
" paid, nor be entitled to the revenue, before they are printed.

" Also I direct and appoint, that no person shall be quali-
" fied to preach the Divinity Lecture Sermons, unless he hath
" taken the degree of Master of Arts at least, in one of the
" two Universities of Oxford or Cambridge; and that the
" same person shall never preach the Divinity Lecture Ser-
" mons twice."

PREFACE.

THE difficulty which attaches to Miracles, in the period of thought through which we are now passing, is one which is concerned not with their evidence, but with their intrinsic credibility. There has risen in a certain class of minds an apparent perception of the impossibility of suspensions of physical law. This is one peculiarity of the present time : another is a disposition to maintain the disbelief of miracles upon a religious basis, and in connexion with a declared belief in the Christian revelation.

The following Lectures, therefore, are addressed mainly to the fundamental question of the credibility of Miracles ; their use, and the evidences of of them, being only touched on subordinately and collaterally. It was thought that such an aim, though in itself a narrow and confined one, was most adapted to the particular need of the day.

CONTENTS.

LECTURE I.

MIRACLES NECESSARY FOR A REVELATION.

St. John xv. 24.

If I had not done among them the works that none other man did, they had not had sin.

How is it that sometimes when the same facts and truths have been before men all their lives, and produced but one impression, a moment comes when they look different from what they did? Some minds may abandon, while others retain, their fundamental position with respect to those facts and truths, but to both they look stranger; they excite a certain surprise which they did not once do. The reasons of this change then it is not always easy for the persons themselves to trace, but of the result they are conscious; and in some this result is a change of belief.

An inward process of this kind has been going on recently in many minds on the subject of miracles; and in some with the latter result. When it came to the question—which every one must sooner or later put to himself on this subject—did these things

B

really take place? are they matters of fact? they have appeared to themselves to be brought to a standstill, and to be obliged to own an inner refusal of their whole reason to admit them among the actual events of the past. This strong repugnance seemed to be the witness of its own truth, to be accompanied by a clear and vivid light, to be a law to the understanding, and to rule without appeal the question of fact.

This intellectual movement against miracles is partly owing, doubtless, to the advance of science withdrawing minds from moral grounds and fixing them too exclusively upon physical. I am not sure, however, that too much has not been made of science as the cause in this case; because, as a matter of fact, we see persons who are but little acquainted with physical science just as much opposed to miracles as those who know most about it, and for a very good reason. For it is evident that the objection which is felt against miracles does not arise from any minute knowledge of the laws of nature, or any elaborate analysis which has shewn the connexion of those laws, traced them farther back, and resolved them into higher and simpler laws; but simply because they are opposed to that plain and obvious order of nature which everybody sees. That •a man should rise from the dead, e. g. is plainly contradictory to our experience; therein lies the difficulty of believing it; and that experience belongs to everybody as much as to the deepest philosopher.

A cause, which has had just as much to do with it as science, is what I may call the historical imagination. By the historical imagination I mean the habit of realizing past time, of putting history before ourselves in such a light that the persons and events figuring in it are seen as once-living persons and once-present events. This is in itself a high and valuable power, and it is evident that there is too little of it in the mass of men, to whom the past is a figured surface rather than an actual extension backward of time, in which the actors had all the feelings of the hour and saw it passing by them as we do,—the men who were then alive in the world, the men of the day. The past is an inanimate image in their minds, which does not beat with the pulse of life. And this want of reality attaching to the *time*, certain occurrences *in* it do not raise the questionings, which those very occurrences realized would raise. But a more powerful imagination enables a man in some way to realize the past, and to see in it the once-living present; so that when he comes across any scene of history, he can bring it home to himself that this scene was once present, that this was the then living world. But when the reality of the past is once apprehended and embraced, then the miraculous occurrences in it are realized too : being realized they excite surprise ; and surprise, when it once comes in, takes two directions ; it either makes belief more real, or it destroys belief. There is an element of doubt in surprise ; for this emotion arises *because* an event is strange, and an event is strange because it goes counter to and jars with presumption. Shall surprise then give life to belief or

stimulus to doubt ?   The road of belief and unbelief
in the history of some minds thus partly lies over
common ground ; the two go part of their journey
together ; they have a common perception in the
insight into the real astonishing nature of the facts
with which they deal.   The majority of mankind
perhaps owe their belief rather to the outward influence of custom and education than to any strong
principle of faith within ; and it is to be feared that
many if they came to perceive how wonderful what
they believed was, would not find their belief so easy
and so matter-of-course a thing as they appear to
find it.   Custom throws a film over the great facts
of religion, and interposes a veil between the mind
and truth, which, by preventing wonder, intercepts
doubt too, and at the same time excludes from
deep belief and protects from disbelief.   But deeper
faith and disbelief throw off in common the dependence on mere custom, draw aside the inter-
posing veil, place themselves face to face with the
contents of the past, and expose themselves alike to
the ordeal of wonder.

I would, however, give a passing caution against
one mistake which a mind gifted with an historical
imagination is apt to commit.   Such a mind raises
a clear and vivid picture of a particular period,
imagines the persons acting and speaking, calls up
a perfect scene and fills it with the detail of actual
life.   The world which it thus pictures, it then
assimilates, with allowance for externals, to the
world of the present day, translating character and

motives, actions and events into a modern type, in
order to make them look real and living. If the
period, then, into which this mind has transported
itself be that of the first promulgation of the Gospel,
the miraculous events of that epoch are imagined
and pictured as the kind of supernatural events
which, if they made their appearance at the present
day, would receive a natural explanation. He has
hitherto, then, made no mistake of fact, because he
has only raised a picture, and only professed to do
so. But just at this juncture he is apt to make,
unawares, a mistake of fact ; i. e. to suppose, because he has transported himself in imagination
to the world of a distant age, that therefore he
has *seen* that world and its contents, and to mistake a picture for reality. It seems to him as if
he could bring back a report from thence, and
assure us that nothing really took place in that
world of the nature that we suppose. But in truth
he no more knows by this process of the imagination what took place in that world, than another
person knows : for we cannot in this way ascertain
facts. The imagination assumes knowledge, and
does not make it : it vivifies the stock we have,
but does not add one item to it. The supposition
—'Had we lived in the world at that time we
should have seen that there was nothing more miraculous in it then than there is now'—carries a
certain persuasiveness with it to some ; but it is
a mere supposition. They may by an effort of
mind have raised a vivid image of the past, but

they have not gained the least knowledge of its events by this act. That world has now passed away and cannot be recalled. But certain things are said to have taken place in it. Whether those events did take place or not must depend on the testimony which has come down to us.

With this prefatory notice of a prevalent intellectual feature of the day,—for this effort to realize the past, to make it look like yesterday, does not only characterize individual writers, but is part of the thought of the age,—I enter upon the consideration of the position which I have chosen as the subject of these Lectures; viz. that Miracles, or visible suspensions of the order of nature for a providential purpose, are not in contradiction to reason. And, first of all, I shall enquire into the use and purpose of miracles,—especially with a view to ascertain whether in the execution of the Divine intentions toward mankind, they do not answer a *necessary* purpose, and supply a want which could not be supplied in any other way.

There is one great necessary purpose, then, which divines assign to miracles, viz. the proof of a revelation. And certainly, if it was the will of God to give a revelation, there are plain and obvious reasons for asserting that miracles are necessary as the guarantee and voucher for that revelation. A revelation is, properly speaking, such only by virtue of telling us something which we could not know without it. But how do we know that that communication of what is undiscoverable by human reason

is true? Our reason cannot prove the truth of it,
for it is by the very supposition beyond our reason.
There must be, then, some note or sign to certify
to it and distinguish it as a true communication
from God, which note can be nothing else than a
miracle.

The evidential function of a miracle is based upon
the common argument of design, as proved by coincidence. The greatest marvel or interruption of
the order of nature occurring by itself, as the very
consequence of being connected with nothing, proves
nothing ; but if it takes place in connexion with
the word or act of a person, that coincidence proves
design in the marvel, and makes it a miracle ; and
if that person professes to report a message or
revelation from heaven, the coincidence again of
the miracle with the professed message from God
proves design on the part of God to warrant and
authorize the message. The mode in which a miracle acts as evidence is thus exactly the same in
which any extraordinary coincidence acts : it rests
upon the general argument of design, though the
particular design is special and appropriate to the
miracle. And hence we may see that the evidence
of a Divine communication cannot in the nature
of the case be an ordinary event. For no event
in the common order of nature is in the first place
in any *coincidence* with the Divine communication :
it is explained by its own place in nature, and is
connected with its own antecedents and consequents
only, having no allusion or bearing out of them.

It does not either in itself, or to human eye, contain
any relation to the special communication from God
at the time. But if there is no coincidence, there
is no appearance of design, and therefore no attestation. It is true that prophecy is such an attestation, but though the event which fulfils prophecy
need not be itself out of the order of nature, it is
an indication of a fact which is; viz. an act of
superhuman knowledge. And this remark would
apply to a miracle which was only miraculous
upon the prophetical principle, or from the extraordinary coincidence which was contained in it. And
hence it follows that could a complete physical
solution be given of a whole miracle, both the
marvel and the coincidence too, it would cease from
that moment to perform its function of evidence.
Apparent evidence to those who had made the mistake, it could be none to us who had corrected it.

It will be urged, perhaps, that extraordinary
coincidences take place in the natural course of
providence, which are called special providences ;
and that these are regarded as signs and tokens of
the Divine will, though they are not visible interferences with the order of nature. But special
providences, though they convey *some*, do not convey *full* evidence of, design. Coincidence is a
matter of degree, and varies from the lowest degree
possible to t' e fullest and highest. In whatever
degree, therefore, a coincidence may appear in the
events of the world, or in the events of private
life, in that degree it is a direction, to whomsoever

it is evident, to see the finger of God either in
public affairs or in his own, and to draw a lesson,
or it may be to adopt a particular course of conduct, in consequence. But it is of the nature of
a miracle to give <u>proof</u>, as distinguished from mere
surmise, of a Divine design ; and therefore the most
complete and decisive kind of coincidence alone is
miraculous.

It must be observed, however, that a special providence is an indication of a special Divine design,
to whatever extent it is so, only as being an indication of extraordinary Divine agency somewhere,
which agency partakes substantially of a miraculous
character ; though that character is not placed directly before our eyes, but is only gathered from
such marks of coincidence as the events in the case
exhibit. The point at which the Divine power comes
into contact with the chain of natural causation is remote, and comparatively hidden ; but still however
high up in the succession of nature, such extraordinary agency is, at the point at which it does occur,
preternatural ; because by nature we mean God's
general law, or usual acts. A special providence
thus differs from a miracle in its evidence, not in
its nature ; it is an invisible miracle, though not
so absolutely so as not to be indirectly traceable
by means of such indications as the events afford.
If a marvel is commanded or announced, or even
what is not a marvel but only a striking event
(such as sudden cure of a bad disease), and it takes
place immediately, the coincidence is too remark-

able to be accounted for in any other way than
design. The destruction of Sodom and Gomorrah,
the dividing of the Red Sea, and other miracles
which were wrought by the medium of natural
agency, were miracles for this reason. But in the
case of a special providence, the coincidence suggests but does not compel this interpretation. The
death of Arius, e. g. was not miraculous, because
the coincidence of the death of an heresiarch taking
place when it was peculiarly advantageous to the
orthodox faith, to which it would have been advantageous at any time, was not such as to compel
the inference of extraordinary Divine agency ; but
it was a special providence because it carried a
reasonable appearance of it. The miracle of the
Thundering Legion was a special providence, but
not a miracle for the same reason, because the coincidence of an instantaneous fall of rain in answer
to prayer carried some appearance, but not proof,
of preternatural agency, especially in the climate
where the occurrence happened. Where there is
no violation of physical law, the more inexplicable
must be the coincidence in order to constitute
the proof of extraordinary Divine agency ; and
therefore in that class of miracles which consists
of answers to prayer, the most unaccountable kind
of coincidence alone can answer the purpose. And
the same principle applies to other miracles. The
appearance of the cross to Constantine was a miracle
or a special providence, according to which account
of it we adopt. As only a meteoric appearance in

the shape of a cross, without the adjuncts, it gave some token of preternatural agency, but not full evidence.

It may be conceded, indeed, that the truths which are communicated in a revelation might be conveyed to the human mind without a visible miracle : and upon this ground it has appeared to some that a revelation does not absolutely require miracles, but might be imparted to the mind of the person chosen to be the recipient of it by an inward and invisible process alone. But to suppose upon this ground that miracles are not necessary for a revelation is to confound two things which are perfectly distinct ; viz. the ideas themselves which are communicated in a revelation, and the proof that those ideas are true. For simply imparting ideas to the human mind, or causing ideas to arise in the human mind, an ordinary act of Divine power is sufficient, for God can put thoughts into men's minds by a process altogether secret, and without the accompaniment of any external sign, and it is a part of His ordinary providence to do so. And in the same way in which He causes an idea of an ordinary kind to arise in a person's mind, He could also cause to arise an extraordinary idea ; for though the character of the ideas themselves would differ, the process of imparting them would be the same. But, then, when the extraordinary idea was there, what evidence would there be that it was true ? None : for the process of imparting it being wholly secret, all that the recipient of it could possibly then know, would be that he had the idea, that it was in his mind ; but that the idea was in his mind would not prove in the least that it was true. Let us suppose, e. g. that the idea was imparted to the mind of a particular person that *an atonement had been made for the sins of the whole world*, and that the Divine power stopped with the act of imparting that idea and went no further. The idea, then, of a certain mysterious event having taken place has been imparted to him and he has it, but so far from that person being able to give proof of that event to others, he would not even have received evidence of it himself. In an enthusiastic mind, indeed, the rise, without anything to account for it, of the idea that such an event had taken place, might of itself produce the *belief* that it had, and be taken as witness to its own truth ; but it could not reasonably constitute such a guarantee, even to himself, and still less to others.

The distinction may be illustrated by a case of prophecy. It was divinely communicated to the ancient prophet that Tyre or Babylon should be destroyed, or that Israel should be carried into captivity ; and in this communication itself there was nothing miraculous, because the idea of the future destruction of a city, and of the future captivity of a people, could be raised in the mind of a prophet by the same process by which God causes a natural thought to arise in a person's mind. But then the mere occurrence of this idea to the prophet would be no proof that it was true. In the case of prophecy, then, the simple event which fulfils it is the proof of the truth of that idea ; but this kind of proof does not apply to the case of a revelation of a doctrine, which must therefore have another sort of guarantee.

If, then, a person of evident integrity and loftiness of character rose into notice in a particular country and community eighteen centuries ago, who made these communications about himself—that he had existed before his natural birth, from all eternity, and before the world was, in a state of glory with God ; that he was the only-begotten Son of God ; that the world itself had been made by him ; that he had, however, come down from heaven and assumed the form and nature of man for a particular purpose, viz. to be the Lamb of God that taketh away the sins of the world ; that he thus stood in a mysterious and supernatural relation to the whole of mankind ; that through him alone mankind had access to God ; that he was the head of an invisible kingdom, into which he should gather all the generations of righteous men who had lived in the world ; that on his departure from hence he should return to heaven to prepare mansions there for them ; and lastly, that he should descend again at the end of the world to judge the whole human race, on which occasion all that were in their graves should hear his voice and come forth, they that had done good unto the resurrection of life, and they that had done evil unto the resurrection of damnation,—if this person made these assertions about himself, and all that was done was to make the assertions ; what would be the inevitable conclusion of sober reason respecting that person ? The necessary conclusion of sober reason respecting that person would be that he was disordered in his understanding. What other decision could we come to when a man, looking like one of ourselves and only exemplifying in his life and circumstances the ordinary course of nature, said this about himself, but that when reason had lost its balance, a dream of extraordinary and unearthly grandeur might be the result ? By no rational being could a just and benevolent life be accepted as proof of such astonishing announcements. Miracles are the necessary complement then of the truth of such announcements, which without them are purposeless and abortive, the unfinished fragments of a design which is nothing unless it is the whole. They are necessary to the justification of such announcements, which indeed, unless they are supernatural truths, are the wildest delusions. The matter and its guarantee are the two parts of a revelation, the absence of either of which neutralizes and undoes it.

But would not a perfectly sinless character be proof of a revelation ? Undoubtedly that would be as great a miracle as any that could be conceived ; but where is the proof of perfect sinlessness ? No outward life and conduct, however just, benevolent, and irreproachable, could prove this, because goodness depends upon the inward motive, and the perfection of the inward motive is not proved by the outward act. Exactly the same act may be perfect or imperfect according to the spirit of the doer. The same language of indignation against the wicked which issues from our Lord's mouth might be uttered by an imperfect good man, who mixed human frailty with the emotion. We accept our Lord's perfect goodness then upon the same evidence upon which we admit the rest of His supernatural character; but not as proved by the outward goodness of His life, by His character, sublime as that was, as it presented itself to the eye.

On the subject, however, of the necessity of miracles to a revelation, the ground has been taken by some that this necessity is displaced by the strength of the *internal* evidence of Christianity. And first, it is urged that the intrinsic nature of the doctrines, and their adaptation to the human heart, supplies of itself the proof of their truth.

But the proof of a revelation which is contained in the substance of a revelation has this inherent check or limit in it, viz. that it cannot reach to what is undiscoverable by reason. Internal evidence is itself an appeal to reason, because at every step the test is our own appreciation of such and such an idea or doctrine, our own perception of its fitness; but human reason cannot in the nature of the case prove that which, by the very hypothesis, lies beyond human reason.

Let us take, e. g. the doctrine of the Incarnation. The idea of a union of the Divine nature with the human has approved itself to the mind of mankind as a grand and sublime idea; in debased shapes it has prevailed in almost every religion of the heathen world, and it occupies a marked space in the history of human thought. The Christian doctrine appeals to every lofty aspiration of the human heart ; it exalts our nature, places us in intimate relation to God, and inspires us with a sense of His love. The human heart therefore responds to the doctrine of the Incarnation, and feels that doctrine to be adapted to it. But because the idea is thus adapted to it, is that a proof that it has been chosen in the Divine counsels to be put into execution? No: it would be wild reasoning to infer from the sublimity of a supposition, as a mere conception of the mind, that that conception had been embodied in a Divine dispensation, and to conclude from a thought of man an act of God. To do this is to attribute to ourselves perceptions of the Divine will beyond our conscience ; i. e. to attribute to ourselves supernatural perceptions. So, again, that the human heart responds to an Atonement supposed to be revealed, is no proof that that Divine act has taken place ; because the human heart has no power by its mere longings of penetrating into the supernatural world, and seeing what takes place there.

But the internal evidences of Christianity include, beside the intrinsic nature of the doctrines, the fruits of Christianity—its historical development. However necessary, it is said, the evidence of miracles was upon the first promulgation of the Gospel, when the new faith was but just sown, and its marvellous growth, its great results, its mighty conquests over the human heart were not yet before the eye, it is

no longer necessary now, when we have these effects
before us. This is a kind of proof then of a revelation
which is peculiarly adapted to produce inward conviction—a persuasion of the truth of that religion which
produces such results. No member of the Christian
evidence taken singly has perhaps so much strength
as this ; nor can we well rest too much upon it, so
long as we do not charge it with more of the burden
of proof than it is in its own nature equal to—viz.
the whole. But that it cannot bear. If the sincere
belief of persons in something does not prove that
thing, can the natural consequences of that belief
of themselves prove it ? If I am asked for the proof
of a doctrine, and I say simply, ' I believe it,' that
is obviously no proof; but if I go on to say, ' This
belief has had in my own case a connexion with
devout practice,' that alone is not adequate proof
either, even though this connexion has taken place
in others as well on a large scale. We can indeed
in imagination conceive such a universal spread of
individual holiness and goodness as would amount
to a supernatural manifestation : as, e. g. if we supposed that the description of the Christian Church
given in parts of prophecy was literally fulfilled, and
" the people were *all* righteous[a]." But the actual
result of Christianity is very different from this.
There are two sides of the historical development of
Christianity; one of success and one of failure. What
proportion of nominal Christians in every age have
been real Christians ? Has Christianity stopped war,

[a] Isaiah lx. 21.

persecution, tyranny, injustice, and the dominion of
selfish passion in the world which it has professedly
converted ? No ; nor is that the fault of Christianity,
but of man.   But if the appeal is made to the result
of Christianity as the proof of the supernatural truths
of Christianity, we must take that result as it stands.
What *is* that result ?   It is that amidst the general
deflection of Christians from the Gospel standard, a
certain number—so large indeed in comparison with
the corresponding class among the heathen as to
surprise us, but small as compared with the whole
body—are seen in every age directing their lives upon
religious principles and motives.   But we cannot
safely pronounce this to be a standing supernatural
phenomenon, equivalent to, and superseding the need
of, miraculous evidence.   Taken indeed in connexion
with prophecy, the results of Christianity stand upon
a stronger ground as Christian evidence ; but it must
be remembered that this connexion introduces another element into the argument, different from and
additional to the simple fact of the results, viz.
the fulfilment of prophecy contained in them,—an
element of proof which is in essence *miraculous*
proof. (Note i.)

It must be remembered that when this part of
Christian evidence comes so forcibly home to us, and
creates that inward assurance which it does, it does
this in connexion with the proof of miracles in the
background, which though it may not for the time
be brought into actual view, is still known to be
there, and to be ready for use upon being wanted.

The *in*direct proof from results has the greater force, and carries with it the deeper persuasion, because it is additional and auxiliary to the *direct* proof behind it, upon which it leans all the time, though we may not distinctly notice and estimate this advantage. Were the evidence of moral result to be taken rigidly alone, as the one single guarantee for a Divine revelation, it would then be seen that we had calculated its single strength too highly. If there is a species of evidence which is directly appropriate to the thing believed, we cannot suppose, on the strength of the indirect evidence we possess, that we can do without the direct. But miracles are the direct credentials of a revelation ; the visible supernatural is the appropriate witness to the invisible supernatural—that proof which goes straight to the point, and, a token being wanted of a Divine communication, is that token. We cannot, therefore, dispense with this evidence. The position that the revelation proves the miracles, and not the miracles the revelation, admits of a good qualified meaning ; but taken literally, it is a double offence against the rule, that things are properly proved by the proper proof of them ; for a supernatural fact *is* the proper proof of a supernatural doctrine ; while a supernatural doctrine, on the other hand, is certainly *not* the proper proof of a supernatural fact.

But suppose a person to say, and to say with truth, that his own individual faith does not rest upon miracles ; is he therefore released from the

defence of miracles? Is the question of their truth
or falsehood an irrelevant one to him? Is his faith
secure if they are disproved? By no means : if
miracles were, although only at the commencement,
necessary to Christianity, and were actually wrought,
and therefore form part of the Gospel record and
are bound up with the Gospel scheme and doctrines ;
this part of the structure cannot be abandoned without the sacrifice of the other too. To shake the
authority of one-half of this body of statement is
to shake the authority of the whole. Whether or
not the individual makes *use* of them for the support of his own faith, the miracles are there ; and
if they are there they must be there either as
true miracles or as false ones. If he does not avail
himself of their evidence, his belief is still affected
by their refutation. Accepting as he does the supernatural truths of Christianity and its miracles
upon the same report from the same witnesses,
upon the authority of the same documents, he cannot help having at any rate this negative interest
in them. For if those witnesses and documents
deceive us with regard to the miracles, how can
we trust them with regard to the doctrines? If
they are wrong upon the evidences of a revelation, how can we depend upon their being right
as to the nature of that revelation? If their account of visible facts is to be received with an
explanation, is not their account of doctrines liable
to a like explanation? Revelation then, even if it
does not need the truth of miracles for the benefit

of their proof, still requires it in order not to be
crushed under the weight of their falsehood.

Or do persons prefer resting doctrine upon the
ground more particularly of tradition? The result
is still the same. For the Christian miracles are
bound up inseparably with the whole *corpus* of
Christian tradition. But if tradition has been mistaken with respect to facts, how can we trust it
with respect to doctrines? Indeed, not only are
miracles *conjoined* with doctrine in Christianity,
but miracles are inserted *in* the doctrine and are
part of its contents. A man cannot state his belief
as a Christian in the terms of the Apostles' Creed
without asserting them. Can the doctrine of our
Lord's Incarnation be disjoined from one physical
miracle? Can the doctrine of His justification of us,
and intercession for us, be disjoined from another?

This insertion of the great miracles of our Lord's
life in the Christian Creed itself serves to explain
some language in the Fathers which otherwise might
be thought to indicate an inferior and ambiguous
estimate of the effect of miracles as evidence. They
sometimes speak of the miracles performed by our
Lord during His ministry as if they were evidence
of His mission rather as the fulfilment of prophecy,
than upon their own account. Upon this head, then,
it must be remembered, first, that to subordinate
miracles as evidence to prophecy is not to supersede
miraculous evidence; for prophecy is one department of the miraculous. But, in the next place, the
miraculous Birth of our Lord, His Resurrection and

Ascension, were inserted in the Christian Creed; which cardinal miracles being accepted, the lesser miracles of our Lord's ministry had naturally a subordinate place as evidence. If a miracle is incorporated as an article in a creed, that article of the creed, the miracle, and the proof of it by a miracle, are all one thing. The great miracles therefore, upon the evidence of which the Christian scheme rested, being thus inserted in the Christian Creed, the belief in the Creed was of itself the belief in the miraculous evidence of it. The doctrine of the Atonement, its acceptance, and the return of the Son of God to heaven to sit at His Father's right hand, are indeed in the abstract separable from the visible miracles of the Resurrection and Ascension which were the evidence of it; but actually in the Christian Church this *evidence* of the doctrine is the very *form* of the doctrine too; and the Fathers in holding the doctrine held the evidence of miracles to it. (Note 2.)

Thus miracles and the supernatural contents of Christianity must stand or fall together. These two questions—the *nature* of the revelation, and the *evidence* of the revelation—cannot be disjoined. Christianity as a dispensation undiscoverable by human reason, and Christianity as a dispensation authenticated by miracles—these two are in necessary combination. If any do not include the supernatural character of Christianity in their definition of it, regarding the former only as one interpretation of it or one particular traditional form

of it, which is separable from the essence,— for
Christianity as thus defined, the support of miracles
is not wanted, because the moral truths are their
own evidence. But Christianity cannot be maintained as a revelation undiscoverable by human
reason, a revelation of a supernatural scheme for
man's salvation, without the evidence of miracles.

And hence it follows that upon the supposition
of the Divine design of a revelation, a miracle is not
an anomaly or irregularity, but part of the system
of the universe ; because, though an irregularity
and an anomaly in relation to either part, it has
a complete adaptation to the whole. There being
two worlds, a visible and invisible, and a communication between the two being wanted, a miracle
is the instrument of that communication. An exception to each order of things separately, it is in
perfect keeping with both taken together, as being
the link or medium between them. This is, indeed,
the form and mode of order which belongs to *instruments* as a class. A key is out of relation,
either to the inside or outside taken separately of
the inclosure which it opens ; but it is in relation
to both taken together as being the instrument of
admission from the one to the other. Take any
tool or implement of art, handicraft, or husbandry,
and look at it by itself ; what an eccentric and
unmeaning thing it is, wholly out of order and
place ; but it is in exact order and place as the
medium between the workman and the material.
And a miracle is in perfect order and place as the

medium between two worlds, though it is an anomaly with respect to one of them alone.

Spinoza, indeed, upon this ground of order, That nothing can be out of the order of the universe that takes place *in* the universe, denies the possibility of a miracle ; but the truth of this inference depends entirely on the definition we give of a miracle. If a miracle is defined to be something which contradicts the order of the whole, then, upon the principle that nothing which is out of the order of the whole can exist or take place, there can *be* no such thing as a miracle. But if a miracle is only a contradiction to one part, i. e. the visible portion of the whole, this conclusion does not follow. And thus, according as we define a miracle, this ground of universal order becomes either a ground for refuting the miraculous or a ground for defending it. The defect of Spinoza's view is that he will not look upon a miracle as an *instrument*, a means to an end, but will only look upon it as a marvel beginning and ending with itself. "A miracle," he says, "as an interruption to the order of nature, cannot give us any knowledge of God, nor can we understand anything from it." (Note 3.) It is true we cannot understand anything from an interruption of the order of nature, simply as such ; but if this interruption has an evidential function attaching to it, then something may be understood from it, and something of vast importance.

We must admit, indeed, an inherent modification in the function of a miracle as an instrument of

proof. To a simple religious mind not acquainted
with ulterior considerations, a miracle appears to be
immediate, conclusive, unconditional proof of the doctrine for which it is wrought ; but, on reflexion, we
see that it is checked by conditions ; that it cannot
oblige us to accept any doctrine which is contrary
to our moral nature, or to a fundamental principle
of religion. But this is only a limitation of the
function of a miracle as evidence, and no disproof
of it ; for conditions, though they interfere with the
force of a principle where they are *not* complied with,
do not detract from it where they *are*. We have
constantly to limit the force of particular principles,
whether of evidence, or morals, or law, which at first
strike us as absolute, but which upon examination
are seen to be checked ; but these principles still
remain in substantial strength. Has not the authority of conscience itself checks and qualifications ?
And were a person so disposed, could he not make
out an apparent case against the use of conscience
at all—that there were so many conditions from this
quarter and the other quarter limiting it, that it
was really left almost without value as a guide ?
The same remark applies to some extent to the
evidence of memory. The evidence of miracles, then,
is not negatived because it has conditions. The
question may at first sight create a dilemma—If a
miracle is nugatory on the side of one doctrine,
what cogency has it on the side of another ? Is it
legitimate to accept its evidence when we please,
and reject it when we please ? But in truth, a

miracle is never without an argumentative force, although that force may be counterbalanced. Any physical force may be counteracted by an impediment, but it exists all the while, and resumes its action upon that impediment being removed. A miracle has a natural argumentative force on the side of that doctrine for which it is wrought ; if the doctrine is such that we cannot accept it, we resist the force of a miracle in that instance ; still that force remains and produces its natural effect when there is no such obstruction. If I am obliged by the incredible nature of an assertion to explain the miracle for it upon another principle than the evidential, I do so ; but in the absence of this necesssity, I give it its natural explanation. A rule gives way when there is an exception to it made out ; but otherwise it stands. When we know upon antecedent grounds that the doctrine is false, the miracle admits of a secondary explanation, viz. as a trial of faith ; but the first and most natural explanation of it is still as evidence of the doctrine, and that remains in force when there is no intrinsic objection to the doctrine.

When, then, a revelation is made to man by the only instrument by which it can be made, that that instrument should be an anomaly, an irregularity relatively to this visible order of things, is *necessary;* and all we are concerned with is its competency. Is it a good instrument ? is it effective ? does it answer its purpose ? does it do what it is wanted to do ?

This instrument, then, has certainly one important note or token of a *Divine* instrument ;—it bears upon it the stamp of *power*. Does a miracle, regarded as a mere prodigy or portent, appear to be a mean, rude, petty, and childish thing? Turn away from that untrue because inadequate aspect of it, to that which is indeed the true aspect of a miracle. Look at it as an instrument, as a powerful instrument, as an instrument which has shewn and proved its power in the actual result of Christendom. Christianity is the religion of the civilized world, and it is believed upon its miraculous evidence. Now for a set of miracles to be accepted in a rude age, and to retain their authority throughout a succession of such ages, and over the ignorant and superstitious part of mankind, may be no such great result for the miracle to accomplish, because it is easy to satisfy those who do not inquire. But this is not the state of the case which we have to meet on the subject of the Christian miracles. The Christian being the most intelligent, the civilized portion of the world, these miracles are accepted by the Christian body as a whole, by the thinking and educated as well as the uneducated part of it, and the Gospel is believed upon that evidence. Allowance made for certain schools of thought in it, this age in which we live accepts the Christian miracles as the foundation of its faith. But this is a great result—the establishment and the continuance of a religion in the world,—as the religion too of the intelligent as well as of the simpler portion of society. Indeed, in connexion with this point, may we not observe that the evidence of miracles has been taken up by the most inquiring and considerate portion of the Christian body ; by that portion especially which was anxious that its belief should be rational, and should rest upon evidence ? Of that great school of writers which has dealt with miracles, the conspicuous characteristics have been certainly no childish or superstitious love of the marvellous, but the judicial faculty, strong reasoning powers, strong critical powers, the power of estimating and weighing evidence. May we not then, when the miracle is represented as a mere childish desideratum, take these important circumstances into consideration,— the object which the Christian miracles have actually effected ; their actual result in the world ; the use which has been made of them by reasonable and reflecting minds ; the source which they have been of reasonable and reflecting belief ; their whole history, in short, as the basis, along with other considerations, of the Christian belief of the civilized world, educated and uneducated ? May we not call attention to the Gospel miracle in its actual working,— that it has been connected not with fanciful, childish, credulous, and superstitious, but with rational religion ; that it has been accepted by those whose determination it has been only to believe upon rational grounds ; that indeed, if there is a difference, it has been the instrument of conviction rather to the reasoning class of minds than the unreasoning. A miracle is in its own nature an

appeal to the reason ; and its evidence contrasts
in this respect with the mere influence of sentiment
and tradition.   These are strong witnesses to the
nature of a miracle as an instrument, and shew
that a miracle is a great instrument, and worthy
of the Divine employment.

For—and this largely constitutes the greatness
and efficacy of the instrument—the evidence of a
miracle is not only contemporary with the miracle,
but extends in the nature of the case through all
subsequent ages into which the original testimony
to such miracle is transmitted.   The chain of testimony is indeed more and more lengthened out, and
every fresh link which is added is a step further from
the starting-point, but so long as the original testimony reaches us, through however many links, the
miracle which it attests is the same evidence that it
ever was.   Scientific men have sometimes, indeed,
speculated upon the effect of time upon the value
of historical evidence ; practically speaking, however,
between an event's first standing in regular history,
and its very latest which is at this very moment,
we see no difference.   The testimony to the battle
of Pharsalia is as strong now, as at its first insertion
in the page of history ; nor can we entertain the
notion of a time, however remote, when it will not be
as strong as it is now.   Whatever value, then, the testimony to the Christian miracles had when that testimony first took its place in public records, that it has
now, and that it will continue to have so long as the
world lasts.   But such a prospect raises our estimate

of the importance and the greatness of a miracle as an instrument indefinitely, for indeed we do not know its full effects, we are in the middle, or perhaps only as yet in the very beginning of its history as a providential engine for the preservation of a religion in the world. A miracle is remarkably adapted for the original propagation of a religion, but this is only its first work. The question must still always arise, and must be always rising *afresh* in every generation afterwards,—Why must I believe in this revelation ? So far, then, from the use of miracles being limited to a first start, even supposing a religion could spread at first by excitement and sympathy without them, a time must come when rational and inquiring minds would demand a guarantee ; and when that demand was made a miracle alone could answer it. The miracle, then, enters at its birth upon a long career, to supply ground for rational belief throughout all time.

Mahometanism, indeed, established itself in the world without even any pretence on the part of its founder to miraculous powers. But the triumph of Mahometanism over human belief, striking as it has been, cannot blind us to the fact that the belief of the Mahometan is in its very principle irrational, because he accepts Mahomet's supernatural account of himself, as the conductor of a new dispensation, upon Mahomet's own assertion simply, joined to his success. (Note 4.) But this belief is in its very form irrational ; and whatever may be the apparent present strength and prospects of Mahometanism, this defect must cling to its very foundation, with this corollary attaching to it, viz. that *if* the law of reason is allowed to work itself out in the history of human religions, the ultimate dissolution of the Mahometan fabric of belief is certain, because its very existence is an offence against that law. But the belief of the Christian is, at all events in form, a rational belief, which the Mahometan's is not; because the Christian believes in a supernatural dispensation, upon the proper evidence of such a dispensation, viz. the miraculous. Antecedently, indeed, to all examination into the particulars of the Christian evidence, Christianity is the only religion in the world which professes to possess a body of direct external evidence to its having come from God. Mahometanism avows the want of this; and the pretensions of other religions to it are mockery. One religion alone produces a body of testimony—testimony doubtless open to criticism—but still solid, authentic, contemporaneous testimony, to miracles —a body of evidence which makes a stand, and upholds with a natural and genuine strength certain facts.

And in this distinction alone between Mahometanism and Christianity, we see a different estimate of the claims of reason, lying at the foundation of these two religions and entertained by their respective founders. Doubtless the founder of Mahometanism could have contrived false miracles had he chosen, but the fact that he did not consider miraculous evidence at all wanted to attest a supernatural dis-

pensation, but that his word was enough, shews an
utterly barbarous idea of evidence and a total mis-
calculation of the claims of reason which unfits his
religion for the acceptance of an enlightened age
and people ; whereas the Gospel is adapted to perpetuity for this cause especially, with others, that
it was founded upon a true calculation, and a foresight of the permanent need of evidence ; our Lord
admitting the inadequacy of His own mere word,
and the necessity of a rational guarantee to His
revelation of His own nature and commission. " If
I had not done among them the works that none
other man did, they had not had sin[b] ;" " The works
that I do bear witness of Me, that the Father hath
sent Me[c]."

[b] St. John xv. 24.   [c] Ibid. v. 36.

LECTURE II.

ORDER OF NATURE.

GEN. VIII. 22.

While the earth remaineth, seedtime and harvest, and cold and heat, and summer and winter, and day and night shall not cease.

WHATEVER difficulty there is in believing in miracles in general arises from the circumstance that they are in contradiction to or unlike the order of nature. To estimate the force of this difficulty, then, we must first understand what kind of belief it is which we have in the order of nature; for the weight of the objection to the miraculous must depend on the nature of the belief to which the miraculous is opposed.

And first, what is meant by the order of nature? It will be answered, That succession and recurrence of physical events of which we have had experience. But this, though true as far as it goes, would be a very *inadequate* definition of what we mean by that important phrase—just omitting indeed the main point. For that order of nature which we assume in all

D

our purposes and plans in life is not a past but a future. That which is actually known and has been observed is over and gone, and we have nothing more to do with it : it is that which has not come under our observation, and which is as yet no part of our knowledge, which concerns us ; not yesterday's but to-morrow's state of the case. We entertain a certain belief respecting what will be the state of the case to-morrow with reference to the rising of the sun and other things : and that is the order of nature with which we are practically concerned, not that part of it which we know but that part of it of which we are ignorant.

What we mean, then, by the phrase 'order of nature' is the *connexion* of that part of the order of nature of which we are ignorant with that part of it which we know—the former being expected to be such and such *because* the latter is. But this being the case, how do we justify this expectation, i. e. how do we account for the belief in the order of nature ?

This belief, then, is defined as consisting in an expectation of *likeness*—that the unknown is *like* the known, that the utterly invisible future will be *like* the past. "This," says Bishop Butler, "is that presumption or probability from analogy expressed in the very word continuance which seems our only natural reason for believing the course of the world will continue to-morrow as it has done, so far as our experience and knowledge of history can carry us back." (Note I.)

But though the fact is very obvious that we *do*
expect the unknown to be like the known, the future
like the past, why is it that we do ? on what ground
does this expectation arise ? whence is it " that
likeness should beget this presumption ?" The answer to this question will decide the mental character
of our belief in the uniformity of nature, and so
enable us to estimate the weight of the objection
to the miraculous thence arising.

On asking ourselves the question, then, why we
believe that the future order of nature will be like
the past, why such and such a physical fact will
go on repeating itself as it has done, say the rising
of the sun, or the ebb and flow of the tide, our first
impulse is to say that it is self-evident it will do
so. But such a ground gives way upon a moment's
reflexion. We mean by self-evident that of which
the opposite is self-contradictory ; but though the
fact that the sun rose to-day would be contradicted
by the fact that it did not rise to-day, it is in no
way contradicted by the fact that it will not rise
to-morrow. These two facts are quite consistent
with each other, as much so as any other two facts
that could be mentioned.

But though the connexion in our minds between
the past recurrence of a physical fact up to this very
day, and its future recurrence to-morrow, is not a self-
evident one, is there any reason of any kind that
can be assigned for it ? I apprehend that when we
examine the different reasons which may be assigned
for this connexion, i. e. for this belief that the future

will be like the past, they all come at last to be mere statements of the belief itself, and not reasons to account for it.

It may be said, e. g. that when a fact of nature has gone on repeating itself a certain time, such repetition shews that there is a permanent cause at work ; and that a permanent cause produces permanently recurring effects. But what is there to shew the existence of a permanent cause ? Nothing. The effects which have taken place shew a cause at work to the extent of those effects, and those particular instances of repetition, but not at all further. That this cause is of a nature more permanent than its existing or known effects, extending further, and about to produce other and more instances besides those it has produced already, we have no evidence. Why then do we expect with such certainty the further continuance of them ? We can only say, because we believe the future will be like the past. We have professed, then, to give a reason why we believe this, and we have only at last stated the fact that we do.

Let us imagine the occurrence of a particular physical phenomenon for the first time. Upon that single occurrence we should have but the very faintest expectation of another. If it did occur again once or twice, so far from counting on another recurrence, a cessation would come as the more natural event to us. But let it occur a hundred times and we should feel no hesitation in inviting persons from a distance to see it ; and if it occurred every day for years, its

recurrence would then be a certainty to us, its cessation a marvel. But what has taken place in the
interim to produce this total change in our belief?
From the mere repetition do we know anything more
about its cause? No. Then what have we got besides
the past repetition itself? Nothing. Why then are
we so certain of its *future* repetition? All we can
say is that the known casts its shadow before ;
we project into unborn time the existing types, and
the secret skill of nature intercepts the darkness of
the future by ever suspending before our eyes, as it
were in a mirror, a reflexion of the past. We really
look at a blank before us, but the mind, full of the
scene behind, sees it again in front.

Or is it to give a reason why we believe that the
order of nature will be like what it has been to say
that we do not know of this constancy of nature at
first, but that we get to know it by *experience*?
What do we mean by knowing from experience?
We cannot mean that the future facts of nature have
fallen within our experience, or under our cognizance ; for that would be to say that a future fact
is a past fact. We can only mean, then, that from
our past experience of the facts of nature, we form
our *expectation* of the future ; which is the same as
saying that we believe the future will be like the
past : but to say this is not to give a reason for this
belief but only to state it.

Or do we think it giving a reason for our confidence in the future to say that though "no man has
had experience of what *is* future, every man has had

experience of what *was* future ?" This is a true
assertion, but it does not help us at all out of the
present difficulty, because the confidence of which
we speak relates not to what *was* future, but to
what *is* future. It is true, indeed, that what *is*
future becomes at every step of our advance what
was future, but that which is now *still* future, is not
the least altered by that circumstance, it is as invisible, as unknown, and as unexplored as if not
one single moment of the past had preceded it,
and as if it were the very beginning and the very
starting-point of nature. Let any one place himself in imagination at the first commencement of
this course of nature, at the very first opening of
the great roll of time, before any of its contents
had been disclosed,—what would he *know* of the
then future course of nature ? Nothing. At this
moment he *knows* no more of its future course
dating from this moment. However at each present instant the future emerges into light, this only
moves forward the starting-point of darkness ; at
every fresh step into the future the future begins
afresh, and is as unknown a future as ever, behind
the same impenetrable veil which has always hid
it. Whatever time converts into the known we
are always on the confines of the unknown ; and
whatever tracts of this country we discover, the
rest is as much undiscovered ground as ever. That
" every man then has had experience of what was
future," is no reason for his confidence in what *is*
future, *except* upon one assumption, viz. that the

future will be like the past. But, such being so, this professed reason for the belief in question does not account for it, but assumes it.

What ground of reason, then, can we assign for our expectation that any part of the course of nature will the *next* moment be like what it has been up to *this* moment, i. e. for our belief in the uniformity of nature? None. No demonstrative reason can be given, for the contrary to the recurrence of a fact of nature is no contradiction. No probable reason can be given, for all probable reasoning respecting the course of nature is founded *upon* this presumption of likeness, and therefore cannot be the foundation of it. No reason can be given for this belief. It is without a reason. It rests upon no rational ground and can be traced to no rational principle. Everything connected with human life depends upon this belief, every practical plan or purpose that we form implies it, every provision we make for the future, every safeguard and caution we employ against it, all calculation, all adjustment of means to ends, supposes this belief ; it is this principle alone which renders our experience of the slightest use to us, and without it there would be, so far as we are concerned, no order of nature and no laws of nature ; and yet this belief has no more producible reason for it, than a speculation of fancy. A natural fact has been repeated ; it will be repeated :—I am conscious of utter darkness when I try to see why one of these follows from the other : I not only see no reason, but I perceive that I see none, though I can no more help the expectation than I can stop the circulation of my blood. There is a premiss and there is a conclusion, but there is a total want of connexion between the two. The inference, then, from the one of these to the other rests upon no ground of the understanding; by no search or analysis, however subtle or minute, can we extract from any corner of the human mind and intelligence, however remote, the very faintest reason for it.

Such was the conclusion of a great philosopher of the last century, after an examination of the foundation upon which the belief in the order of nature rested. " When it is asked," says Hume, " what is the foundation of all our reasonings and conclusions concerning the relation of cause and effect, it may be replied in one word—Experience. But if we ask, What is the foundation of all conclusions from experience ? this implies a new question, which may be of more difficult solution. . . . Experience can be allowed to give direct and certain information of those precise objects only, and that precise period of time which fell under its cognizance ; but why should this experience be extended to future times and to other objects ? It must be acknowledged that there is here a consequence drawn by the mind, that there is a certain step taken, a process of thought and an inference which wants to be explained. These two propositions are far from the same. I have found that such and such an object has always been attended with such an effect, and I foresee that other objects which are in appearance similar will be attended with similar effects. I shall allow, if you please, that the one proposition may justly be inferred from the other : I know in fact that it always is inferred : but if you insist that the inference is made by a chain of reasoning, I desire you to produce that reasoning. The connexion between these propositions is not intuitive. There is required a medium which may enable the mind to draw such an inference, if, indeed, it can be drawn by reasoning and argument. What that medium is I must confess passes my comprehension. I cannot find, I cannot imagine any such reasoning. You say that the one proposition is an inference from the other ; but you must confess that the inference is not intuitive, neither is it demonstrative. Of what nature is it then ? To say it is experimental is begging the question. For all inferences from experience *suppose* as their foundation that the future will resemble the past : it is impossible therefore that any arguments from experience can prove this resemblance. Let the course of things be allowed hitherto ever so regular, that alone, without some new argument or inference, proves not that for the future it will continue so. As an agent I am quite satisfied on the point, but as a philosopher I want to learn the foundation of this inference. No reading, no inquiry has yet been able to remove my difficulty. Can I do more than propose it to the public, even though perhaps I have small hopes of obtaining a solution ? We shall at all events by this means be sensible of our ignorance, if we do not augment our knowledge[a]."

Such is the nature of this remarkable and momentous inference and belief—necessary, all important for the purposes of life, but solely practical and possessing no intellectual character. Will it be said that this unintellectual and unreasoning character belongs to it in common with all the original perceptions of our nature, which cannot, as being original, rest upon any argumentative foundation? This would not be a true or correct account of the character of this particular inference, and the absence of the rational quality in it. For there is this important difference between the rational or intellectual perceptions which cannot be traced further back than themselves, and this inference we are speaking of, viz. that those perceptions cannot be contradicted without an absolute absurdity, whereas an event in contradiction to this inference is no absurdity at all. The truth of a mathematical axiom cannot be traced further back than itself; but then an axiom is self-evidently true, and a contradiction to it is as self-evidently false. And, to go out of the sphere of strict demonstration, the inference from the coincidence of one part with another in organized matter, to design or law as distinguished from chance, is an inference which cannot be traced further back than itself, but then this inference cannot be contradicted without a shock to reason. The

[a] Enquiry concerning the Human Understanding, sect. iv.

supposition that this whole world came together by chance is an absurdity. But the inference from the past to the future wants this intrinsic note and test of an inference of reason, that the contradictory to it is in no collision with reason. There is no violence to reason in the supposition that the world will come to an end and the sun will one day not rise, notwithstanding the increasing presumption from repetition up to that very day that it will rise. Indeed, it is not wholly unmeaning to observe that the great metaphysician himself, who analyzed the argument from experience, has unconsciously tested that argument by this very case. Two famous atheistical philosophers have predicted the end of the world and the dissolution of all things. The grand and striking prophecy of Lucretius is given with an almost oracular solemnity; but the vaticination of our own philosopher, based upon hints and analogies in nature, is also delivered with a grave and serious voice, which arrests attention. "Suppose," says Hume, "all authors in all languages agree that from the first of January, 1600, there was a total darkness over the whole earth for eight days : suppose that the tradition of this extraordinary event is still strong and lively among the people : that all travellers who return from foreign countries bring us accounts of the same tradition, without the least variation or contradiction : it is evident that our present philosophers, instead of doubting the fact, ought to receive it as certain, and ought to search for the causes whence it might be derived. The

decay, corruption, and dissolution of nature is an
event rendered probable by so many analogies, that
any phenomenon which seems to have a tendency
towards that catastrophe comes within the reach of
human testimony[b]." The end of the world, then,
so far from being impossible, is here contemplated
as likely ; and yet up to the very moment of the
end—for if it comes at all, it may come in a moment
—the argument from experience that it will *continue*
will be in full force,—nay, in the very greatest force
that it has ever been in since the beginning of things.
The argument from mere experience, then, intrinsically differs in the quality of reasoning, not only
from mathematical reasoning, but even, as has been
noticed, from the other great department of *probable*
reasoning.

Indeed, that this belief in the uniformity of
nature is not a part of reason is shewn by the circumstance that even the brute animals are possessed
with it, apparently quite as much as man is. This
is indeed the very first and most obvious trait of
their instinct ; for it must strike the most ordinary
observers that all animals shew by their actions that
from the past they infer the future, and that they
calculate, just in the same way in which we do, upon
the constancy of that part of the course of nature
with which they are concerned. Nor can we by
the very minutest analysis discover the slightest
difference in the nature of this particular instinct in

[b] Essay on Miracles.

the two cases, however different may be the range and rank of the facts to which it is applied. However limited the experience of animals as compared with man's, the inference *from* experience is the same in them as in man. "We admire," says Hume, "the instincts of animals as something very extraordinary and inexplicable by all the disquisitions of the human understanding. But our wonder will perhaps cease or diminish, when we consider that experimental reasoning itself, which we possess in common with beasts, is nothing but a species of instinct or mechanical power, that acts in us unknown to ourselves." I would add to this statement one remark. Some faint elements of reason being discernible in. the brute, it is not enough to prove that a process is not a process of reason, that something approaching to it is seen in the brute. But allowing this, still a mental act which an animal performs in a mode which we cannot see to differ from the human mode of it, however valuable an act, is not what we popularly call and mean by an act of reason.

Under what head, then, shall we bring this mysterious and incomprehensible inference from the known to the unknown, from the objects and time of which we have had experience to other objects and other times of which we have none ;—that which we call belief in the order of nature ? To what general principle shall we refer this common primordial property of rational and irrational natures which lies at the basement of the whole pyramid of life ? It

is not of importance to bring it under any regular
head, so long as we understand its general character.
We may observe that our nature, though endowed
with reason, contains constitutionally large irrational
departments, and includes within it, as a true and
genuine part of itself, nay, and a most valuable part,
many processes which are entirely spontaneous, irresistible, and, so to call it, of the *automaton* kind.
Such, e.g. is the impression which time makes upon us,
by which it relieves our sorrows and moderates our
joys. The loss of a relative or friend is in point of
reason the same loss years hence that it is now, but
we can no more prevent the effect of time upon our
mind, than we can the spontaneous action of an
internal bodily organ. So, again, the force of association is an irresistible principle. The ties of place
and of country are in one respect irresistible ; men
may act against them, but can never cancel or anni-
hilate them in their own minds. And—to take a
signal instance—custom or habit is an irresistible
principle. No *reason* can be given why acts should
become easier by repetition, i. e. for the force of
habit. The acts, however, being done, the formation of a habit is s spontaneous and irresistible
a process as the growth of a vegetable. Under
which head the belief now spoken of would appear to come. "Whenever," says the philosopher
I have quoted, " the repetition of any particular
act or operation produces a propensity to renew the
same act or operation, without being impelled by
any reasoning or process of the understanding, we

always say that this propensity is the effect of
custom. By employing that word we do not pretend
to have given the ultimate reason of such a propensity. We only point out a principle which is
universally acknowledged, and which is well known
by its effects. Perhaps we can push our inquiries
no further, or pretend to give the cause of this cause;
but must rest contented with it as the ultimate
principle which we can assign to all our conclusions
from experience. This hypothesis seems even the
only one which explains the difficulty why we draw
from a thousand instances an inference which we are
not able to draw from one instance [c]."

[c] Enquiry concerning the Human Understanding, sect. 5. It
will be observed that this argument from experience of which we
are speaking, is different from, and must not be confounded with,
what we call the argument of analogy. The term analogy itself
may indeed be applied to any case of likeness: on which account
the inference from like past to like future, or the argument of experience, may be and is sometimes called an argument of analogy.
But it must be seen that it makes all the difference in the nature
of the argument whether it is applied to like *physical* facts or like
acts of a *moral* being. What we call by distinction the argument
of analogy is concerned with the latter: it is an argument from
an act of the Divine Being in one case to the probability of a like
act in another which appears to us a similar case. The validity
of this argument, then, depends entirely upon the similarity of these
two cases; the resemblance in the two sets of circumstances and
nature of the two objects to which the two acts belong—the two
acts from the one of which we argue to the other. Nothing could
be more absurd than to argue from one act to another like it, if
there were no resemblance in the cases in and objects for which the
two acts were performed. And the same with respect to the negative side of analogy. Nothing could be more absurd than to
suppose that, to prove the tenableness of one course of action,

And now, the belief in the order of nature being thus, however powerful and useful, an unintelligent impulse of which we can give no rational account, in what way does this discovery affect the question of miracles? In this way: that this belief not having itself its foundation in reason, the ground is gone upon which it could be maintained that miracles as opposed to the order of nature were opposed to reason. There being no producible reason why a new event should be like the hitherto course of nature, no decision of reason is contradicted by its unlikeness. A miracle in being opposed to our experience is not only not opposed to necessary reasoning, but to any reasoning. Do I see by a certain perception the connexion between these two—It *has* happened so: it *will* happen so; then may I reject a new reported fact which has *not* happened so as an impossibility. But if I do not see the connexion between these two by a certain perception, or by any

attributed to the Deity, in *one* case, it was enough to point to even the most admitted similar course of Divine action in a totally *different* case. The whole validity, then, of the argument of analogy depends upon the establishment of a parallel case, i. e. though not absolutely identical, substantially similar: and for the correctness of this resemblance in the two cases we make ourselves responsible when we use the argument. But the selection of a real parallel or like case, such as this argument stands in need of, is an act of reason and judgment, requiring thought and comparison; it is indeed an act which exercises the utmost discrimination; and is therefore an act of another kind wholly to the mechanical expectation of like events or recurrences in nature. Whence it appears that the argument of analogy, as it is called, is a fundamentally different argument from the argument of experience.

perception, I cannot. For a miracle to be rejected as such there must at any rate be some proposition in the mind of man which is opposed to it : and that proposition can only spring from the quarter to which we have been referring, viz. that of elementary experimental reasoning. But if this experimental reasoning is of that nature which philosophy describes it as being of, i. e. if it is not itself a process of reason, how can there from an irrational process of the mind arise a proposition at all,—to make which is the function of the rational faculty alone ? There cannot ; and it is evident that the miraculous does not stand in any opposition whatever to reason.

I have spoken throughout this argument of the belief in the order of nature as the expectation of *continuance, of a like future ;* but it makes no difference whether the unlike event is a future or a reported past one : in either case it comes into collision with the expectation of likeness, which takes within its scope alike the future and the past. The report of a past unlike event encounters the same resistance in the mind as the idea of a future one.

Thus step by step has philosophy loosened the connexion of the order of nature with the ground of reason, befriending, in exact proportion as it has done this, the principle of miracles. In the argument against miracles the first objection is that they are against *law ;* and this is answered by saying that we know nothing in nature of law in the sense in which it prevents miracles. Law can only prevent miracles by *compelling* and making necessary the succession of nature, i. e. in the sense of causation; but science has itself proclaimed the truth that we see no causes in nature[d], that the whole chain of physical succession is to the eye of reason a rope of sand, consisting of antecedents and consequents, but without a rational link or trace of necessary connexion between them. We only know of law in nature in the sense of recurrences in nature, classes of facts, *like* facts in nature—a chain of which, the junction not being reducible to reason, the interruption is not against reason. The claim of law settled, the next objection in the argument against miracles is that they are against *experience;* because we expect facts *like* to those of our experience, and miracles are *unlike* ones. The weight, then, of the objection of unlikeness to experience depends on the reason which can be produced for the expectation of likeness: and to this call philosophy has replied by the summary confession that we have *no* reason. Philosophy, then, could not have overthrown more thoroughly than it has done the order of nature as a necessary course of things, or cleared the ground more effectually for the principle of miracles.

Hitherto, however, we have been dealing with the inference from the known to the unknown, or the belief in the uniformity of nature, in connexion only

[d] Taking "cause" not in an absolute sense as necessarily containing its effect, but in the popular sense of secondary cause, which may be suspended by a higher cause, the idea of real causation in nature is not opposed to the miraculous, and general belief has united the two.

with the facts of vulgar sensible experience. Let us now regard the same inference and principle in connexion with science ; in which connexion it receives a more imposing name, and is called the inductive principle. The inductive inference or principle is that act of the mind by which, when the philosopher has ascertained by discovery a particular fact in nature, and its recurrence in the same connexion within his own observation, he forthwith infers that this fact will universally take place, or converts it into a law. Does this inference from past experience, then, in connexion with science pass into a new phase and become luminous and intellectual, or does it remain the same blind and unreasoning instinct as before ?

When we examine, then, what it is which composes that process which is called inductive reasoning, we find that it consists of two parts, and that the first of these two parts is the simple discovery of a fact. There is wanted the physical cause of some known fact, and this cause is another fact not known as yet in this relation, for which accordingly the philosopher institutes a search. It must be a fact which fulfils certain conditions, must always precede the known fact when the latter takes place, and always omit this precedence when it does not take place. The test of invariable antecedence puts aside as causes on the one hand all the facts which the event *takes* place *without,* and on the other hand all which the event does *not* take place *with,* till it gets at the residuum which is the physical cause. The sagacity of the man of science, then, is shewn in hitting upon and singling out the fact which fulfils these conditions from the midst of the whole promiscuous crowd of facts which surround the phenomenon before him—a process which severely tries his powers of observation, force and steadiness of attention, quickness of apprehension, watchfulness, accuracy ; his powers of comparison, of seeing things in relation, and detecting hidden relationships and connexions in things. He has to extract the real key to the enigma out of a quantity of deceptive and misleading promises of solution, which take him in different directions only to retrace his steps ; he has to repeat again and again the selection of facts which he brings to the test, to see if they answer to it ; he has to carry in his mind a large body of old observations, in order to provide connexion and productiveness to the new.

This is the first part, then, of the inductive process ; but as yet we have only ascertained a fact—a fact indeed which fulfils peculiar conditions, and therefore has not been observed by the ordinary use of the eyes, but by a process of selection, but still no more than a fact, that is to say, a particular past occurrence which has been often repeated : that the pursuit of it has been regular and systematic does not alter the particularity of the fact, or make it at all the more a universal or a law. To take the familiar instance of the discovery of vaccination. In this instance it was discovered that in all the observed cases of freedom from a particular complaint, à certain fact *preceded* that fact ; but that was only a particular observation : how was it converted into a universal, or into the law that, where that fact or something equivalent to it preceded, that freedom would *always* follow ?

The inference, then, which converts scientific observation into law, which we call the inductive principle, and is the second part of the inductive process, is exactly the same instinct which converts ordinary and common experience into law ; viz. that habit by which we always extend any existing recurrent fact of nature into the future. The inductive principle is only this unreasoning impulse applied to a scientifically ascertained fact, instead of to a vulgarly ascertained fact. Science is only a method of ascertaining the fact, which when once ascertained is the same as any common fact, and dealt with by our nature in the same way. Science has led up to the fact, but there it stops, and for converting the fact into a law, a totally unscientific principle comes in, the same as that which generalizes the commonest observation in nature. The one is a selected fact indeed, the other an obvious palpable fact, but that which gives constancy and future recurrence to each—the *prediction* attaching to them, is a simple impression of which we can give no rational account, which likens the future to the past. The naturalist obtains his fact by his own sagacity, but the generalization of it is done for him, and this spontaneous addition is the same in the discovery of a philosopher and the observation of a savage. There is all the difference in the philosophical rank of the two *observations*, their transition from fact into law is one common mechanical appendage. That which stereotypes them both is the same, and for his future or universal the scientific man falls back upon the same instinct as that which supplies the physical prospect of the peasant. (Note 2.)

And here it may be remarked by the way, that what is called inductive reasoning is not, strictly speaking, reasoning. It is called so because an inference is made in it, a general conclusion is drawn from particulars. But the first part of the inductive process is not reasoning but observation; the second part is not reasoning but instinct: the scientific part is not inductive, the inductive part is not scientific. Hence we cannot attribute to scientific men, by however penetrating and lofty faculties they may have discovered *facts*, any peculiar perception of recurrence or *law*. Language has been used as if science generated a perception of mathematical or necessary sequence in the order of nature. (Note 3.) But science has herself proclaimed the truth that there *is no* necessary connexion in nature; nor has science to do with generalization at all, but only with discovery. And I may add, that though science avails herself of the inductive principle and depends for all her utility upon it, still to ascertain the nature of this principle is not the province of physical but of mental science.

It must be observed, again, that the inductive principle thus spoken of as unscientific, upon which the *order* of nature is founded, is totally different from the perception of *harmony and relation* in nature. We use the phrase 'order of nature' in two senses ; that of arrangement, and that of recurrence. I see relation amongst different things, and I call that the order of nature ; and I see the repetition of the same thing, and I call that the order of nature too. I examine the component parts, and see their wonderful and subtle adjustment ; and I take every-thing in a lump, and expect its uniform continuance ; and both of these I call the order of nature. But in one of these senses order is a scientific perception, in the other it is not : and though philosophers have a far deeper insight into the order of nature in the one sense than common people have, they have not in the other. Their knowledge of nature enables them to unravel the multiplicity of relations in her, and so to see a more wonderful and nicer agreement or system in her ; but gives them no greater light whereby to prophesy her continuance or repetition. While we also remark that it is not in the sense of harmony and system that the order of nature is opposed to the miraculous at all. The action of some intricate engine is interrupted designedly for some purpose ; is the admirable perfection of the machinery at all interfered with by that fact ? Do I see its order and arrangement the less ? Does even an injurious interruption of the relations of the internal organs of the body, as disease is, make our bodily structure at all less wonderful a contrivance ? The order of nature, then, in the sense of its harmony, is not disturbed by a miracle; the interruption of a train of relations in one instance leaves them standing in every other, i. e. leaves the system as such untouched. Nature is the same surprising exhibition of mutual relation and adjustment, whether in one instance or so the action of the machine is or is not interrupted. What *is* disturbed by a miracle is the mechanical expectation of recurrence, from which, and not from the *system* and arrangement in nature, the notion of immutability proceeds.

What is the conclusion, then, to be drawn from this statement of the process of induction? It is this. The scientific part of induction being only the pursuit of a particular fact, miracles cannot in the nature of the case receive any blow from the scientific part of induction; because the existence of one fact does not interfere with the existence of another dissimilar fact. That which *does* resist the miraculous is the *un*scientific part of induction, or the instinctive generalization upon this fact. The inductive principle being that which assimilates the unknown to the known, or establishes the order of nature, is opposed to any dissimilar fact or interruption of that order, whether we think of it as going to be, or whether we think of it as having by report taken place. A reported miracle is a reported case in which the order of nature did not for that instance continue, but was interrupted. The inductive principle therefore resists that miracle. But what *is* the inductive principle? What is its nature? what is its force? what is its weight upon such a question? The inductive principle is simply the mechanical expectation of the likeness of the unknown to the known, not become any more luminous than it was before because its subject-matter is higher, but being in the most vulgar and the most scientific material alike unreasoning, i. e. no part of the distinctive reason of man. When, then, there is nothing on the side of reason opposed to it, as is the case commonly, we follow it absolutely. But supposing there should arise a call of reason to us to believe what is opposite to it; supposing there is the evidence of testimony, which is an appeal to our proper reason, that an event has taken place which is opposed to this impression—it is evident then that our reason must prevail in the encounter, i. e. that if there is on one side positive evidence, the antecedent counter expectation of instinct must give way. And thus we come round to Butler's statement of the ground of experience, that there is a probability that all things will continue as we experience they are, except in those in which we have some reason to think they will be altered. This definition of the force of experience is an appeal to our consciousness, and our consciousness responds to it, recognising no other belief in the order of nature but the one thus described. But as thus described this belief is self-limited, and intrinsically admits of events contrary to it; within its very body and substance is contained the confession of its own possible error, the anticipation of reasonable contradiction to it.

The proper function of the inductive principle, the argument from experience, or the belief in the order of nature—by whatever phrase we designate the same instinct—is to operate as a practical basis for the affairs of life and the carrying on of human society. Without it it would be impossible for the world to go on, because without it we should have no future before us to calculate upon; we should not feel any assurance of the continuance of the world itself from moment to moment. This principle it is, then, which makes human life practicable; which utilizes all our knowledge; which makes the past anything more than an irrelevant picture to us; for of what use is the experience of the past to us unless we believe the future will be like it? But it is also evident what is *not* the proper function of this principle. It does not belong to this principle to lay down speculative positions, and to say what can or cannot take place in the world. It does not belong to it to control religious belief, or to determine that certain acts of God for the revelation of His will to man, reported to have taken place, have not taken place. Such decisions are totally out of its sphere; it can assert the universal as a *law;* but the universal as a law and the universal as a proposition are wholly distinct. The one asserts the universal as a fact, the other as a presumption; the one as an absolute certainty, the other as a practical certainty, when there is no reason to expect the contrary. The one contains and includes the particular, the other does not: from the one we argue mathematically to the falsehood of any opposite particular ; from the other we do not. Yet there has existed virtually in the speculations of some philosophers an identification of a universal as a law, with a universal proposition ; by which summary expedient they enclosed the world in iron, and bound the Deity in adamantine fetters ; for *such* a law forestalls all exception to it. An apparently counterprocess has indeed accompanied this elevation of induction to mathematics, viz. the lowering of mathematics to induction. But either form of identification has the same result, and is an alchemical process for transmuting the blind inference from experience into demonstration, and thus endowing the order of nature which rests upon that experience with the character of immutable and necessary law. (Note 4.)

For example, one signal miracle, pre-eminent for its grandeur, crowned the evidence of the supernatural character and office of our Lord—our Lord's ascension—His going up with His body of flesh and bones into the sky, in the presence of His disciples. " He lifted up His hands, and blessed them. And while He blessed them, He was parted from them, and carried up into heaven. And they looked steadfastly toward heaven as He went up, and a cloud received Him out of their sight[e]."

Here is an amazing scene, which strikes even the devout believer, coming across it in the sacred page suddenly or by chance, amid the routine of life,

[e] Luke xxiv. 50, 51 ; Acts i. 9, 10.

with a fresh surprise. Did, then, this event really take place ? Or is the evidence of it forestalled by the inductive principle compelling us to remove the scene *as such* out of the category of matters of fact ? The answer is, that the inductive principle is in its own nature only an *expectation ;* and that the expectation, that what is unlike our experience will not happen, is quite consistent. with its occurrence in fact. This principle does not pretend to decide the question of fact ; which is wholly out of its province and beyond its function. It can only decide the fact by the medium of a universal ; the universal proposition that no man has ascended to heaven. But this is a statement which exceeds its power ; it is as radically incompetent to pronounce it as the taste or smell is to decide on matters of sight ; its function is practical, not logical. No antecedent statement, then, which touches my belief in this scene, is allowed by the laws of thought. Converted indeed into a universal proposition, the inductive principle is omnipotent, and totally annihilates every particular which does not come within its range. The universal statement that no man has ascended into heaven, absolutely falsifies the fact that One Man has. But thus transmuted, the inductive principle issues out of this metamorphose, a fiction not a truth ; a weapon of air, which even in the hand of a giant can inflict no blow because it is itself a shadow. The object of assault receives the unsubstantial thrust without a shock, only exposing the want of solidity in the implement of war.' The battle against the supernatural has been going on long, and strong men have conducted it and are conducting it—but what they want is a weapon. The logic of unbelief wants a universal. But no real universal is forthcoming, and it only wastes its strength in wielding a fictitious one.

LECTURE III.

PSALM CXXXIX. 14.

Marvellous are Thy works, and that my soul knoweth right well.

IT is evident that the effect which the visible order of nature has upon some minds is, that as soon as they realize what a miracle is, they are stopped by what appears to them a simple sense of its impossibility. So long as they only believe by habit and education, they accept a miracle without difficulty, because they do not realize it as an event which actually took place in the world; the alteration of the face of the world, and the whole growth of intervening history, throw the miracles of the Gospel into a remote perspective in which they are rather seen as a picture than real occurrences. But as soon as they see that, if these miracles are true, they once really happened, what they feel then is the apparent sense of their impossibility. It is not a question of evidence with them: when they realize, e. g. that our Lord's re-

surrection, if true, was a visible fact or occurrence,
they have the seeming certain perception that it
is an impossible occurrence. 'I cannot,' a person
says to himself in effect, 'tear myself from the type
of experience, and join myself to another. I cannot
quit order and law for what is eccentric. There
is a repulsion between such facts and my belief as
strong as that between physical substances. In the
mere effort to conceive these amazing scenes as real
ones, I fall back upon myself and upon that type
of reality which the order of nature has impressed
upon me.'

Now when such a person proceeds to probe the
ground of his deep objection to a miracle, the first
thing, I think, that cannot but strike him is how
very poor any reason he can allege and specify
is, compared with the amount of his own inward
feeling of certainty. If he is a reflecting person,
he cannot but be struck of his own accord with
this singular disproportion between the two—on
the one hand an overpowering prepossession, on the
other hardly anything to sustain it. The form in
which he will first put his reason to himself will
perhaps be that miracles are inconceivable to him.
But what is meant by this assertion? That the
causes are inconceivable? But the causes of the
commonest physical facts are the same. That the
facts are inconceivable? But the facts are not inconceivable, but conceivable. I can conceive the
change of water into wine just as easily as I can
conceive any chemical conversion ; i. e. I can first

conceive water, and then I can conceive wine in the place of water ; and that is all I can do in the case of any change of one substance into another in chemistry. The absence of the medium of an artificial process only makes the cause inconceivable, not the fact. So I can form the idea of a dead man alive again, just as easily as I can of the process of decay ; one fact is as conceivable as another, while the causes are alike inconceivable of both.

We cannot rest, then, at the reason of inconceivableness, but must go on to some further one. Is it that miracles are physical results produced without means, without a physical medium intervening between the Divine will and the result ? But we cannot pronounce upon the fact of the total absence of means, but only on their invisibility, which belongs to many steps and media in nature. Nor can we pronounce upon the necessity of physical means ; for even in the natural action of will or spirit upon matter, there must be a point at which the one acts on the other without a medium, however inconceivable that may be ; otherwise, if the media never end, the one never gets at the other at all.

The reason then against miracles that we come to at last, and in which all these vaguer reasons end, is simply their *unlikeness* to the order of nature. A *suspension* of the order of nature is the ordinary phrase in which we express this unlikeness to the order of nature ; but whether or not we call unlikeness by this term, the fact itself is the ultimate objection to a miracle.   It was shewn, however, in my last Lecture, what the expectation of likeness was, and that no reason against an unlike event as such was producible or even imaginable.

The .rejector of miracles has indeed, in the over-powering force of an impression upon his mind, something to which argument is hardly adapted. Every time he recals a miracle to his imagination, he recals a felt something at the bottom which in his own idea closes the door against it ; something at the root of the matter which is untouched, a true cause of conviction which is unanswered : he cannot conceive that so strong a rejecting influence as he feels can be without rational necessity ; that the force of the resistance in his mind is not its own vindication.

And yet the question of the possibility of any-thing—possibility, i. e. as far as we know—is a judicial question which must be decided in the same way as a question of fact.   There is a court which decides this question—the inner court of our own mind, in which witnesses are cited and evidence is heard.   The witnesses cited into this court are all the faculties and perceptions of our minds ; and when they have answered to the summons, one question is put to them, — Does any reason exist why a miracle is impossible ?   If they know of none, the case is over.   The court of possibility decides in the same way in which a court of fact does.   It is an open court into which all mankind are admitted, for indeed the witness in that court is the collective reason of mankind, which appears there to give an account of itself, to declare to its own known contents, and whether amongst them all there is found a reason for the impossibility of a miracle. Science has its summary evidence of fact by which it challenges foregone conclusions; and reason has the same.

What has been, then, in the present instance the cause at work—that which has made a reason, when there was none, against the miraculous as such? I cannot but think that under an intellectual disguise it is the imagination. The design, as I have stated, of the inductive principle or belief in the order of nature is a practical one—to enable provision to be made for human life and welfare ; which could not be done unless we could reckon upon the likeness of the past to the future. For without this expectation, what would be our prospect? Every moment of nature might be its last, and we should live upon the constant brink of utter change and dissolution, which would paralyse all action in us. But the impression as it exists in us by nature, being entirely a practical one, and this being its legitimate and constitutional scope, imagination seizes hold of it and diverts it from its scope ; by brooding upon it exaggerates it ; converts a practical expectation into a scientific truth, and extracts from an unreasoning instinct what it cannot by its very nature contain—a universal intellectual proposition, that the order of nature is immutable.

We apply the term imagination to denote that faculty by which the mind adds anything *out of*

itself to a fact or truth, whether that fact or truth
be a visible object, or an idea or motive within us.
Being such, however, the imagination has a very
different moral aspect according as it acts in one
or other of two ways ; that is to say, actively by
energy and self-exertion from within, or passively
by yielding to an impulse or impression from without.   In either case it adds to a fact something
which that fact does not supply of itself; for to
yield too much to an impression is to exaggerate
it : but the two cases of addition widely differ.
When the imagination acts by energy from within,
when it enables us to see the force and extent of
some truth, to grasp a condition of things external
to ourselves, to understand the feelings and the
wants of others, to admire nature, to sympathise
with man ; or when it aids in the work of combination, construction, invention ; in thus *actively*
imparting meaning and life to facts, imagination
is a noble and effective instrument, if indeed we
may not call it a part, of reason.   But when the
imagination exaggerates an impression by passively
submitting and surrendering itself to it, when it
gives way to the mere force of attraction, and
instead of grasping something else, is itself grasped
and mastered by some dominant idea—it is then
not a power, but a failing and a weakness of nature.
We may call these respectively active and passive
imagination.   When imagination is spoken of in
books of morals as a common source of delusion
and unhappiness in men, who are carried away by

their joys and griefs, their hopes and fears, and allow impressions to fasten upon them till they cannot shake them off, it is not the active imagination which is meant, but the passive.

The passive imagination, then, in the present case exaggerates a practical expectation of the uniformity of nature, implanted in us for practical ends, into a scientific or universal proposition; and it does this by surrendering itself to the impression produced by the constant spectacle of the regularity of visible nature. By such a course a person allows the weight and pressure of this idea to grow upon him till it reaches the point of actually restricting his sense of possibility to the mould of physical order. It is a common remark that repetition as such tends to make itself believed; and that if an assertion is simply reiterated often enough it makes its way to acceptance; which is to say that the force of impression produces belief independently of reason. The order of nature thus stamps upon some minds the idea of its immutability simply by its repetition. The imagination we usually indeed associate with the acceptance of the supernatural rather than with the denial of it; but the passive imagination is in truth neutral; it only increases the force and tightens the hold of any impression upon us, to whatever class the impression may belong, and surrenders itself to a superstitious or a physical idea, as it may be. Materialism itself is the result of imagination, which is so impressed by matter that it cannot realise the existence of spirit.

The passive imagination thus accounts for the rise of the apparent perception of the impossibility of a miracle. For what is this perception in those who have it, and what is the actual form which it takes? The form which it takes is this, that, upon the image of a miracle occurring to the mind, there is at once an entire starting back and repulsion from it, as from something radically antagonistic to the very type of reality and matter of fact. Now, that a contradiction to the order of nature should excite a provisionary resistance in our minds is inevitable, because we possess the instinctive expectation of uniformity, unlikeness disagrees with that expectation, this disagreement creates surprise, and surprise is provisionary resistance. But what is it that makes this provisionary resistance final? Is it reason? No. Reason imposes no veto upon unlikeness. Then it is the imagination. Reason may reject that unlike event for want of evidence, imagination alone can reject it as such.

Is it not true, indeed, that the intellect, like the feelings and affections, is capable of contracting bad habits, which need not at all interfere with the soundness and acuteness of it in general, but may only corrupt and disable the judgment upon particular subjects? If then, when there is no producible reason why a miracle should be impossible, a person appears to himself to perceive that it is; if the intellect is so bound to the order of nature that it rejects by an instantaneous impulse a fact of a contrary type as such, it can only be because the intellect has contracted an unsound habit upon that subject-matter.

It will be replied, however, 'We do not reject strange and anomalous facts as such, we receive many such ; and therefore our disbelief in miracles is not the effect of imagination starting back from an eccentric type.' But I answer, that the acceptance of eccentric facts solely upon the hypothesis that they are ultimately reducible to the order of nature, is not an acceptance of really eccentric facts. They are admitted and receive assent only upon the idea that their eccentricity is a temporary mask, underneath which really lie facts which come under the head of existing classes and known laws. They are accepted as hypothetically *like* facts to known ones, not as unlike ones. Notwithstanding all the admission which is extended to such phenomena, facts ultimately eccentric excite as such a final resistance in the minds to which we are alluding, although no reason for their impossibility is forthcoming.

And yet we may see how the imagination is compelled to confront and consent to the most inconceivable things, because it is dragged by the reason to do it. Two great counteracting influences appeal to it to preserve its balance against the impression from the uniformity of nature, and to rouse it from its lethargic submission to custom and recurrence. One is the wonders of the visible world, the other is—for in this discussion I assume the doctrines of natural religion—the wonders of the invisible world.

First the wonders of nature appeal to the imagination, in counteraction to the yoke of physical law. If we examine into the nature of the sense of wonder, we see that it implies a kind of *resistance* in the mind,—often, indeed more generally, a pleased resistance,—but still a resistance to the facts which excite it. There is an element of doubt in wonder, an hesitation, a difficulty in taking in the new material and incorporating it in the existing body of belief. There is a sense of strangeness in wonder, of something to overcome in the character of the fact presented to it. All wonder therefore, where the facts are, as they are in the case of natural marvels, admitted, is a precedent for facts resisted and yet believed, resisted on one side of our nature, believed on another. We see that in nature God acts in modes which astonish us, which startle us. On every side are seeming incredibilities. Why should this be so? Why is nature such a dispensation of surprises? Why is it that no processes, no methods, no means to ends go on in her which do not contain this element? Is it the unavoidable condition of existence at all that it should be wonderful, and that all its mechanism should be wonderful? Whether it is or no, the wonders of nature are precedents of the kind which I mention.

But we have no sooner said thus much than we are immediately met by the fact that many men who have had the deepest sense of the wonderful in nature have been disbelievers in the supernatural: and the names of some great poets, and men of powerful imagination in the realm of science, will occur as familiar instances of this. What, then, is the difference in the sense of wonder in these two spheres, and what is the relation in which the wonderful in nature stands to the supernatural ?

The old saying, then, that nature is as wonderful really as any miracle, were we not so accustomed to her, omits the task of comparison, and does not bring out an important distinction which exists between these two kinds of the wonderful. A wonder of natural science is wonderful on its own account, and by reason of what is actually seen in it. In some vast disposition of nature for supplying the eye with light, or the vegetable with proper nutriment, or the limbs with active power, or for providing the breath of life itself, or for communicating heat, or distributing colour, or for sustaining the motions of the heavens, or for any of those innumerable purposes for which the physical universe is adapted and contrived—it is the incredible power which *comes out* and exhibits and expresses itself in the arrangement which constitutes the subject of wonder. The effect is like that of looking on some gigantic machine in motion : it is the regulated force in action before our eyes that arrests us, which we admire for its own sake. The greatness lies in what is present and addresses itself to our perceptions, as power in execution. This is the case especially in the impression made upon us by those extraordinary revelations of science which divulge as it were the miracles of nature,—the disclosures, e. g. of the velocity of some of the motions of nature, or the magic of her metamorphoses and conversions. Even in the region of rude nature the source of wonder is in this respect the same, that that emotion arises in consequence of some signal force of nature which *comes out* and is manifested and expressed; which thus strikes us with astonishment on its own account. Such is the impression produced by the speed of lightning, the rage of winds, the weight of waters, even the great sounds of nature. And the same remark applies to the perception of the obvious and palpable features of order, beauty, and grandeur in nature; viz. that the effect which they produce upon our minds is an effect arising from something which is expressed and which comes out before our eyes.

But while the marvel of nature surprises on account of what is visible and expressed in it, a miracle, on the other hand, excites our wonder less as a visible fact than as the sign of an invisible one : the wonderful really lies behind it; for that which lies behind a miracle, the true reality of which the eccentric sign is but the veil and front, is the world supernatural. A miracle shews design and intention, i.e. is the act of a Personal Being. Some one, therefore, there is who is moving behind it, with whom it brings us in relation, a spiritual agent of whose presence it speaks. A miracle is thus, if true, an indication of another world, and an unseen state of being, containing personality and will; of another world of moral being besides this visible one; and this is the overawing and impressing consideration in it; in the wonder excited by it, the mind rests only momentarily on the external fact, and passes on immediately to that mysterious personal power out of nature of which it is the token.

Hence we obtain the true scope and character of that affection or propensity of the human mind which we call the love of the supernatural. It is impossible to question the existence and universality of this affection, and that it is an affection which is productive of a characteristic sensation of pleasure. And when we examine and analyse this sensation, and investigate the source of this gratification—one instance of which indeed we may say we have even in the interest which attaches to those reported cases of supernatural communications and visits from the unseen world, upon whatever evidence resting, which we have all heard in conversation—when we trace, I say, this emotion to its source, we find it deeply and intimately connected with the sense of eternity in our minds, the desire for our own future existence. Any communication from the unseen world—supposing it for an instant to be true—is a token of personal existence going on in that world, and so a pledge, as it were, of the continuation of our own personal life when we depart hence. We are interested parties therefore. How indeed do we see people superstitiously, fancifully, and therefore wrongly, catching at such signs of another world as if for safety; at anything which promises a rescue from the absorption of the grave. But the very morbid excess of such longings shews that the love

of the supernatural is no fictitious feeling. A miracle
then, besides all the other purposes which it serves,
is an answer to this affection; it speaks to us of a
power out of this order of things, of will, of Moral
Being, of Personal Being in another world—of *His*
existence, whose existence, according to our Lord's
argument, is a security for the continuance of our
own. Thus a miracle has an awe and a wonder
attaching to it which is peculiarly its own, and is in
marked contrast with physical wonder ; because it is
a sign of an invisible world. It speaks to us in a
manner and to a purpose, which all the astonishing
forces of nature collected together cannot reach to :
because it is addressed immediately to the soul, to
the sense of immortality. The marvels of nature do
not address themselves immediately to this part of
us. Physical wonder is simply entering into present
reality, into *what things are;* the sense is part of
our very understanding ; for though great intellects
have it most, a man must be without intellect at
all who has *no* wonder. And therefore all the marvels and all the stupendous facts in nature do not
speak to us in that way in which *one miracle* speaks
to us; because *they* do not speak to us directly of eternity; *they* do not tell us that we are not like themselves—passing waves of the vast tide of physical life.

And here I will just remark upon the perverse
determination of Spinoza to look at miracles in that
aspect which does not belong to them, and not to
look at them in that aspect which does. He compares miracles with nature, and then says how wise

is the order of nature, how meaningless the violation
of it; how expressive of the Almighty Mind the one,
what a concealment of it the other! But no one
pretends to say that a miracle competes with nature,
in physical purpose and effectiveness. That is not
its object. But a miracle, though it does not profess
to compete with nature upon its rival's own ground,
has a ghostly force and import which nature has not.
If real, it is a token, more pointed and direct than
physical order can be, of another world, and of Moral
Being and Will in that world. And I may add, that
for this effect of a miracle the benevolent and philanthropical type is not necessary, however befitting
such miracles as are intended to be emblems of
Divine love : it is enough for this function of a
miracle that *power* is shewn : nor do we on that
account bow down to the *mere* power in a miracle,
but only to that power as the sign and evidence of
a truth beyond it.

Wonder in the natural world, then, differs from that
wonder which has for its object the supernatural; but
it is not the less true that physical wonder is *an introduction* to the belief in the supernatural—in this way,
that it tends to raise in the mind a larger idea of
possibility—that idea which is expressed in the old
quotation, that "there are more things in heaven
and earth than are dreamed of in our philosophy;"
the notion of the potential as distinguished from
what is actual ; the sense of the unknown. The same
imagination which causes wonder also naturally produces this larger sense of possibility ; for indeed this

latter is a kind of *negative* imagination ; which without framing positive images or figures of things, or putting contingencies into shape, distinctly contemplates the idea of what is out of sight, and raises up a vivid sense of an unknown region. This negative imagination is in the affairs of this world the groundwork of a worldly sagacity ; for those who are conscious of surrounding darkness, though they do not shape to themselves the contents of it, catch the more readily at such facts as emerge to light, and are more cautious under their concealment ; and in spiritual things partakes of the nature of faith ; for a sense of the possible unknown enters largely into our notion of faith.

Nor is this connexion of the sense of wonder with this sense of possibility shewn by a common source only ; it is also proved by a common foe, which acts as the stupifier and suppressor of them both—viz. *custom.* Custom proverbially diminishes wonder. It is commonly noticed as a deteriorating effect of custom, that it benumbs the faculty of admiration. The case has been often put, that could we imagine ourselves with our mature faculties seeing nature for the first time, the sight of her glory would act irresistibly upon us like a splendid vision, and raise the most powerful emotions, but that we are accustomed to her and therefore our perception of her sublimity is deadened[a]. We would fain re-

[a] " Nil adeo magnum nec tam mirabile quicquam
Principio, quod non minuant mirarier omnes
Paulatim ; ut cœli clarum purumque colorem

lease ourselves from the thraldom of this stupor, unwind to its very last link the chain of custom by which we are bound, and win back the original perception; but we are held in the iron grasp of necessity. The effect of constant repetition is that the impression wears off, and our admiration becomes not so much admiring as the consciousness that we ought to admire. And yet if God, in planting us here, has set us down before a spectacle which is designed to elicit our admiration, it is plain that this defect of it is a confession that we are so far inadequate to the situation in which we are placed. I do not say that it may not be partially remedied by effort and culture. So the awe which moral and religious truths inspire wears off by repetition, till they become mere words; unless a counteracting force is found in our own minds. And thus the same person may exemplify the simultaneous growth of the strengthening and weakening effect of custom; deriving from this power an extraordinary facility and readiness in the use of particular faculties, while the same power has deadened in him the impression of every high truth.

> Quemque in se cohibent palantia sidera passim
> Lunæque et solis præclara luce nitorem :
> Omnia quæ si nunc primum mortalibus adsint
> Ex improviso ceu sint objecta repente ;
> Quid magis his rebus poterat mirabile dici,
> Aut minus ante quod auderent fore credere gentes ?
> Nil ut opinor, ita hæc species miranda fuisset ;
> Quom tibi jam nemo fessus satiate videndi
> Suspicere in cœli dignatur lucida templa."
>
> *Lucretius*, ii. 1027.

But if custom proverbially diminishes wonder, its effect in limiting the idea of possibility is equally proverbial : for it is the most familiar observation, that when we are accustomed to certain modes of doing things we get to think no other mode possible.   No incongruity so glaring but that it is harmony itself to the eye of custom ; no combination so true but that it looks to it an impossibility : because the mind has surrendered itself captive to one form and mould, and cannot conceive anything different from what it is.   And here I observe the questionable company in which the impression of immutability in the order of nature, i. e. of the possibility of nothing out of it, comes ; for the same principle that limits the sense of possibility also deadens the sense of wonder, and blunts the perception of beauty and truth.   There is an evident analogy in these two effects of custom ; its effect upon sensibility, and its effect upon belief. For I have shewn that the immutability of the order of nature is the decision of *custom,* only custom operating on the area of all nature instead of a small and local scale[b].

The sense of wonder then and the larger sense of possibility are connected together, as shewn both by a common source and common foe, while it is also

[b] " Quelle raison ont-ils de dire qu'on ne peut resusciter ? Quel est plus difficile de naître ou de resusciter, que ce qui n'a jamais été soit, ou que ce qui a été soit encore ? Est il plus difficile de venir en être que d'y revenir ? La coutume nous rend l'un facile ; le manque de coutume rend l'autre impossible. Populaire façon de juger."—*Pascal, ed. Faugere,* vol. ii. p. 323.

evident that the sense of possibility has a great deal
to do with the belief in the supernatural. The sense
of physical wonder therefore is through this medium intrinsically allied to and introductory to the
belief in the supernatural. It is an attitude of mind
which favours the latter belief. We may observe
that some old religions, e. g. the Scandinavian, and
the still earlier Aryan, seem to have been almost
founded upon the sense of physical wonder. At the
same time the sense of wonder in nature *may* stop
at a first stage, and not reach this further one which
naturally succeeds to it. Having followed its object
up to the gates of darkness, there it may rest, and it
is the more likely to do so if the mind of the poet is
under the influence of sensual passion or—what is a
better though still a bad reason—a deep prejudice
against the supernatural arising from passionate
indignation at the abuses of religion, and hypocrisy
in the profession of it.

But the miraculous having a natural ally in the
marvels of nature, has in the next place a still
stronger support and a more direct parallel in the
wonderful truths of the invisible world, which in
this inquiry we assume.

Upon this head, then, a ground has been recently
taken which deserves notice. "We are ready," it
has been said, "to admit the existence of an invisible
world totally different from this visible one ; we do
not object to anything inconceivable in that world ;
to the most mysterious and incomprehensible doctrines relating to it ; we leave untouched the whole

domain of the spiritual and invisible. But the existence of *another* world or order of things is another
thing altogether from the interruption of *this*. What
staggers our reason is not the invisible supernatural,
but the violation of physical law." (Note 1.)

This position, then, breaks down with respect to
the *doctrines* of revelation, for the simple reason that
those doctrines require miracles for their proof, and
therefore cannot consist with the rejection of the
miraculous. But how does it stand as a simple
comparison of the belief in the *miraculous* with
the belief in an *invisible* world?

It is quite true, then, that if there is any intrinsic
absurdity in the interruption of order as such, the
absurdity of the interruption of order in one world
is not cancelled by the existence of another and a
second world: and it is irrelevant to bring forward
the latter fact as any extenuation of the former.
But if the objection to the interruption of order is
only a certain resistance of the mind, in that case, in
admitting so astonishing a conception as the existence
of an invisible world we have already got over the
resistance of our minds in one most signal and remarkable instance; which is a precedent for our
getting over it in another instance. The natural
effect of the mind taking in one strange and surprising truth, is that it entertains less opposition to
another truth, on account of its being strange and surprising. The parallel holds in this important respect,
even if the two instances are distinguished from each
other in some points.

For what image can be presented to the mind which more confounds the imagination than personal existence after the body's dissolution ? What can go more counter to the impress of experience ? What, if we did not believe it to be the most serious of all facts, would be a more wild and eccentric conception, more like a dream of imagination, and a visionary creation of the poet, than the existence of another invisible world of created beings ? If a reflecting person is asked what it is absolutely easy to believe in, his answer is short,—Matter, and life connected with matter. If he is asked what it is not absolutely easy to believe in, his answer is equally short,—Everything else. The real belief in invisible things is, and is intended to be, and is represented in Scripture as being, not entirely easy, but requiring an effort and ascent of the mind. To a carnal imagination an invisible world is a contradiction in terms—another world besides the *whole* world. Nor is there much difference upon this head between the unseen world of natural religion and the unseen world of the Nicene Creed. The notion of a fixed and final state which absorbs all transitory life ; of an eternal world and consummation of all things which gathers into itself the whole spiritual population of the universe, and distributes into its infinite realms of endless life the countless millions of personal beings who pass into it out of this state of mortality—this or the Christian doctrine of another .world is a far sublimer conception than any pagan one ; but another world at all is a marvellous,

astonishing, and supernatural conception. And if we
go into particulars, we know that there must be forms
of life in that world, conditions of intelligence, sights
and objects in it which follow inconceivable types.
And we allow all this to be a reality, and innumerable hosts to be living now in that unseen sphere
which is only divided from us by the veil of the
flesh.   Now a person may say that a marvellous
condition of things in another world is not the same
with the miraculous in this, but can he embrace
the former conception as an actual truth, without a
general effect on his standard of credibility ?   Could
he avoid, while this idea was vividly upon him, feeling *less* resistance in the mind to the miraculous ?
Could a miracle look otherwise than *less* strange
to him with the strong impression of an existing
different world at the moment upon his mind ?   Has
not the obstacle of unlikeness to the known had to
give way, and has there not been already introduced
into his mind something wholly alien to the experimental contents of it ?   That which is repulsive in
a miracle is the eccentricity of type in the fact ; this
provokes the rejecting instinct, the antagonism of
custom or experience ; but in the admission of another
world he has already passed through the shock of
this collision.   If an eternal invisible world indeed
is admitted at all, it is so vast a conception, that this
visible world floats like a mere fragment upon the
unfathomable depths of that great mystery ; and its
laws assume a subordinate rank.

  When, then, the distinction is drawn between the

existence of another world and the violation of order in this world, between the invisible and inconceivable, and the miraculous, it must be remembered that in both cases alike there is a difficulty of belief, arising from the common source of that mental habit which visible order engenders. If, then, I yield to this habit in the one instance, why may I not yield to it in the other, and an invisible world become an unreal conception to me ? An historical imagination throws itself back into the Gospel era, pictures the people, the city, the passing day of the time and country; then when it has made that time as real as possible, as truly present time once as to-day is now, the doubt arises—How can I believe that this stupendous miracle was a real occurrence ? But exactly the same ordeal will disturb the belief in the invisible world. Let a person try to think *it* real ; let him say to himself—' Is the whole multitude that has passed away from this earthly scene since the race of man existed, in existence now, every one of them a living person in the realms of spirit ; is this person, is that person at this moment living, this great monarch, that sagacious statesman, that sublime philosopher or poet, that heroic soldier of antiquity ? Are the men of all ages, from the earliest pastoral tribe to the generation that has only just departed from us, enjoying a simultaneous existence in that world ? Are such things conceivable ?' As such thoughts crowd upon his mind will he not find it as difficult to think all this a reality, as he does the miraculous to be such ? And

yet if he does not think it a reality, what has he
to look forward to himself when this passing scene
is over ? This resistance, then, of the imagination
to the miraculous is either no test of its truth, or
a test which endangers the existence of the invisible
world as well.

When we reduce the broad distinction drawn between the invisible world and the miraculous as objects of belief to its first principle, that principle would
seem to be the principle of unity, or, if *we* may so
express it, *one world at a time*—that the two worlds
admitted to exist, must exist in absolute discon-
nexion. The objection felt against a miracle is that
it offends against this principle, that it puts the two
worlds into communication and junction with each
other, whereas they are intrinsically separate ; that
it is an interpolation from one order of things into
another, an injection of the supernatural into the
sphere of the natural, thus confounding two systems
which are perfectly distinct. Can the Supreme Mind
or Will in the invisible world declare itself by the
insertion of an anomalous fact in nature ? It is
boldly answered, No.

With respect, then, to this objection to a miracle,
that it is a transgression against the unity of nature,
I observe that nature, so far from being constructed
upon any principle of unity, or simplicity in its
contents, is itself the first great transgressor of that
principle, being as mixed and heterogeneous a composition as can be imagined ; and that therefore the
introduction of a miracle into this scene is not a

sudden incongruity, but that we are prepared for it by the miscellaneous and dissimilar physical and spiritual material of this world itself. It would indeed be a contradiction in terms to say that nature had anything in it *supernatural;* because the fact of the constant appearance of anything in nature makes it natural, and that only is supernatural which is out of the order of nature [c]. But though the contents of nature are all in common natural, as being its contents, they are of such totally different types, and some so much higher than others, that some as compared to and in relation to others are supernatural. A miracle is therefore no discordant isolation in a system of mere matter, but blends with and carries out the diversity of nature, which takes off the edge of the resistance to it.

It would be cognate to this observation to notice that which has been so much dwelt upon by many, that nature *borders* everywhere upon the supernatural; that the supernatural is not removed to an impassable distance from her, but stands at her very portals and touches her very outskirts. God is not *in* nature; nevertheless the evidence of a God is. But what does evidence imply? It im-

---

[c] We mean by the supernatural that which is out of the order of nature. God, angels, departed spirits, heaven and hell, are out of the order of nature because they are not in nature at all; a miracle is in nature in the sense of visibility, but is not in the order of nature; the invisible world therefore, and miracles, are supernatural. But life, the human soul, conscience, reason, will, are natural, because they are in the order of nature or part of our constant experience.

plies a light breaking through nature, revealing that which is the subject of this light; that nature is tracked to the edge of an incomprehensible truth. Wherever evidences of design, then, appear in the world, there nature borders upon mystery — the mystery of the Universal Mind and Will. And what, again, is the very infinity of the material world? Do we not think of it as a kind of impossibility, so extravagant and eccentric a fact it is, and replete with extravagant results? (Note 2.) Space itself, divested of the limit of sense, seems incredible. Yet this space is not a mere idea but a *fact* of this world; for not anywhere out of nature, but in whatever direction I point my finger, lies that enigma of infinite space which is as insoluble and mysterious as an apparition. But I revert to the topic of the mixed physical and spiritual contents of nature; which comes to a head in the situation of *man* in nature.

The record which this earth gives of itself shews that after a succession of stages and periods of vegetable and animal change, a new being made his appearance in nature. Those who profess to trace the bodily frame of man to a common animal source, still admit that the *rational and moral being* man is separated from all other animal natures by a chasm in the chain of causation which cannot be filled up; and that even if such a transition is only conceived as a leap from a lower to a higher level in the same species, such a leap is only another word for an inexplicable mystery. But such a

change cuts asunder the identity of the being
which precedes it and the being which succeeds it.
(Note 3.)

The first appearance, then, of man in nature was the
appearance of a new being in nature ; and this fact
was relatively to the then order of things miraculous;
no more physical account can be given of it than
could be given of a resurrection to life now.   What
more entirely new and eccentric fact indeed can be
imagined than a human soul first rising up amidst
an animal and vegetable world ? Mere consciousness—
was not that of itself a new world within the old
one ? Mere knowledge—that nature herself became
known to a being within herself, was not that the
same ? Certainly man was not all at once the skilled
interpreter of nature, and yet there is some interpretation of nature to which man as such is equal in
some degree.   He derives an impression from the
sight of nature which an animal does not derive ;
for though the material spectacle is imprinted on its
retina, as it is on man's, it does not see what man sees.
The sun rose, then, and the sun descended, the stars
looked down upon the earth, the mountains climbed
to heaven, the cliffs stood upon the shore, the same
as now, countless ages before a single being existed
who *saw* it.   The counterpart of this whole scene
was wanting—the understanding mind; that mirror
in which the whole was to be reflected ; and when
this arose, it was a new birth for creation itself, that
it became *known*,—an image in the mind of a conscious
being.   But even consciousness and knowledge were

a less strange and miraculous introduction into the world than conscience.

Thus wholly mysterious in his entrance into this scene, man is *now* an insulation in it : he came in by no physical law, and his freewill is in utter contrast to that law. What can be more incomprehensible, more heterogeneous, a more ghostly resident in nature, than the sense of right and wrong ? What is it ? whence is it ? The obligation of man to sacrifice himself for right is a truth which springs out of an abyss, the mere attempt to look down into which confuses the reason. (Note 4.) Such is the juxtaposition of mysterious and physical contents in the same system. Man is alone, then, in nature ; he alone of all the creatures communes with a Being out of nature ; and he divides himself from all other physical life by prophesying, in the face of universal visible decay, his own immortality.

But man's situation in nature being such, his original entrance a miracle, his sojourn an interpolation in the physical system, a world within a world—a life of consciousness, freewill, conscience, reason, communion with God, sense of immortality insulated as an anomaly in the midst of matter and material law ; is it otherwise than in accordance with this fact that the Divine method of training and educating this creature should be marked by distinctive and anomalous features ? If man himself is an exception to nature, why should not his providential treatment be the same ? Why should that not be upon occasions divided from the order of nature by the same mystery and chasm which divides its subject from it ? The being is an isolated being—isolated in his commencement and in his destiny—for whom miracles are designed. These Divine acts are concerned with the *education of man*, his instruction, the revelation of important truths to him, and his whole preparation and training for another world ; but this being the case, what does such a dispensation of miracles amount to but this, that the education of man has been conducted by communications with the mysterious fountain-head of his being, with the same extraordinary agency which produced his first entrance into the world. An anomalous situation bears corresponding fruits. " The soul of man," says Lord Bacon, " was not produced by heaven or earth, but was breathed immediately from God : so that the ways and proceedings of God with spirits are not included in nature ; that is in the laws of heaven and earth ; but are reserved to the law of His secret will and grace[d]."

It is indeed avowed by those who reduce man in common with matter to law, and abolish his insulation in nature, that upon the admission of freewill, the objection to the miraculous is over, and that it is absurd to allow exception to law in man, and reject it in nature.

What has been said may be collected and abridged in one pregnant position—that man while in this world is placed *in relations to another ;* which is a supernatural relationship within nature. Could we

[d] A Confession of Faith, vol. ii. p. 482.

imagine a person, who had not conceived the idea of religion, seeing for the first time the act of prayer —his surprise and perplexity at the sight would truly indicate what a remarkable insertion in nature this relationship to the unseen world was. So far from the two worlds standing totally apart, human reason itself places them in connexion ; and this connexion naturalizes a miracle. The same Divine policy which has imparted this double scope to reason, and instituted in this world our relations to another, only goes a step further when it gives us a message or communication from that world. The school which calls itself Secularist sees this result involved in this premiss, and therefore cuts off revelation at the root by denying that we have any relations to another world at all, by the maxim, " Act for the world in which you live ; while you are in this world you have nothing to do with another." (Note 5.)

To conclude, then, let us suppose an intelligent Christian of the present day asked, not what evidence he has of miracles, but how he can antecedently to all evidence think such amazing occurrences *possible ;* he would reply, ' You refer me to a certain sense of impossibility which you suppose me to possess, applying not to mathematics but to facts. Now on this head I am conscious of a certain natural resistance in my mind to events unlike the order of nature. But I resist many things which I know to be certain ; infinity of space, infinity of time, eternity past, eternity future, the very idea of a God

and another world. If I take mere resistance therefore for denial, I am confined in every quarter of
my mind, I cannot carry out the very laws of reason,
I am placed under conditions which are obviously
false. I conclude, therefore, that I may resist and
believe at the same time. If Providence has implanted in me a certain expectation of uniformity
or likeness in nature, there is implied in that very
expectation resistance to an *un*like event, which
resistance does not cease even when upon evidence
I *believe* the event, but goes on as a mechanical
impression, though the reason counterbalances it.
Resistance therefore is not disbelief, unless by an
act of my own reason I *give* it an absolute veto,
which I do *not* do. My reason is clear upon the
point, that there is no disagreement between itself
and a miracle as such.'

Such a reply would be both true itself, and also
a caution against a mistake which both younger
and older minds are apt to fall into, that of confounding the resistance of impression to a miracle
with the veto of reason. Upon the facts of the
Gospel history being first realised, they necessarily
excite this resistance to a greater extent than they
did when they were mainly accepted by habit; but
this resistance is in itself no disbelief, though some
by the very mistake of confounding it with disbelief
at last make it such, when in consequence of this
misconception they begin to doubt about their own
faith.

Nor is it dealing artificially with ourselves to exert

a force upon our minds against the false certainty of the resisting imagination—such a force as is necessary to enable reason to stand its ground, and bend back again that spring of impression against the miraculous which has illegally tightened itself into a law to the understanding. Reason does not always prevail spontaneously and without effort even in questions of belief; so far from it, that the question of faith against reason may often be more properly termed the question of reason against imagination. It does not seldom require faith to believe reason, isolated as she may be amid vast irrational influences, the weight of custom, the power of association, the strength of passion, the vis inertiæ of sense, the mere force of the uniformity of nature as a spectacle—those influences which make up that power of the world which Scripture always speaks of as the antagonist of faith.

LECTURE IV.

HEBREWS XI. 3.

Through faith we understand that the worlds were framed by the word of God.

THE peculiarity of the argument of miracles is that it begins and ends with an assumption; I mean an assumption relatively to that argument. We assume the existence of a personal Deity prior to the proof of miracles in the religious sense; but with this assumption the question of miracles is at an end; because such a Being has necessarily the power to suspend those laws of nature which He has Himself enacted.

For the Divine *power* assumed, vain would it be to throw the impossibility of such an interruption on the Divine will—as if the act were contrary to the Divine perfections; and as if it argued inconsistency and unsteadiness in the Deity, having established the order of nature, to disturb it by exceptional acts. For it can argue no inconstancy in the Divine will to institute an order of nature for one purpose and

suspend it for another. The essential uniformity
and regularity of Divine action is a purely arbitrary
conception, and certainly one not borrowed from
any criterion of excellence in human conduct. God
cannot depart indeed from His absolute purpose,
but it does not follow from that, that an unvaried
course of action *is* His purpose. The order of nature is not founded upon a theatrical principle, as
if it were a grand procession, any interruption of
which was in itself desecration : its merit lies in
its utility ; it is necessary for human life, and animal life too, which otherwise could not be sustained,
because there would be no knowing what to expect
or what to provide against from hour to hour. But
for this practical use, nothing would signify less than
whether the whole material universe were in order
or disorder. But if the merit of the order of nature
lies in its use, there is no reason why it should not
be suspended, if there is use in suspending it.

The question of miracles is thus shut up within
the inclosure of one assumption, viz. that of the
existence of a God. When we state this, however,
it is replied that this very conception of God, as
a personal omnipotent Being, is a peculiar conception
for which there is no evidence in material nature.
'Everybody,' it is said, 'must collect from the order
and harmony of the physical universe the existence
of a God, but in acknowledging a God, we do
not thereby acknowledge this peculiar or doctrinal
conception of a God. We see in the structure of
nature a Mind, a universal Mind, but still a Mind

which only operates and expresses itself by law. Nature only does and only can inform us of mind *in* nature, the partner and correlative of organized matter.   Nature, therefore, can speak to the existence of a God in this sense, and can speak to the omnipotence of God in a sense coinciding with the actual facts of nature; but in no other sense does nature witness to the existence of an Omnipotent Supreme Being.   Of a Universal Mind out of nature nature says nothing, and of an Omnipotence which does not possess an inherent limit in nature, she says nothing either.   And therefore that conception of a Supreme Being which represents Him as a Spirit independent of the physical universe, and able from a standing-place external to nature to interrupt its order, is a conception of God for which we must go elsewhere.   That conception is obtained from revelation, which is asserted to be proved by miracles.   But that being the case, this doctrine of Theism rests itself upon miracles, and therefore miracles cannot rest upon this doctrine of Theism.' (Note i.)

If the premiss then of this argument is correct, and this doctrine of Theism is from its standing-ground in nature thrown back upon the ground of revelation, this consequence follows; and more, for miracles being thrown back upon the same ground on which Theism is, the whole evidence of revelation becomes a vicious circle; and the fabric is left suspended in space, revelation resting on miracles and miracles resting on revelation.   But is this premiss correct?

It is then to be admitted that historically, and looking to the general actual reception of it, this conception of God was obtained from revelation. Not from
the first dawn of history to the spread of revelation in
the world, do we see in mankind at large any belief
in such a Being. The vulgar believed in many gods,
the philosopher believed in a Universal Cause ; but
neither believed in God. The philosopher only
regarded the Universal Cause as the spring of
the Universal machine, which was necessary to the
working of all the parts, but was not thereby raised
to a separate order of being from them. Theism
was discussed as a philosophical not as a religious
question, as one rationale among others of the origin
of the material universe, but as no more affecting
practice than any great scientific hypothesis does
now. Theism was not a test which separated the
orthodox philosopher from the heterodox, which
distinguished belief from disbelief ; it established no
breach between the two opposing theorists ; it was
discussed amicably as an open question ; and well
it might be, for of all questions there was not one
which could make less practical difference to the
philosopher, or, upon his view, to anybody, than
whether there was or was not a God. Nothing
would have astonished him more than, when he had
proved in the lecture hall the existence of a God,
to have been told to worship Him. 'Worship whom?'
he would have exclaimed : 'worship what ? worship
how ?' Would you picture him indignant at the
polytheistic superstition of the crowd and mani-

festing some spark of the fire of St. Paul, " when he saw the city wholly given to idolatry," you could not be more mistaken. He would have said that you did not see a plain distinction ; that the crowd was right on the religious question, and the philosopher right on the philosophical ; that however men might uphold in argument an infinite abstraction, they could not worship it ; and that the hero was much better fitted for worship than the Universal Cause ; fitted for it not in spite of but in consequence of his want of true divinity. The same question was decided in the same way in the speculations of the Brahmans. There the Supreme Being figures as a characterless impersonal essence, the mere residuum of intellectual analysis, pure unity, pure simplicity. No temple is raised to him, no knee is bended to him. Without action, without will, without affection, without thought, he is the substratum of everything, himself a nothing. The Universal Soul is the unconscious Omnipresent *Looker-on ;* the complement, as co-extensive spectator, of the universal drama of nature ; the motionless mirror upon which her boundless play and sport, her versatile postures, her multitudinous evolutions are reflected, as the image of the rich and changing sky is received into the passive bosom of the lake. Thus the idea of God, so far from calling forth in the ancient world the idea of worship, ever stood in antagonism with it : the idol was worshipped because he was not God, God was not worshipped because He was. One small nation alone out of all antiquity worshipped God, believed the universal Being to be a personal Being. That nation was looked upon as a most eccentric and unintelligible specimen of humanity for doing so; but this whimsical fancy, as it appeared in the eyes of the rest, was cherished by it as the most sacred deposit, it was the foundation of its laws and polity; and from this narrow stock this conception was engrafted upon the human race.

But although this conception of the Deity has been received through the channel of the Bible, what communicates a truth is one thing, what proves it is another : the truth once possessed is seen to rest upon grounds of natural reason. The theory of a blind plastic nature might account for some imaginable world, but does not account for this world. For we naturally attribute to the design of a personal Being, a contrivance which is directed to the existence of a personal Being ; if an elaborate bodily organization issues in the life of myself—a person, I cannot avoid concluding that there is at the bottom of it the intention of a personal Being that I should live. From personality at one end, I infer personality at the other ; and cannot suppose that the existence which is contrived should be intelligent and moral, and the contriver of it a blind irrational force. The proof of a personal Deity does not rest upon physical organization alone, but on physical organization adapted to the wants of moral beings. The Bible therefore *assumes* this truth rather than formally communicates it ; the first chapter of Genesis proceeds upon it as proved ; and the prophet though he speaks as a prophet, still also speaks as a man on this subject. He proclaims this idea of God as a plain truth of human reason, which the world did not see only because it was blinded by folly; he ridicules polytheism with indignation and sarcasm; he foretells the ultimate universal worship of the One God. He sees with the eye of prophecy, and of reason too, that the true idea of God cannot remain for ever in a corner, but must some day find access to the whole mind of the human race, which is made for its reception; to the expulsion of the false religions of the world.

Not, however, that the existence of a God is so clearly seen by reason as to dispense with faith (Note 2); not from any want of cogency in the reasons, but from the amazing nature of the conclusion —that it is so unparalleled, transcendent, and inconceivable a truth to believe. It requires trust to commit oneself to the conclusion of any reasoning, however strong, when such as this is the conclusion; to put enough dependence and reliance upon any premisses to accept upon the strength of them so immense a result. The issue of the argument is so astonishing, that if we do not tremble for its safety, it must be on account of a practical principle in our minds which enables us to *confide* and trust in reasons, when they are really strong and good ones. Which principle of trust is faith—the same principle by which we repose in a witness of good character who informs us of a marvellous occurrence—so marvellous that the trust in his testimony has to be sustained by a certain effort of the reasonable will.

The belief, therefore, in the existence of a God is not because it is an act of reason, any the less an act of faith.   Because faith *is* reason, only reason acting under particular circumstances.   When reason draws conclusions which are in accordance with experience, which have their parallels in the facts which we are conversant with in the order of nature and in common life, then reason is called reason : when reason draws conclusions which are not backed by experience, and which are not paralleled by similar facts within our ordinary cognizance, then reason is called faith.   Faith, when for convenience' sake we do distinguish it from reason, is not distinguished from reason by the want of premisses, but by the nature of the conclusions.   Are our conclusions of the customary type ?   Then custom imparts the full sense of security.   Are they not of the customary but of a strange and unknown type ?   Then the mechanical sense 'of security is wanting, and a certain trust is required for reposing in them, which we call faith. But that which draws these conclusions is in either case reason.   We infer, we go upon reasons, we use premisses in either case.   The premisses of faith are not so palpable as those of ordinary reason, but they are as real and solid premisses all the same.   Our faith in the existence of a God and a future state is founded upon reasons, as much so as the belief in the commonest kind of facts.   The reasons are in themselves as strong, but because the conclusions are marvellous and are not seconded and backed by known parallels or by experience, we do not so passively

acquiesce in them : there is an exertion of confidence
in depending upon them and assuring ourselves of
their force. The inward energy of the reason has to
be evoked, when she can no longer lean upon the
outward prop of custom, but is thrown back upon
herself, and the intrinsic force of her premisses. Which
reason not leaning upon custom is faith : she obtains
the latter name when she depends entirely upon her
own insight into certain grounds, premisses, and evidences, and follows it, though it leads to transcendent, unparalleled, and supernatural conclusions.

We may remark that when reason even in ordinary
life or in physical inquiry is placed under circumstances at all analogous to those of religion, reason
becomes, as a consequence of that situation, a kind of
faith. We have a very different way of yielding to
reasons in common life, according as the conclusions
to which they lead accord with or diverge from the
type of custom. We accept them as a matter of
course in the former case, it requires an effort to
accept them and place dependence upon them in the
latter; which dependence upon them in the latter case
therefore is a kind of faith. Indeed, the remark may
be made that a kind of faith appears to be essential
for practical confidence in any reasoning whatever
and any premisses, when we are thrown back upon
ourselves and do not act mechanically in concert with
others. And we frequently see persons who, when
they are in possession of the best arguments, and,
what is more, understand those arguments, are still
shaken by almost any opposition, because they want

the faculty to *trust* an argument, when they have got
one ; which is not the case with those who can both
understand and trust too ; wherein we see the link
which connects faith with self-confidence and strength
of will.   In religion, then, where conclusions are so
totally removed from the type of custom, and are so
vast and stupendous, this applies the more strongly ;
but in truth *all* untried conclusions need faith, whatever strong arguments there may be for them.   When
a scientific man sees various premises conspiring to
direct him to some new truth or law in nature, the
aptness with which these coincide and fall in with
each other may amount to such strong evidence, that
he may feel virtually certain of his discovery, and yet
he does not feel it quite secure till it has stood the
test of some crowning experiment.   His reason, then,
in the interim is faith, he trusts his premises, he
feels practically sure that they cannot mislead him,
he sees in their whole mode of combining and con-
curring a warrant for the issue, although the final
criterion is still in prospect.   Such a condition of
mind is analogous to that of the religious believer,
who perceives in nature, moral and physical, (for we
are speaking only of natural religion at present,) the
strongest arguments for certain religious conclusions
—such as the existence of a God, and a future life ;
and yet waits for that final certification of these
great truths, which will be given in another world.
" For we are saved by hope, but hope that is seen is
not hope : for what a man seeth, why doth he yet
hope for ?   But if we hope for that we see not, then

do we with patience wait for it." Faith, then, is *unverified* reason ; reason which has not yet received the verification of the final test, but is still expectant.

Indeed, does not our heart bear witness to the fact that to believe in a God is an exercise of faith? That the universe was produced by the will of a personal Being, that its infinite forces are all the power of that one Being, its infinite relations the perception of one Mind—would not this, if any truth could, demand the application of the maxim—*Credo quia impossibile?* Look at it only as a conception, and does the wildest fiction of the imagination equal it? No premisses, no arguments therefore, can so accommodate this truth to us, as not to leave the belief in it an act of mental ascent and trust; of faith as distinguished from sight. *Divest* reason of its trust, and the universe stops at the impersonal stage—there is no God. And yet if the first step in religion is the greatest, how is it that the freest and boldest speculator rarely declines it? How is it that the most mysterious of all truths is a universally accepted one? What is it which guards this truth? What is it which makes men shrink from denying it? Why is atheism a crime? Is it that authority still reigns upon one question, and that the voice of all ages is too potent to be withstood?

But this belief, however obtained, being assumed in the argument of miracles, in discussing this argument we have to do not with the proof of a personal Deity, but only with the natural consequences of this belief, supposed to be true. To ex-

tract consequences indeed out of admissions before
the sense of such admissions is defined or understood,
is an illegitimate proceeding; and from the mere
admission of a God in some sense, we could not
thus argue. But if not only the existence of a Deity
in some sense is admitted, but if that sense is defined,
and the religious conception of the Deity as a moral
and personal Being is admitted to be true; this is a
ground upon which we may fairly argue, and from
which we may deduce consequences; that is to say,
we may examine what the belief means, and what is
necessarily and naturally implied in this belief supposed to be true.

But this conception of a God necessarily implies
omnipotence; because the Universal Cause must have
power, and universal power, if He has will; which,
according to this religious and moral conception of
Him, He *has*. No will, no power indeed, for our very
idea of power implies will; but together with will
the Universal Being possesses power, and power com-
mensurate with Himself; including the particular
power involved in a miracle. For any cause has *as
such* the power to suspend its own effects, depending
as these do altogether upon it, provided only it has
the *will;* if voluntary power set them going the
same power can stop them. The Universal Cause
therefore has the same power; and either God has will
and He can interrupt the order of nature; or He has
not a will and He is not in the religious sense God.

A personal Deity, therefore, can suspend the order
of nature; but all admit a personal Deity who admit

the principle of religious worship. We use the word 'personal' only to denote that in the Deity which constitutes Him more than a force, to express that He is a moral Being, a Being with will. All worship implies such a personal Being to whom it is addressed. For I do not, of course, include under worship that passionate contemplation of nature which is sometimes called worship. The ecstasy of atheistic poets at the sight of nature was the effect, indeed, of beholding a real manifestation of the Divine glory; nor can we witness without emotion their absorption in the sublime vision and spectacle, which transfixed them and made them mute, imparting to their wild insatiable life its one solitary rest; but this ecstasy was not worship, because it only contemplated the Divine glory as impressed upon matter, and not in relation to its Fountainhead. Worship as a religious act implies a personal object. *Can* we—I do not say ought, but can we worship a force, a law, a principle? One who professed to do so would stand convicted not of a foolish act, or of a fanciful act, or of a superstitious act, but of a total mistake in imagining that he had done the act at all. Because it is an impossible act. If men worship then, if they pray, if they address themselves to the Deity, if they make petitions to Him, they acknowledge Him in that very act as a personal Deity. Whatever doubts mere philosophers and inquirers may entertain, believers and worshippers, those who admit, rather I should say who demand religion, who feel it to be necessary for them, a want of their nature, which nothing else can supply—in a word, religious men— grant a Deity in the special sense now mentioned ; but in this special sense is involved tl.e consequence now mentioned, viz. that a Deity in this sense must possess omnipotence, and power over nature, to suspend her laws.

The primary difficulty of philosophy indeed relating to the Deity is action at all ; from the inconceivableness of which, in connexion with the Divine nature, it was that the ancient subtle philosophical conception of God as a mere universal *substratum* arose. If action is conceded at all, there is no difficulty about miraculous action. But prayer certainly implies a Deity who can act, who can do something for us ; prayer, therefore, concedes the first great point relating to the Deity, and in conceding that concedes the whole. What, indeed, is a Deity deprived of miraculous action but a Deity deprived of action ; and what is a Deity deprived of action but an impersonal force which is no object of prayer ? (Note 3.)

Is this consequence then of the acceptance of a personal Deity intercepted by saying that this special conception of a Deity is derived from " mystery and faith," and that "all religion as such ever has been and must be a thing entirely *sui generis?"* (Note 4.) No : because the evidence or the foundation of a conception has nothing to do with the natural consequence of that conception if admitted ; the pledge which is contained in believing and acting upon that conception. Let the believer say that his belief in such a Being is founded upon "mystery and faith;" well, but upon whatever ground he believes this truth, he believes it; and if he believes it, he believes it with its natural consequence involved in it. Can it be said that religion does not interfere with physics? (Note 5.) Not, if religion be the belief here mentioned; for this belief is the belief in a God who *can* interfere with nature,—in a Universal Cause who has a *will;* and who has, with that will, the *power* to suspend physical effects.

On the fundamental question, indeed, of the Divine Omnipotence, we assent to some known familiar limitations; such as that God cannot do what is contrary to His will and nature, and cannot do what is contradictory to necessary truth: but these are no precedents for the kind of limitation which the withdrawal of an interrupting physical power from the Divine Omnipotence is. Because these are only verbal and apparent limitations; power implying will, it is no real restraint upon Divine power that it cannot oppose will; and a contradiction to necessary truth being nothing, nothing is taken away in the abstraction of the power to effect it. Whereas the other is a real and actual limitâtion of the Divine power—unless indeed it is assumed that the order of nature is necessary, and therefore its case a case of necessary or mathematical truth. Upon the assumption that these two cases stand upon the same ground, it would indeed follow that the denial of the Divine power to interrupt the order of nature was no more a real limitation of it, than the denial of the power to contradict a mathematical truth. But this assumption is self-evidently untenable and absurd.

If, therefore, the power of interrupting the order of nature is to be severed from the stock of the Divine Omnipotence, it can only be done by one of two conceptions, either the conception of an *impersonal* Deity, or the conception of a confessedly and avowedly *limited* Deity—limited in reality, I mean, and not only verbally. With the former I have upon my assumption nothing to do. The latter is an attempted compromise between an Omnipotent God and no God : denying Him absolute power over the material universe, while professing to leave Him such power as to constitute Him an object of prayer and worship.

A limited Deity was a recognised conception of antiquity. Confounded and astonished by the vastness of a real Omnipotence and the inconceivableness of the acts involved in it, the ancients took refuge in this idea as all that reason could afford of that Godship which reason could not deny. Two great difficulties lay at the bottom of this conception, the creation of matter and the existence of evil; the former producing the doctrine of the coeternity of matter with the Deity; the latter producing the doctrine of the coeternity of evil with the Deity, as a rival, antagonist, and check upon Him : whether in the modified form of an original irrational soul or refractoriness of matter; or the more developed form of Ditheism and Manichæanism. Of these two great ancient difficulties one is now obsolete. A man of science now only professes to ground an hesitation to admit a *beginning* in nature upon observation, not upon any antecedent objection to creation. It is indeed an instructive fact, and shews how little dependence can be placed upon first-sight notions of impossibility which reign supreme in many minds for their day, that this great impossibility of antiquity, the difficulty of difficulties which had brooded like a nightmare upon the philosophers of ages, was dismissed by Hume in these two words of a footnote,— " That impious maxim of ancient philosophy *ex nihilo nihil fit*, by which the creation of matter was excluded, ceases to be a maxim according to this philosophy[b]." The existence of evil, however, is no obsolete difficulty, but still retains its ground, and suggests even to modern perplexity the idea of a limited Deity. One who excepts the physical world from the Divine power may still appeal to the alleged parallel of evil. ' Here, at any rate,' he may say, ' is no shadow or fiction, or empty abstraction ; evil is not, like a mathematical contradiction, a *nothing*, however called so by the Schoolmen, but plainly something, a fact, a palpable fact. The inability to prevent evil, therefore, cannot be dealt with as a verbal limit only to the Divine power, like the inability to accomplish a mathematical contradiction ; it is a real limit : and one real limit is a precedent for another.'

[b] Enquiry concerning the Human Understanding, sect. 12.

But the answer to this is, that with reference to the higher ends of the universe, we do not know that evil is *not* necessary, and its prevention a contradiction to necessary truth—that we do not know, therefore, that the inability to dispense with it does *not* come under the head of a verbal limit to Divine omnipotence, like the inability to accomplish a mathematical contradiction.

Assuming the existing constitution of man, we *see* the necessity here mentioned for evil. Any plain man would say that for high moral virtue to be produced without evil, either as a contingency in the shape of trial or a fact in the shape of suffering, was upon the existing constitution of man an utter impossibility : that upon this datum evil was a condition of the problem.

Nor is this only a didactic truth of the moralist, but a descriptive one of poetry. Dramatic poetry, by which I mean all which takes man and human character as its subject, produces its captivating impression and effect, by a representation of the issue of the struggle with evil ; by the final image which it leaves on the mind of the human character as it comes out of that struggle, strengthened by difficulty, softened by grief, or calmed by misfortune. The truth it communicates is the same as the moralist's, only put into a pictorial instead of a disciplinarian form, and intended mainly to impart not the sense of responsibility, but pleasure. The spectacle which delights is a human character which is the production of trial.

Secure for the moment ourselves, we enjoy the
sight of the sublime result of the contest with evil
in others, the conclusion in which the process of pain
issues.   And thus it is that men admire the very
opposites of themselves.   The proud who shrink
as from a knife from their own slightest humiliation,
are captivated by the spectacle of humility in another.   The moral images of the ambitious man,
which he raises in his own mind to look at with
affection, are they likenesses of himself?   No: they
are the suffering, the sad, the fallen, those who by
adversity have been raised above the world.   He is
a pleased beholder of the moral effect of life's evils,
himself only grasping at its prizes;   and the very
deprivations which are death to himself, are his
gratification in their result upon the character of
another.   He bears witness against himself, and " delights in the law of God after the inner man, but
sees another law in his members."

Assuming the existing constitution then of man,
we *account* for evil—for evil in the general, though
the particulars are beyond us—as a necessary contingency attaching to trial, a necessary fact for discipline.   The Bible in assuming this constitution of
man, assumes with it this solution of evil, and in-
corporates evil in the Divine scheme.   The ancient
philosopher had but an imperfect discernment of the
necessity of evil even *upon* this assumption, even
under the actual conditions of man's nature;   not
being able to rid himself completely of the idea
that human nature could be cured by philosophy,

instead of by the chastening rod. He did but half see that which the Christian philosopher sees with the utmost distinctness—the use *in fact* of evil; the want of which partial satisfaction was the cause of the desperateness of his rationale of evil, as a rival of the Deity; for had he distinctly seen its *conditional* necessity, he would not have despaired about the *root* of the enigma.

It is indeed true that to the question why man *was* so constituted as to render evil thus necessary, no answer can be given. *Upon* this condition evil is no insoluble mystery, but is accounted for; upon abstract grounds it *is* an insoluble mystery. The argument, however, of the Divine Omnipotence does not require that we should know that evil *is* necessary; but only that we should not know that it is *not:* because even in the latter case we are under the check of a prohibition; we cannot assert that the existence of evil does *not* stand upon the same grounds as necessary truth, and therefore that the inability to dispense with it is *not*, like the inability to contradict necessary truth, a mere verbal limitation of the Divine power.

The same answer applies to the objection to the Divine Omnipotence arising from man's free-will. Is a physical limitation of that Divine attribute, it may be asked, any greater limitation than the moral one involved in the power of the human will to resist the Divine? But although the existence o. such a power in the creature is incomprehensible to us, we do not know that his possession of this liberty is not necessary for the ultimate formation of his moral character; and therefore that the formation of that character without it is not a contradiction to necessary truth; analogous to a mathematical absurdity.

Does an opponent demand the same rights of ignorance on the side of his own position? They are not enough for him; for his argument requires that he should make the positive assertion of a contradiction to necessary truth in a suspension of physical law; nor indeed can he claim them, for by our reason we see there is no such contradiction.

The conception of a limited Deity then, i.e. a Being really circumscribed in power, and not verbally only by a confinement to necessary truth, is at variance with our fundamental idea of a God; to depart from which is to retrograde from modern thought to ancient, and to go from Christianity back again to Paganism. The God of ancient religion was either not a personal Being or not an omnipotent Being; the God of modern religion is both. For, indeed, civilization is not opposed to faith. The idea of the Supreme Being in the mind of European society now is more primitive, more childlike, more imaginative, than the idea of the ancient Brahman or Alexandrian philosopher: it is an idea which both of these would have derided as the notion of a child—a *negotiosus Deus*, who interposes in human affairs and answers prayers. So far from the philosophical conception of the Deity having advanced with civilization, and the poetical receded, the philosophical has receded and the poetical advanced. The God of whom it is said, "Are not five sparrows sold for two farthings, and not one of them is forgotten before God; but even the very hairs of your head are numbered," is the object of modern worship. Nor, again, has civilization shewn any signs of rejecting doctrine. Certain ages are indeed called the ages of faith; but the bulk of society in *this* age believes that it lives under a supernatural dispensation; and accepts truths which are not less supernatural, though they have more proof, than some doctrines of the middle ages: and if so, *this* is an age of faith. It is true most people do not live up to their faith now; neither did they in the middle ages.

Has not modern philosophy, again, shewn both more strength and acuteness, and also more faith, than the ancient? I speak of the main current. Those ancient thinkers who reduced the Supreme Being to a negation, with all their subtlety wanted strength, and settled questions by an easier test than that of modern philosophy. The merit of a modern metaphysician is, like that of a good chemist or naturalist, accurate observation in noting the facts of mind. Is there a contradiction in the idea of creation? Is there a contradiction in the idea of a personal Infinite Being? He examines his own mind, and if he does not see one, he passes the idea. But the ancient speculators decided, without examination of the true facts of mind, by a kind of philosophical fancy; and according to this loose criterion, the creation of matter and a personal Infinite Being were impossibilities ; for they mistook the inconceivable for the impossible. And thus a stringent test has admitted what a loose but capricious test discarded ; and the true notion of God has issued safe out of the crucible of modern metaphysics. Reason has shewn its strength, but then it has turned that strength back upon itself ; it has become its own critic ; and in becoming its own critic it has become its own check.

If the belief then in a personal Deity lies at the bottom of all religious and virtuous practice, and if the removal of it would be a descent for human nature, the withdrawal of its inspiration and sup-port, and a fall in its whole standard ; the failure of the very breath of moral life in the individual and in society ; the decay and degeneration of the very stock of mankind ;—does a theory which would withdraw miraculous action from the Deity interfere with that belief? If it would, it is but prudent to count the cost of that interference. Would a Deity deprived of miraculous action pos-sess action at all? And would a God who cannot act be a God ? If this would be the issue, such an issue is the very last which religious men can desire. The question here has been all throughout, not whe-ther upon any ground, but whether upon a religious ground and by religious believers, the miraculous as such could be rejected. But to that there is but one answer, that it is impossible in reason to separate religion from the supernatural, and upon a religious basis to overthrow miracles.

LECTURE V.

ACTS I. 8.

*Ye shall be witnesses unto Me both in Jerusalem, and in all
Judæa, and in Samaria, and unto the uttermost parts of the
earth.*

THE force of testimony rests upon a ground of
reason ; because our reason enables us to discern
men's characters and understandings—that they are
honest men and men of sufficient understanding ;
which being assumed, the truth of their reports is
implied and included in this original observation
respecting the men themselves, and may be depended
upon so far as this observation may be depended
upon.   It is true we believe many things which
are told us without previous knowledge of the
persons who are our informants, but ordinarily
we assume honesty and competency in men, unless
we have reason to suppose the contrary.

But such being the nature of testimony, it may
be asked, ' Do we receive through this second-hand
channel of knowledge, truths upon which our eternal
interests depend ?   In other words, can we suppose

that these truths would be embodied in visible occurrences, which can only reach us through testimony ? Can we think that our own relations to
the Divine Being depend upon such a medium,
that is to say, upon facts brought to us through
it ? that human testimony interposes between ourselves and God, and that His communications to us
travel by this circuitous route, going back to a
distant point in history, and returning thence to
us by a train of historical evidence ?' The answer
to this is, that certainly testimony does not satisfy
all the wants of the human mind in the matter of
evidence, because upon the supposition that a most
wonderful event of the deepest importance to us
has taken place, we have naturally a longing for
direct and immediate knowledge of that event, as
distinguished from knowing of it through the
medium of other persons, especially if the intervening chain of testimony is long. In the matter
of evidence, however, the question is not what
satisfies, but what is sufficient ; and therefore if God
has adopted any medium or channel of evidence by
which to convey His communications to us, all that
we are practically concerned to ask is—is it a *reasonable* one ? is it a proof of a natural force and
weight, such as is accommodated to the constitution
of our minds ? If testimony be this kind of proof,
there is nothing incongruous in its being chosen to
convey even the most important spiritual truths to
us ; it is enough if, however secondary a channel, it
does convey them to us.

It is to be admitted, however, that the force of testimony has certain inherent limits or conditions when applied to the proof of miracles. And first, I would observe *in limine*, that that which testimony is capable of proving must be something within the bounds of reason; i. e. something which, in the fair exercise of reasonable supposition, we can imagine possible. The question is sometimes put—'What if so many apparently competent witnesses were to assure you that they had seen such and such a miracle—mentioning the most monstrous, absurd, fantastic, and ludicrous confusion of nature, of which mere arbitrary conception could raise the idea in the mind—would you believe them?' But the test of mere conception is not in its own nature a legitimate test of the force of testimony; because conception or fancy is a simply wild and unlimited power of imagining anything whatever, and putting together any forms we please in our minds; but such a power is in no sort of correspondence with actual possibility in nature. In the universe, under the Divine government, there can be nothing absolutely wild or outlandish: if physical law does not constitute the bound of possibility, some measure of possibility there must be, and our very idea of God is such a measure. Pure, boundless enormity, then, is itself incredible, and therefore out of the reach of testimony, *although* it is imaginable. Nor indeed is the supposition of sound and competent testimony to such merely imaginable extravagancies and excesses of deviation from order a lawful one, because it is practically impossible that there should be a body of men of good repute for understanding and honesty to witness to what is intrinsically incredible. We are only concerned with the miraculous under that form and those conditions under which it has actually by trustworthy report taken place, as subordinated to what has been called " a general law of wisdom," i. e. to a wise plan and design in the Divine Mind ; under which check the course of miracles has, so to speak, kept near to nature, just diverging enough for the purpose and no more.

But besides this preliminary limit to the force of testimony, which excludes simple monstrosity and absurdity, another condition has also been attached to it by divines, which applies to it in the case of any miracle whatever, viz. that all evidence of miracles assumes the belief in the existence of a God. (Note 1.) It may be urged that, according to the argument of design (which does not apply to the coincidences in nature only, but to any case of coincidence whatever), a miracle, supposing it true, *proves* and need not assume a supernatural agent. But were this granted, the evidence of a Universal Being must still rest on a universal basis ; a miracle being only a particular local occurrence ; and therefore for the proof of a God we should still have to fall back upon the evidence of nature. Even the imaginary case, which has been put, of its being written in our very sight on the sky by a wonder-working agency—There is a God, could not upon this account prove the existence of a God. But even could a miracle legitimately prove it, it must still assume the belief in it to begin with ; because it could not prove it to an atheist who had *already withstood* the proof of it in nature. A mind that had not been convinced by the primary evidence of a Deity, must consistently reject such a second evidence, and therefore unless a man brings the belief in a God to a miracle, he does not get it from the miracle.

But the admission of divines that the evidence of miracles assumes the belief in a God was not made with a view to an imaginary instance, but with reference to the actual situation of mankind at large upon this subject, and the medium through which in the nature of the case the evidence of miracles must ordinarily be received, which is testimony. This admission is based upon the relations in which an atheist necessarily stands to human *testimony* upon this subject, and the mode in which his want of belief in a God affects the value of that testimony.

The effect, then, of atheism upon the value and weight of human testimony to miracles must be, as regards the atheist himself, that of invalidating such testimony, and depriving it of all cogency. For consider the light in which an atheist must regard the whole body and system of religious belief in the world, and the whole mass of religious believers, so far as they are affected by their belief. What other view can he take of religion but that it is simple fanaticism, or of religious men but that they are well meaning but unreasonable and mistaken enthusiasts ? Let a man decide, not that

there is not a God, but only that there is no evidence
that there is one, and what is the immediate result?
He looks around him, and he sees that a conclusion
which in his own judgment stands upon no rational
grounds, is embraced by all religious people with the
firmest practical certainty, and treated as a truth,
which it is almost madness to doubt of. But though
he could not condemn men as enthusiasts for taking
a different view of evidence from himself, provided
they only maintained their own view of the question
as the preferable and more probable one, he must
look upon this absolute unhesitating and vehement
faith in that which he considers to be without rational proof, as passionate and blind zeal. He must
regard systematic devotion, constant addresses, prayer
and service to a Being of whose existence there is
not evidence, as downright fanaticism. But this
being the case, he must necessarily estimate the
testimony of such persons in matters specially *connected with* this credulous belief of theirs, at a very
light rate : upon his own ground it is only reasonable
that he should treat with the greatest suspicion all
reports of miraculous occurrences from religious believers ; whose evidence upon ordinary subjects he
will admit to be as sound as his own, inasmuch
as in the common affairs of life they shew discretion
enough ; but whom he must, upon his own hypothesis, regard as utterly untrustworthy upon the
particular topic of religion. *That* is their weak
point, the subject upon which they go wild. Are
we to believe a man upon the very theme upon

which he is deluded ?   No : upon other questions
he may be as competent a witness as anybody else,
but upon this particular one he is the victim of
hallucinations. Such is the unavoidable judgment of
an atheist, and upon his own ground a correct judgment, upon the testimony of religious and devout
men to miraculous interpositions of the Deity.
Suppose one of these to come to him and say, 'I
have seen a miracle ;' he would reply, ' I will believe you or not according to what you mean by a
miracle : if this miracle which you come to tell me
of is only an extraordinary natural fact, and has
nothing to do with religion, I will believe you as
readily as I would anybody else ; but if it is a
miracle in a religious sense, I do not consider you
a trustworthy witness to such a fact ; you are
in an unreasonable condition of mind upon the
question of religion altogether, and being under a
delusion upon the very evidence of a God at all, you
are not likely to possess discretion or sobriety as a
spectator, of what you call an interposition of His.
Upon that subject you are a partial, fanciful, and
flighty witness.'

The evidence of miracles thus assumes the belief
in a God, because in the absence of that belief all
the testimony upon which miracles are received la-
bours under an incurable stigma.   And this it is
which constitutes the real argument of the celebrated
Essay of Hume. This Essay is a philosophical
attempt, indeed, to decide the question whether
certain events took place eighteen centuries ago by

a *formula;* and as the inductive formula places a miracle outside of *possibility,* Hume's evidential formula secures a balance of *evidence* against it. It does this by establishing a common measure and criterion of probability, by which both the miracle and the testimony to it are to be tried, viz. experience. Because, although this philosopher has expunged the argument of experience out of the tablet of human reason, he professes that he has no other test of truth to fall back upon but that, and that he must take either that or none. Testimony is therefore reduced from an original principle to a mere derivative of experience; and then the formula, that the falsehood of the testimony is less contradictory to experience than the truth of the miracle, settles the question. But a rule which would oblige everybody to disbelieve fresh intelligence, whenever the facts were unprecedented, is an impossible one; it could not work in human affairs; and it in fact breaks down in the writer's own hands; who gives in an hypothetical instance a formal specimen of that kind of marvel which is capable of being proved by testimony; and in so doing describes a fact which is totally contrary to human experience. But though his formula encounters the natural fate of infallible recipes and solutions, every reflecting reader must see the force and the truth, upon the writer's own ground, of his assertion of the obliquity, the exaggeration, and the passion of religious testimony; and must admit that a philosopher who thinks that mankind are under a delusion in worshipping God, has a right to think them under an equal delusion when they testify to Divine interpositions.

Having stated the fundamental admission of divines that the evidence of miracles assumes the belief in Supernatural Power, I next observe that this condition of miraculous evidence gives us the distinction between miracles and ordinary facts as matters of credit. A miracle differs from an ordinary fact in the first place as a subject of credit, simply as being an extraordinary fact, and we naturally require a greater amount of evidence for it on that account. There is, indeed, the greatest unlikeliness that *any* occurrence whatever, which comes into our head by chance or intentional conception, though it is of the commonest kind, will really happen as it is imagined; and from this great antecedent improbability of the most ordinary events, it has been inferred that no calculable difference exists between the improbability of ordinary facts and the improbability of miracles; or therefore in the amount of evidence required for them. But to draw such an inference is to confound two totally distinct grounds of improbability. If all that I can say of the likelihood of an event's occurrence is that it comes into my head to imagine it, that is no reason whatever for it, and the absence of all reason for expecting an event constitutes of itself the improbability of that event. But this kind of antecedent improbability being simply the absence of evidence, is immediately neutralized by the ap-

pearance of evidence, to which it offers no resistance :
while that improbability which arises from the marvellous character of an event naturally offers a resistance to evidence, which must therefore be the stronger
in order to overcome such resistance. (Note 2.)

But if we take in the whole notion of a miracle
not as a marvellous event only, but the act of a
Supernatural Being, a miracle is still more widely
distinguished from an ordinary event as a subject
of credit and evidence.   The evidence of an ordinary
fact does not assume any ground or principle of *faith*
for the reception of it.   It is true that all belief in
testimony implies faith in this sense, that we accept
upon the report of other persons the occurrence of
some event or the existence of some object which we
have not seen with our own eyes.   But common
testimony is so complete a part of the present order
of things and of the whole agency by which natural
life is conducted, and the belief in it is so necessary
and so matter-of-course an act in us, that we cannot
regard the mere belief in testimony as faith in the
received sense of that word.   We may never have seen
a well-known place in our own country or abroad,
but if the place is universally talked of, if it appears
in all maps and books of travels and geography, and
if anybody would be considered to be out of his
mind if he doubted its existence ; it would be a mis-
application of language to call the journey thither
an act of faith.   The very merit of faith is that we
make something of a venture in it ; which we do
when we believe in testimony *against* our expe-

rience. But when the facts which are the subject
of testimony are in full accordance with our experience, then, the testimony being competent and
sufficient, belief is unavoidable, it is as natural to
an atheist or a materialist as it is to a believer;
and therefore in such cases belief in testimony
does not involve the principle of faith. But a
miracle in assuming the existence of supernatural
power, assumes a basis of faith. A miracle has
a foot, so to speak, in each world; one part of it
resting upon earth, while the other goes down
beyond our intellectual reach into the depths of
the invisible world. The sensible fact is subject to
the natural law of testimony, the Divine intervention
rests upon another ground. A miracle is both an
outward fact, and also an invisible and spiritual fact,
and to embrace the twofold whole, both testimony
and faith are wanted.

It has been a fault in one school of writers on
evidence, that in urging the just weight of testimony, they have not sufficiently attended to this
distinction, and have overlooked the deep gulf which
divides facts which assume a basis of religious
faith from ordinary facts as subjects of evidence.
These writers are too apt to speak of miracles as if
they stood completely on a par with other events
as matters of credit, and as if the reception of them
only drew upon that usual and acknowledged belief
in testimony by which we accept the facts of ordinary history. But this is to forget the important
point that a miracle is on one side of it not a fact

of this world, but of the invisible world; the Divine interposition in it being a supernatural and mysterious act : that therefore the evidence for a miracle does not stand exactly on the same ground as the evidence of the witness-box, which only appeals to our common sense as men of the world and actors in ordinary life; but that it requires a great religious assumption in our minds to begin with, without which no testimony in the case can avail; and consequently that the acceptance of a miracle exercises more than the ordinary qualities of candour and fairness used in estimating historical evidence generally, having, in the previous admission of a Supernatural Power, first tried our faith.

This admission of divines, again, that the evidence of miracles assumes the belief in a Personal Deity, supplies us with the proper ground on which to judge of some positions which have been recently promulgated on the subject of miracles and their evidence. " No testimony," it has been said, " can reach to the supernatural: testimony can only apply to an apparent sensible fact; that it is due to supernatural causes is entirely dependent on the previous belief and assumption of the parties." (Note 3.)   Does then this statement only mean to distinguish in the case of a miracle between the *fact* and the *cause*, that the fact alone can be a subject of testimony, not the supernatural cause ?   It is, in that case, an undeniably true statement; for the supernatural cause of a fact is a truth which in its own nature cannot be reached by ocular evidence or attestation. Testimony does not pretend to include in its report of an extraordinary fact the rationale of that fact; it does not profess to penetrate beyond the phenomenon, and put itself in contact with the source and original of it, and thence bring back the intelligence that that source lies outside of physical law in a special act of the Divine will. This species of evidence has its own office, which is to attest visible and sensible occurrences; unless it is worthless testimony it can do no less, and if it is the best conceivable testimony it can do no more. What those facts amount to, how they are to be interpreted, what they prove, depends upon another argument altogether than that of testimony. I accept upon the report of eye-witnesses certain miraculous occurrences; that these occurrences are interpositions of the Deity depends upon the existence of a Deity to begin with, and next upon the argument of design or final causes; because the extraordinary coincidence of miraculous occurrences with a professed Divine commission on the part of the person who announces or commands them, proves a Divine intention and act. That which constitutes a miraculous occurrence a miracle in the common or theological acceptation, is therefore not obtained from simple testimony; though it is obtained immediately by our reason from the data which testimony supplies. Thus understood, the position to which I have referred amounts to the statement that testimony is testimony, and not another kind of evidence; it does not deny the supernatural cause of the occurrences in question, but only that testimony itself proves it ; the supernatural explanation of a miracle depending upon reasons which are at hand, but which are not contained within the simple report of the witness.

The position, therefore, that " no testimony can reach to the supernatural," if it accepts recorded miracles as *facts*, and only excludes from the department of testimony their *cause*, is a true though an unpractical distinction. Nor can this position be objected to again if it is only to be understood as meaning that testimony is not sufficient to prove the *facts*, without the previous assumption of Supernatural Power or the existence of God in the mind of the receiver of such testimony. For in that case it only amounts to the admission which divines have always made upon the very threshold of the subject of miracles. The great truth upon which the evidence of all lesser instances of supernatural power depends is the truth of the supernatural origin of this world—that this world is caused by the will of a Personal Being ; that it is sustained by that will, and that therefore there is a God who is the object of prayer and worship. A man who does not hold the existence of this Supernatural Being cannot reasonably be expected to attach much weight to reports of amazing preternatural occurrences, laid before him as *religious* facts *connected with* their own religious interests and feelings and persuasions by earnest believers in religion, who can only figure in his eye as devotees and enthusiasts. And if atheism thus invalidates the testimony to miracles, the belief in a God is wanted as a condition of its validity.

But is the statement that "no testimony can reach to the supernatural" made upon the ground that the miraculous fact is intrinsically incredible and impossible, and that a violation of physical law is no more capable of being proved by testimony than a mathematical absurdity? In that case the position is both religiously and philosophically untenable. Here indeed, again, we are met by a distinction between the miraculous *fact* and the violation of *law;* in accordance with which we should have to interpret this statement as still leaving within the province of testimony the proof of the miraculous fact, and only excluding from it the explanation of that fact as a contradiction to physical law. The miraculous occurrence, it is intimated, even if true, need not be in reality a physical anomaly, but only an instance of an unknown operation of law; and therefore in denying the possibility of a violation of law, and excluding the supernatural as a subject of testimony, we do not disqualify testimony for proving the miraculous occurrence itself. "It is not the mere fact," it is said, "but the cause or explanation of it, which is the point at issue." (Note 4.) But such a distinction is practically untenable, because whatever may be said of some kind of miracles, others are—the *facts themselves* are—plainly violations of physical law, and can be nothing else; they are plainly outstanding and anomalous facts, which

admit of no sort of physical explanation. Admit the
real external occurrence of our Lord's Resurrection
and Ascension, and the interpretation of it as a
miracle or contradiction to the laws of nature is
inevitable. Language has been used indeed as if all
the facts of the Gospel history could be admitted and
the miracles denied ; but when we examine the sense
in which the word 'fact' is used in that language,
we find that it is not used in the ordinary sense but
in the sense of an inexplicable erroneous impression
on the minds of the witnesses.

For, indeed, this distinction is no sooner made than
abandoned ; it is admitted that some kind of miraculous facts are intrinsically as facts incredible ; and
in the place of the distinction between the miraculous
fact and the violation of law, is substituted the distinction between the fact, and the *impression* of the
fact upon the minds of the witnesses. (Note 5.) Testimony, it is said, can prove the impression upon
the minds of the witnesses, but cannot "from the
nature of our antecedent convictions" prove the
real occurrence of the fact, that "the event really
happened in the way assigned." This indeed, upon
the supposition of the intrinsic incredibility of the
facts, is the only hypothesis left to account for honest
testimony to them. We have no alternative then
but to fall back upon something unknown, obscure,
and exceptional in the action of human nature, in
the case of the witnesses ; some hidden root of delusion, some secret disorganization in the structure of
reason itself, or interference with the medium and

channel between it and the organs of sense; whence it must have arisen that those who did not see certain occurrences, were fully persuaded that they did see them. But such an explanation *requires* the intrinsic incredibility of the facts, and is illegitimate without it: because if they are not in their own nature incredible, no occasion has come for resorting to such an explanation; there is no reason why I should resist the natural effect of testimony, and institute this unnatural divorce between the impression and the fact at all.

The position then that "no testimony can reach to the supernatural," is correct or incorrect according as it is based upon the impossibility of the supernatural, or the inadequacy of mere testimony—its inherent defectiveness upon such subject-matter, unless supplemented by a ground of faith within ourselves. We allow the need of a previous assumption to give force to the evidence of miracles; at the same time we are prepared to vindicate the validity and the force of testimony, upon that previous assumption being made. Upon the supposition of the existence of a God and of Supernatural Power in the first instance, competent testimony to miraculous facts possesses an obligatory force; it becomes by virtue of that supposition the testimony of credible witnesses to credible facts; for the facts are credible if there is a power equal to being their cause.; and the witnesses are credible if we assume the truth and reasonableness of their religious faith and worship. Untrustworthy and passionate informants upon the atheistic theory,

liable to any delusion and mistake, because upon
this theory their very belief in religion in the first
instance is a delusion; upon the assumption of the
truth of religion they become sound informants; the
change of the hypothesis is a change in the character
of the testimony; the stigma which attached to it
upon the one basis is reversed upon the other, and
what was bad evidence upon the irreligious is good
upon the religious rationale of the world. In this
state of the case, then, testimony, when it speaks to
the miraculous, has a natural weight and credit of
the same kind as that which it possesses in ordinary
matters: and the attested visible fact is the important thing, upon the truth of which the conclusion that it is a miracle follows by the natural
laws of reasoning. For I have shewn it to be a
practically untenable distinction that "it is not the
mere fact, but the cause or explanation of it, which
is the point at issue."

But if the evidence of miracles demands in the
first instance, as the condition of its validity and
force, the belief in the existence of a God; if it begs
the question at the very outset of Infinite and Supernatural Power, as involved in a personal Author of
the universe; it may be urged that so great, so
inconceivable an assumption as this amounts to
placing miracles upon a ground of faith instead of
a ground of historical evidence. You profess, it may
be said, to prove the credibility of the supernatural,
and you do so by assuming *in limine* the actual
existence of it—the existence of supernatural power.

Let this only be understood then and there need be
no further controversy on this subject. "A miracle
ceases to be capable of investigation by reason or
to own its dominion : it is accepted on religious
grounds, and can appeal only to the principle and
influence of faith." (Note 6.)

I reply that miracles undoubtedly rest upon a
ground of faith so far as they assume a truth which
it requires faith to adopt, viz. the existence of a
God : but that such a ground of faith is compatible
with historical evidence for them. Do we mean by
faith, a faculty wholly distinct from reason, which
without the aid of premisses founds conclusions purely
upon itself, which can give no account of itself, or
its own convictions ? Is faith, in short, only another
word for arbitrary supposition ? In that case to re-
legate miracles to a ground of faith is simply to
deprive them of all character of matters of fact. A
matter of faith is then specially *not* a matter of fact,
and miracles could only take place in the region and
sphere of faith by not taking place at all. The individual uses the totally distinct principles of faith
and reason according to the subject-matter before
him. In the world of reason he judges according
to evidence, he believes whatever he believes on
account of certain reasons ; in the world of faith he
believes because he believes. Faith in this case is
no basis for a matter of fact ; a miracle of this sphere
is not an occurrence of time and place, within the
pale of history and geography, but an airy vision
which evaporates as the eye of reason rests upon

it and melts into space. The fact of faith is adapted to the eye of faith only.

But does faith mean belief upon reasonable grounds? Is it as much reason as the most practical common sense is, though its grounds are less sensible and more connected with our moral nature? In this sense faith can support matter of fact, and a miracle in resting upon it, is not thereby *not* an event of history. If a God who made the world is not a mere supposition, a notion of the mind, but a really existing Being, this Being can act upon matter either in an ordinary way or in an extraordinary way; and His extraordinary action on matter is a visible and historical miracle. " For evidence," it has been said, " of a Deity working miracles, we must go out of nature and beyond reason." (Note 7.) If this is true, a miracle cannot rest upon rational evidence; but if an Omnipotent Deity is a conclusion of reason, it can.

But if a miracle is itself a trial of faith, how, it is asked, can it serve as the evidence of something farther to be believed? " You admit," it is said, " that this evidence of a revelation is itself the subject of evidence, and that not certain but only probable evidence; that it is received through a chain of human testimony; that the belief in it is against all our experience, and demands in the first instance the assumption of the existence of supernatural power; in a word, that a miracle must be proved in spite of difficulties itself, before it can prove anything else. But how can a species of evidence which is thus encumbered itself, be effective as the support of something else? So far from miracles being the evidence of revelation, are they not themselves difficulties attaching to revelation?" (Note 8.)

This double capacity, then, of a miracle as an object of faith and yet evidence of faith, is inherent in the principle of miraculous evidence; for belief in testimony against experience being faith, a miracle which reaches us through testimony is necessarily an *object* of faith; while the very purpose of the miracle being to prove a revelation, the same miracle again is *evidence* of faith. But the objection to this double attitude of a miracle admits of a natural answer. My own reflexion indeed upon my own act of belief here, my own consciousness of the kind of act which it is in me, is witness enough that belief in a miracle is an exercise and a trial of faith. But if faith is not mere supposition, but reasonable belief upon premises, there is no reason why a conclusion of faith should not be itself the evidence of something else. It is sufficient that I am rationally convinced that such an event happened; that whatever difficulties I have had in arriving at it that is my conclusion. That being the case, I cannot help myself, if I would, using it as a true fact, for the proof of something farther of which it is calculated in its own nature to be proof. A probable fact is probable evidence. I may therefore use a miracle as evidence of a revelation, though I have only probable evidence for the miracle. The same fact may try faith in one

stage and ground faith in another, be the conclusion
of certain premisses and the premiss for a further
conclusion ; i. e. may be an object of faith and yet
an evidence of faith.

It is not indeed consistent with truth, nor would
it conduce to the real defence of Christianity, to
underrate the difficulties of the Christian evidence ;
or to disguise this characteristic of it, that the very
facts which constitute the evidence of revelation have
to be accepted by an act of faith themselves, before
they can operate as a proof of that further truth.
More than two centuries ago this subject exercised the
deep thoughts of one whom we may almost call the
founder of the philosophy of Christian evidence ; and
who now in the writings of Bishop Butler rules in
our schools, gives us our point of view, and moulds
our form of reflexion on this subject. The answer
of Pascal to the objection of the difficulties of the
Christian evidence, was that that evidence was not
designed for producing belief as such, but for producing belief in connexion with, and as the token of,
a certain moral disposition ; that that gave a real insight into the reasons for and the marks of truth in the
Christian scheme, and brought out proof which was
hidden without it : which proof therefore, though it
did not answer every purpose which evidence can answer, answered its *designed* purpose : in other words,
that the purpose of evidence was qualified by the
purpose of trial ; it being the Divine intention that
the human heart itself should be the illuminating
principle, throwing light upon that evidence, and

presenting it in its real strength[a]. This position then requires the caution to go along with it, that we have no general liberty in individual cases of unbelief to attribute this result to moral defects, because we do not know what latent obstructions of another kind there may have been to the perception of truth ; but with this caution it is a valid reply to the objection made ; because it supplies a reason which accounts for the want of more full and complete evidence than we possess, and a reason which is in consistency with the Divine attributes. One school of writers on Christian evidence has assumed too confidently that any average man, taken out of the crowd, who has sufficient common sense to conduct his own affairs, is a fit judge of that evidence—such a judge as was contemplated in the original design of it, as under Providence limited and measured for our use. One great writer especially, of matchless argumentative powers, betrays this defect in his point of view ; and in bringing out the common-sense side of the Christian evidence—the value of human testimony—with

[a] " Il n'était donc pas juste qu'il parût d'une manière manifestement divine et absolument capable de convaincre tous les hommes ; mais il n'était pas juste aussi qu'il vînt d'une manière si cachée, qu'il ne pût être reconnu de ceux qui le chercheraient sincèrement. Il a voulu se rendre parfaitement connaissable à ceux-là ; et ainsi, voulant paraitre à découvert à ceux qui le cherchent de tout leur cœur, et caché à ceux qui le fuient de tout leur cœur, il tempère sa connaissance en sorte qu'il a donné des marques de soi visibles à ceux qui le cherchent, et obscures à ceux qui ne le cherchent pas. Il y a assez de lumière pour ceux qui ne désirent que de voir, et assez d'obscurité pour ceux qui ont une disposition contraire."— *Pascal, ed. Faugere,* vol. ii. p. 151.

irresistible truth and force, allows his very success
to conceal from him the insufficiency of common
sense alone.

The ground of Pascal is in effect that, as an
original means of persuasion, the Christian evidence
is designed for the few, and not for the many. Because Christianity is the religion of a large part of
the world, and prophesies its own possession of the
whole world, it does not follow that the evidence
of it must be adapted to convince the mass ;—I mean
to convince them, on the supposition of their coming
without any bias of custom and education to decide
the question by evidence alone. It is enough if that
argument is addressed to the few, and if, as the
few of every generation are convinced, their faith becomes a permanent and hereditary belief by a natural
law of transmission. The Christian body is enlarged
by growth and stationariness combined ; each successive age contributing its quota, and the acquisition
once made remaining. This is the way in which, as
a matter of fact, Christianity became the religion of
the Roman empire. In no age, from the apostolic
downwards, did the evidence of the Gospel profess
to be adapted to convince the mass ; it addressed
itself to the few, and the hereditary belief of the
mass followed. Christianity has indeed at times
spread by other means than its evidences, by the
sword, and by the rude impulse of uncivilized people
to follow their chiefs ; but whenever it has spread by
the power of its evidences, this has been their scope.
The profession of the world has been the result, but the

faith of the few has been the original mark of the Gospel argument ; though doubtless many who would not have had the strength of mind to acknowledge the force of that argument, by an original act of their own, have by a Christian education grown to a real inward perception of it ; and hereditary belief has thus, by providing a more indulgent trial, sheltered individual faith. And the same principle of growth can at last convert the world ; however slow the process, the result will come, if Christianity always keeps the ground it gets ; for that which always gains and never loses must ultimately win the whole.

LECTURE VI.

St. John v. 17.

My Father worketh hitherto, and I work.

MIRACLES are summarily characterized as viola-tions of the laws of nature. But may not the Scrip-ture miracles, however apparently at variance with the laws of nature, be instances of unknown law ? This question is proposed in a different spirit by different persons ; by some as a question upon which their belief in these miracles depends, by others only as a speculative question, though one answer to it would be more in accordance with their intellectual predilections than another.

In entering upon this question, however, we must at the outset settle one important preliminary, viz. what we mean by the Scripture miracles. The dis-tinction proposed in our question is a distinction be-tween those miracles as facts, and those miracles as miracles, in the popular sense ; but if we only call the miracles facts at first, we must still know what

those facts are respecting which the question, whether
they are properly miraculous, i.e. violations of law or
not, is raised. Are we to take those facts as they
stand in Scripture, or as seen to begin with through an
interpretative medium of our own, reduced to certain
supposed true and original events, of which the Scripture narrative is a transcendental representation?
As a previous condition of the consistency of those
facts with law, are the facts themselves to undergo
an alteration? I reply, that in an inquiry into the
particular question whether the Scripture miracles
may or may not be instances of unknown law, the
question whether those miracles originally took place
or not, in the way in which they are recorded, in
other words, the question of the authenticity of those
miracles, is one with which I have nothing to do.
Whether or not the facts of the Scripture narrative
are the true and original facts which took place is
a question which belongs to the department of evidence, and one which must be met in its own place ;
but a philosophical inquiry into the consistency or not
of the Scripture miracles with law must take those
miracles as they stand. If not, what *are* the facts,
the physical interpretation of which is in dispute?
We have not got them before us, and the inquiry
must stop for want of material. It is important to
understand the necessity which there is for separating
these two questions, because the mind of an inquirer
at first is very apt to confuse them, and to suppose
that the speculation upon the question of unknown
law gives him a right in the first instance partially to

reduce the facts of Scripture, in order to accommodate them to the inquiry. It must therefore be
understood that the ulterior question as to law in
miracles assumes the miraculous facts as recorded.
Even if the unknown law affects the *facts themselves*, as, upon the theory that they are only impressions upon the minds of the witnesses, it does,
still the facts which are supposed to be accounted
for *by* impression, are the facts stated in Scripture,
and not other facts.

Upon the question then of the referribleness of
miracles to unknown law, we must first observe that
the expression 'unknown law,' as used here, has two
meanings, between which it is important to distinguish ; i.e. that it means either *unknown law*, or
unknown connexion with *known* law. I will take
the latter of these two meanings first.

1. With respect then to unknown connexion with
known law, the test of the claim of any extraordinary isolated and anomalous fact to this connexion is, whether it admits of any hypothesis being
made respecting it, any po sible physical explanation, which would bring it under the head of any
known law. A law of nature in the scientific sense is
in its very essence incapable of producing single or
insulated facts, because it is the very repetition and
recurrence of the facts which makes the law, which
law therefore implies and is a *class* of facts. It
follows that no single or exceptional event can come
by direct observation under a law of nature ; but
that if it comes under it at all it can only do so

by the medium of some *explanation*, by which it
is brought out of its apparent isolation and singu-
larity into the same situation with a class of facts,
i.e. some explanation which shews that the exceptional character of the fact is owing to a peculiarity
in the situation of its subject-matter, and not in the
laws which act upon it. It may be that there is
something extraordinary in the position of a natural
substance, upon which, however, the known laws of
nature are operating all the time, · producing their
proper effects only under unwonted circumstances ;
as in the case of the explained descent of a meteoric
stone, where the laws which act are on the common
laws of gravity and motion, and the only thing singular
is the situation of the stone. The common current
facts of nature, where not yet reduced to law, are
brought under law, if they *are* brought under it, by
direct observation ; by fixing upon the invariable
conjunctions of antecedent and consequent, which are
really happening, and only are not as yet observed.
The weather, e.g. is part of the order of nature of
which the law alone is unknown to us, the facts
being of constant occurrence ; the weather therefore
comes under law, to whatever extent it does come
under it at present, by direct observation ; the invariable conjunctions being of real occurrence, and
only requiring to be *seen.* By tracing those conjunctions back we should have the law of weather
from that point ; and could we trace them back up
to the point at which they link on to the ascertained
series of natural causes, then we should have the full

law of weather. But single or exceptional facts only come under a law of nature by the medium of an explanation or hypothesis, which connects the deviation with the main line, and engrafts the anomaly upon a known stock.

There is, indeed, besides a regular hypothetical explanation of an anomalous fact in the physical world, another and more obscure condition in which a fact may lie without suffering total disjunction from law :—when no formal hypothesis is at present forthcoming, but the fact holds out a promise of one; presents the hints or beginnings of one, though they cannot yet be worked up into a scientific whole. The phenomenon is not wholly dark and wanting in all trace and vestige of physical type, but is said to *await* solution. It will be enough, however, if without express mention we understand this modification as included under the head of an explanation or hypothesis.

So long then as an eccentric fact admits of an explanation in keeping with known law, we are not justified in pronouncing it to be contradictory to known law ; for though the explanation is hypothetical, so long as it is admissible, we are prohibited from asserting the absolute lawlessness of the fact. But, on the other hand, take a supposed or imaginary anomalous occurrence — and many such are conceivable — to which this whole ground of scientific explanation and anticipation would not apply, and in the case of which it would be all obviously out of place. Such an anomalous occurrence would be lawless, and a con-

tradiction to known law, and must be set down as
such. Thus, according as there is room or no room for
scientific anticipation, one kind of physical miracle
is in latent connexion with the system, another is
not. A scientific judgment discriminates between
different types of physical marvels. An eccentric
phenomenon within the region of man—his bodily
and mental affections and impressions—is set down
as an ultimately natural fact, because there the
system of nature is elastic, and such as by its elas-
ticity to accommodate and afford a place for it ;
while no such prospect is held out to an imagined
instance of irregularity in inanimate nature, because the system there is rigid and inflexible, and
refuses to accommodate the alien. The most extraordinary case of suspended animation is an ultimately
natural fact ; a real violation of the law of gravity,
by the ascent of a human body into the sky, is an
ultimate anomaly and outstanding fact. (Note 1.)

Upon the question, then, whether the Gospel
miracles may have an unknown connexion with
known law, the criterion to be applied is whether
they admit or not of a physical hypothesis being
constructed about them, an explanation being given
of them, *upon* which this connexion would follow.
Upon this question then I observe, to begin with,
that a whole class of Gospel miracles meets us in
which the material result taken by itself, and apart
from the manner and circumstances of its production,
cannot be pronounced absolutely to be incapable
of taking place by the laws of nature. Indeed,

this observation may be said to embrace the largest class of miracles ; I refer to the bodily cures and restorations of the functions of bodily organs, by which the blind received their sight, the lame walked, the lepers were cleansed, and the deaf heard. Suppose in any of these cases the physical result to have taken place as a simple occurrence without any connexion with a personal agent—there is nothing in the nature of the fact itself to exclude the supposition that it was owing to some unknown natural cause. A blind man, even one born blind, suddenly recovers his sight. Were such an occurrence to be reported upon good evidence at the present day, it would not be received as anything physically incredible, but would be set down, however extraordinary, even if quite unique, as referrible to some natural cause : and scientific men might proceed to suggest hypothetical explanations of it. The same may be said of a sudden restoration of hearing, of a sudden recovery of speech, of a sudden recovery of the use of a limb, of a sudden recovery from an issue of blood, from palsy, from madness.

But to say that the material fact which takes place *in* a miracle admits of being referred to an unknown natural cause, is not to say that the miracle itself does. A miracle is the material fact *as* coinciding with an express announcement or with express supernatural pretensions in the agent. It is this correspondence of two facts which constitutes a miracle. If a person says to a blind man, 'See,' and he sees, it is not the sudden return of sight alone that we have to account for, but its return at that particular moment. For it is morally impossible that this exact agreement of an event with a command or notification could have been by a mere chance, or, as we should say, been an extraordinary coincidence, especially if it is repeated in other cases.

The chief characteristic, indeed, of miracles and that which distinguishes them from mere marvels, is this correspondence of the fact with a notification;—what we may call the prophetical principle. For indeed, if a prophecy is a miracle, a miracle too is in essence a prophecy; the essence of which is the correspondence, not the futurity, of the event. And consequently, a miracle can afford to dispense with the full supernatural character of its physical result, in consideration of this other source of the miraculous character. No violation of any law of nature takes place in either of the two parts of prophecy taken separately; none in the prediction of an event, none in its occurrence; but the two taken together are proof of superhuman agency; and the two parts of a miracle, the event and the announcement of it, even if the former be in itself reducible to law, are, taken together, proof of the same.

It is evident then that, supposing the miraculous facts of Scripture to stand as they are recorded, no physical hypothesis can be framed which would account for the knowledge and power involved even in this class of miracles. But it must also be remembered that no hypothesis which even accounted for a certain portion of the Scripture miracles, if one such could be imagined, would be of any service on this side, unless it also accounted for the whole.

But could any scientific hypothesis be constructed, which would account for the conversion of water into wine, the multiplication of the loaves, and the resurrection of dead men to life? Undoubtedly if the supposition could be entertained that these miracles as recorded in the Gospels were untrue and exaggerated representations of the facts which really took place, a physical explanation might be proposed, and might even be accepted as a very probable one, of the facts which were supposed to be the real ones. But in that case the reduction of the Gospel miracles to physical law would have been indebted for its success, not to any hypothesis of philosophy, but simply to an alteration of the facts, in accordance with a supposed more authentic and historical estimate of them.

Upon one theory alone, if a tenable one, could such facts be reconcileable with known law; and that is the theory that they were not facts but impressions upon the minds of the witnesses— though impressions so strong and perfect that they were equivalent to facts to those who had them. This explanation, then, resorts for its ground to that more elastic and obscure department of nature above mentioned — the mixed bodily and mental organization of man with its liability to eccentric

and abnormal conditions, and with them to delusions, and disordered relations to the external world.
But this is a theory which is totally untenable upon
the supposition of the truth of the facts of Scripture
as they are recorded. An abnormal condition of the
senses is in the first place connected with positive
disease, and with particular diseases ; or else—if
such a strange result has really ever arisen from
such processes—with professedly artificial conditions
of the man, produced by premeditated effort and
skill ; of which even the asserted effects are very
limited and fragmentary. But that numbers of men
of serious character, and apparently in their ordinary
natural habit, should be for years in a disordered
state of relations to the outward world ; in particular that they should think that for a certain
period they had been frequently seeing and conversing with a Person, whose disciples they had been,
who had returned to life again after a public death,
when they never saw Him at that time, or spoke
to Him,—this is absolutely incredible. And therefore the theory of impression is untenable upon the
facts of Scripture as they stand, and supposes different facts. I speak of the theory of impression
as a physical theory : some speculative divines have
proposed the hypothesis of a miraculous impression
produced for the occasion upon the minds and senses
of the witnesses, as one mode of the production of
miracles in certain cases ; but such a theory, to whatever criticism it may be open, has nothing in common
with the physical explanation here noticed. (Note 2.)

2. But now let us shift the inquiry from the ground which it has taken hitherto, to the other and different question, whether miracles may not be instances of laws which are as yet wholly unknown ;—this defers the question of the physical explanation of a miracle to another stage, when not only the connexion of a particular fact with law has to be discovered, but the law with which it is connected has to be discovered too.

This question, then, is commonly called a question of " higher law."   " All analogy," we are told, " leads us to infer, and new discoveries direct our expectation to the idea, that the most extensive laws to which we have hitherto attained converge to some few simple and general principles, by which the whole of the material universe is sustained [a]."   A " higher law," then, is a law which comprehends under itself two or more lower or less wide laws : and the way in which such a rationale of higher law would be applicable to a miracle would be this ;—that if any as yet unknown law came to light to which upon its appearance this or that miracle or class of miracles could be referred as instances ; in that case we could entertain the question whether the newly discovered law under which the miracles came, and the old or known law under which the common kind of facts come, were not both reducible to a still more general law, which comprehended them both.   But before we can entertain the question of " higher law " as applicable

[a] Babbage's Ninth Bridgwater Treatise, p. 32.

to miraculous and to common facts, we must first have this lower law of the miraculous ones. Could we suppose, e. g. the possibility of some higher law into which both electricity and gravitation might merge ; yet the laws of electricity and the law of gravitation both exist in readiness to be embraced under such higher law, should it ever be discovered. And in the same way, if miracles and the laws of nature are ever to be comprehended under a higher law, we must first have *both* the laws underneath the latter, both the laws of nature and the laws of the miracles.

Could we then suppose the possibility of any unknown laws coming to light which would embrace and account for miracles, one concomitant of this discovery is inevitable, viz. that those fresh laws will involve fresh facts. A law of nature, in the scientific sense, cannot exist without a class of facts which comes under it ; because it is these facts which *are* the law. A law of nature is a repetition of the same facts with the same conjunctions ; but in order for the facts to take place with the same conjunctions, they must in the first instance take place. A law of miraculous recoveries of sight without such recoveries of sight, a law of real suspensions of gravitation without such suspensions of gravitation, a law of miraculous productions of material substances without such productions, a law of resurrections from the dead without resurrections from the dead,—these laws are absurdities. To make an imaginative supposition—Could we conceive that in a future age of the world it were observed, that persons who had passed through certain extraordinary diseases which had then shewed themselves in the human frame, returned to life again after shewing the certain signs of death ;—this observation, made upon a proper induction from recurring instances, would be a law of resurrection from the dead ; but nothing short of this would be : and this would imply a new class of facts, viz. recurring resurrections.

No new class of facts, indeed, is required when an exceptional phenomenon is explained by a *known* law ; for a known law only involves known facts : and no new class of facts is required when *frequent* phenomena are traced to a new law, because the new discovered law is already provided with the facts which come under it, which have been seen always themselves though their law has been unknown ; but when both the phenomenon is exceptional and its law new, that new law implies a new class of facts ; for facts a law must have ; which therefore if they do not now exist, must come into existence in order to make the law [b].

[b] It is true that old and familiar classes of miraculous facts, so to call them, exist in that constant current of supernatural pretension which is a feature of history, and has been a running accompaniment of human nature. And it is true also that a vague attempt has always been going on to connect this supernaturalism with law. The science of magic in its way made this profession ; it mixed this object indeed with relations to demons and unearthly beings ; but still it treated supernaturalism as a secret of nature, and pretended to search and in some degree to have penetrated into this secret. Again, the more exalted kind of heathen thaumaturgy connected miraculous powers with the development of human nature, and

But such being the case, what does this whole supposition of the discovery of such an unknown law of miracles amount to, but to the supposition of a future new order of nature? It would indeed be difficult to say what was a new order of nature, if recurrent miracles with invariable antecedents did not constitute one. But a new order of nature being involved in this supposition, it immediately follows that this whole supposition is an irrelevant, a futile, and nugatory one as regards the present question. A law of nature in the scientific sense has reference to our experience alone: when I speak of a law of nature, I *mean* a law of nature with this reference. A miracle therefore as a violation of the laws of nature assumes the same condition, and is relative to our knowledge. A miracle is thus not affected by any imaginary supposition of a future different order of nature, of which it would *not* be a violation; it is irrespective of such an idea. For no new order of things could make the present order different: and a miracle is constituted by no ulterior criterion, no criterion which lies beyond the course of nature as it comes under our cognizance, but simply by this

deduced them from a higher humanity, as a specimen of which the celebrated Apollonius Tyanæus had them assigned to him. And the belief of rude tribes has subordinated mystical gifts of prophecy and second sight to the law of family descent. But, making allowance for exceptional cases in which it may have pleased the Divine power to interpose, the mature judgment of mankind has set aside the facts of current supernaturalism, except so far as they are capable of being naturally accounted for; and has, with the facts, set aside all pretension to acquaintance with the law of them.

matter-of-fact test.   It is opposed to custom,—to that universal custom which we call experience.   But experience is the experience which we *have*.   A miracle, could we suppose it becoming the ordinary fact of another different order of nature, would not be the less a violation of the present one ; or therefore the less a violation of the laws of nature in the scientific sense.

Bishop Butler has indeed suggested " that there may be beings in the universe whose capacities and knowledge and views may be so extensive as that the whole Christian dispensation may to them appear *natural*, i. e. analogous or conformable to God's dealings with other parts of His creation, as natural as the visible known course of things appears to us [c]." And with respect to the beings who are here supposed, who have the *knowledge* of other parts of the universe, and of God's dispensations there, this suggestion holds good; for the occurrence of the same dispensations with the same antecedents in the different parts of the universe would constitute an order of nature in the universe to those who were acquainted with it.   But we do not possess this knowledge, and an order of nature being relative to knowledge, in the absence of this condition there does not exist this naturalness.

The relation of a miracle to the *laws of nature* also fixes its relations to *general laws*.   The only intelligible meaning which we can assign to general laws, is that they are the laws of nature with the

[c] Analogy, Part i. ch. i.

addition of a particular theory of the Divine mode of conducting them ; the theory, viz. of secondary causes. The question whether the Deity operates in nature by second causes, or by immediate single acts, is not a question which at all affects the laws of nature in the scientific sense. Those laws being simply recurrent facts, are exactly the same, whatever be the Divine method employed in producing those facts. But divines take up the subject at the point at which natural science stops, and inquire whether the Deity operates in the laws of nature by a constant succession of direct single acts, or through the medium of general laws or secondary causes, which, once set in motion, execute themselves. This is an entirely speculative question then, and, inasmuch as the real mode of the Divine action is inconceivable, an insoluble one. The uniformity of all the facts which constitute a law of nature is suggestive of one originating act on the part of the Deity, but it is also consistent with a series of similar single acts ; nor is a universal action in particulars in the abstract more inconceivable than a Universal Being. The language of religion, however, has been framed upon the principle of what is most becoming to conceive respecting the Deity ; and therefore has not attributed to Him an incessant particular action in the ordinary operations of nature, which it hands over to secondary causes ; but only assigned this direct action to Him in His special interpositions. (Note 3.)

General laws, then, being only the laws of nature

with a particular conception appended to them ; if miracles are not reducible to the laws of nature, they are not reducible to general laws. Nor indeed, considering what has been said, would such a reduction be very consistent with the reason upon which general laws stand. For if general laws have been separated from the direct action of the Deity for the very purpose of reserving the latter as the peculiar mark of His special interpositions, to reduce these special interpositions back again from direct action to general law would be to undo the object of this distinction, and after drawing a line of demarcation to efface it again.

The notion of general laws naturally fits on indeed to God's *uniform* operations, but is a forced addition to irregular and extraordinary acts. The subordination of miracles indeed to " general laws of wisdom[d]," if we understand by that phrase a plan or scheme in the Divine Mind which controls the production of miracles, those considerations of utility which regulate their frequency as well as limit and check their type, may well be allowed ; but this is a different use of the term.

The inquiry has, indeed, been raised whether in the original design and mechanism of creation, the law or principle of the system may not have been

---

[d] Bishop Butler observes that " God's miraculous interpositions have been all along by *general laws of wisdom*. Thus, that miraculous powers should be exerted at such times, upon such occasions, in such degrees and manners, and with regard to such persons rather than to others, &c., all this may have been by general laws."—*Analogy*, Part ii. ch. iv.

so contrived that miracles when they occur are as
much the inevitable consequences of that law as
its regular and ordinary effects ; the same cause
or original plan which produces the order of nature,
producing also the exceptions to it. It is observed,
in the first place, that the history of our planet
being composed of successive stages or periods of
animal and vegetable life widely different from each
other, these several orders of nature may have been
but the gradual evolution of one primary law, impressed upon nature on its first construction ; the
highest law of the system being such that it includes all these changes under it, and that no
one formation singly but the whole series constitute the full and adequate expression of it. And
from this application to successive orders of nature,
the same rationale is then applied to the order
of nature and the deviation from it, or miracle.
Neither the order of nature nor the exception to
it alone, it is suggested, but both together, express
that highest generalization in the structure of nature
which is the law of the system and the whole. A
calculating machine is so adjusted as to produce
one unbroken chain of regularly succeeding numbers, when the law which governed the series fails,
and another law comes in, producing another succession of numbers or operating only in a single
instance ; after which it gives way again to the
first law. Neither of the two successions alone, nor
the succession or the insulation alone, expresses
the highest law of the machine, which includes

them both. So, it is said, the order of nature and the exception to it or miracle may both be included under the original law which was impressed upon the structure of nature. "That one or more men at given times shall be restored to life may be as much a consequence of the law of existence appointed for man at his creation, as the appearance and reappearance of the isolated cases of apparent exception in the arithmetical machine[e]." (Note 4.)

If this hypothesis, then, of the origin of miracles is entertained as a truth of *natural science,* an intermitting law of nature as much implies recurrent facts, with the same invariable antecedents, as any other law of nature does ; for if the exception is not as regular as the rule, the exception is not known as a rule or law at all. A clock is so constructed as to strike every hour but one, when it omits the stroke ; but it always omits the same hour. A calculating engine injects into a lengthened series of regularly succeeding numbers an insulated deviation ; but upon the same adjustment of the machine the deviation is repeated. Upon first seeing the exceptional number our impression would be that the machine was out of order, i. e. that this was an occurrence contrary to the law of the machine, nor should we be persuaded that it was not but by the repetition of the same exception in the same place. But miracles do not thus recur at the same physical junctures, and therefore do not come under an intermitting law of nature.

[e] Passages from the Life of a Philosopher, p. 390.

This hypothesis, then, of the origin of miracles cannot be maintained as a truth of natural science, and can only be entertained ,as a speculation respecting the action of the Deity, the mode of operation attributable to the Universal Cause in the production of a miracle—that His action in the matter is not contemporary but original action. It can only be entertained as a speculation respecting the mode of the *causation* of a miracle : this being a distinct question for that of a miracle's referribleness to a law of nature, which law is concerned not with causation but with facts. But as a speculation respecting the Divine action, and the mode of the causation of a miracle, this hypothesis would not, if adopted, make the slightest difference in the nature and character of a miracle. The date of its causation would be put back, but the miracle itself would remain exactly what it was before upon the ordinary hypothesis ; it would be as much an exception to the order of nature as before ; an exception as much the result of the Divine intention and design as before ; and to answer the same specific object which it answered before. Indeed, it is not the design of this hypothesis to make any difference in the miracle itself, or explain it away, but only, leaving it as miraculous as ever, to suggest a more philosophical rationale of its origin. Nor must such an hypothesis be confounded with attempts at physical explanations of miracles.

I have throughout this inquiry taken the term ' law of nature' in the scientific sense, as referring

to that order of nature of which we have experience ;
but if by the laws of nature we understand the laws
of the universe, we then arrive at a totally different
conclusion upon the question of the contrariety of
miracles to the laws of nature. In that case, " Nothing," as Spinoza says, " can take place in nature
which is contrary to the laws of nature," and a suspension of the laws of nature is a contradiction in
terms. A law cannot be suspended but by a force
which is capable of suspending it ; and that force
must act according to its own nature ; and the
second force cannot suspend the first unless the law
of its nature enables it to do so. The law of the
Divine nature enables it to suspend all physical
laws ; but, the existence of a God assumed, the law
of the Divine nature is as much a law of nature
as the laws which it suspends.

Is the suspension of physical and material laws
by a Spiritual Being inconceivable ? We reply, that
however inconceivable this kind of suspension of
physical law is, it is a fact. Physical laws are
suspended any time an animate being moves any
part of its body ; the laws of matter are suspended
by the laws of life. If there is anything I am
conscious of, it is that I am a spiritual being, that
no part of my tangible body is myself, and that
matter and I are distinct ideas. Yet I move matter,
i. e. my body, and every time I do so I suspend
the laws of matter. The arm that would otherwise
hang down by its own weight, is lifted up by this
spiritual being—myself. It is true my spirit is

connected with the matter which it moves in a
mode in which the Great Spirit who acts upon
matter in a miracle is not; but to what purpose
is this difference so long as any action of spirit
upon matter is incomprehensible.   The action of
God's Spirit in the miracle of walking on the water
is no more inconceivable than the action of my own
spirit in holding up my own hand.   Antecedently
one step on the ground and an ascent to heaven
are alike incredible.   But this appearance of incredibility is answered in one case literally *ambulando.*
How can I place any reliance upon it in the
other?

The constitution of nature, then, disproves the
incredibility of the Divine suspension of physical
law; but more than this, it creates a presumption
for it.   For the laws of which we have experience
are themselves in an ascending scale.   First come
the laws which regulate unorganized matter; next
the laws of vegetation; then, by an enormous leap,
the laws of animal life with its voluntary motion,
desire, expectation, fear; and above these, again, the
laws of moral being which regulate a totally different
order of creatures.   Now suppose an intelligent being
whose experience was limited to one or more lower
classes in this ascending scale of laws,—he would be
totally incapable of conceiving the action of the
higher classes.   A thinking piece of granite would
be totally incapable of conceiving the action of
chemical laws, which produce explosions, contacts,
repulsions.   A thinking mineral would be totally

incapable of conceiving the laws of vegetable growth; a thinking vegetable could not form an idea of the laws of animal life; a thinking animal could not form an idea of moral and intellectual truth. All this progressive succession of laws is perfectly conceivable backward, and an absolute mystery forward; and therefore when in the ascending series we arrive at man, we ask, Is there no higher sphere of law as much above *him* as he is above the lower natures in the scale? The analogy would lead us to expect that there was, and supplies a presumption in favour of such a belief.

And so we arrive again by another route at the old turning question; for the question whether man is or is not the *vertex* of nature, is the question whether there is or is not a God. Does free agency stop at the human stage, or is there a sphere of free-will above the human, in which, as in the human, not physical law but spirit moves matter? And does that free-will penetrate the universal frame invisibly to us, an omnipresent agent? If so, every miracle in Scripture is as natural an event in the universe as any chemical experiment in the physical world; if not, the seat of the great Presiding Will is empty, and nature has no Personal Head: man is her highest point; he finishes her ascent; though by this very supremacy he falls, for under fate he is not free himself; all nature either ascends to God, or descends to law. Is there above the level of material causes a region of Providence? If there is, nature there is moved by the Supreme Free Agent; and of

such a realm a miracle is the natural production.
(Note 5.)

Two rationales of miracles thus present themselves
to our choice ; one more accommodating to the
physical imagination and easy to fall in with, on
a level with custom, common conceptions, and ordinary history, and requiring no ascent of the mind to
embrace, viz. the solution of miracles as the growth of
fancy and legend ; the other requiring an ascent of
the reason to embrace it, viz. the rationale of the
supremacy of a Personal Will in nature.   The one
is the explanation to which we fall when we dare
not trust our reason, but mistake its inconceivable
truths for sublime but unsubstantial visions ; the
other is that to which we rise when we dare trust
our reason, and the evidences which it lays before
us of the existence of a Personal Supreme Being.

LECTURE VII.

MIRACLES REGARDED IN THEIR PRACTICAL RESULT.

ROMANS VI. 17.

But God be thanked, that ye were the servants of sin, but ye have obeyed from the heart that form of doctrine which was delivered you.

IN judging of the truth of miracles the revelation of which they were designed to be the proof necessarily comes into consideration; and specially the practical result of that revelation. Without assuming the truth of revelation, we can consider this result. It is a reasonable inquiry which arises in the mind upon first hearing of an era of miracles—What is the good of them? what end and purpose have they answered? If, then, some who had diseases were cured, that is something. But if there has been a permanent, enormous, and incalculable practical result, such a result that no other change in the world is to be compared with it, that is a very serious thing to take into account. We cannot avoid attaching weight to it, giving it a place in the proof, and feeling impressed by the importance of such a circumstance, in relation to the question. Without using—which we have no right to do—this result as direct evidence of the facts in dispute, if the miraculous system has been a practical one, with immense practical effects upon mankind, it plainly ought to have the benefit of this consideration in the estimate of its claims to be received as true.

It is admitted, then, that Christianity has produced the greatest change that has been ever known in the world, with reference to moral standard and moral practice ; and when we inquire further, we find this change attributed by universal consent to the power of the great doctrines of Christianity upon the human heart ; which doctrines could not have been communicated without the evidence of miracles.

And, first, a religion founded on miracles as compared with a religion founded upon the evidences of a God in nature, has a much superior motive power in the very fact of its supernatural origin. Undoubtedly the love of the supernatural may become a mere idle pleasure, and when it does it is condemned in Scripture. " If they hear not Moses and the Prophets, neither will they be persuaded though one rose from the dead." But, on the other hand, this affection is in itself religious, and a powerful instrument of religion. A supernatural fact, a communication from the other world, is a potent influence ; it rouses, it solemnizes ; it is a strong motive to serious action. The other world stands before us in a more real aspect immediately. Thè notion of God as a Personal Being must be beyond all comparison greater in a religion founded upon miracles, than in one founded upon nature : because a miracle is itself a token of personal agency, of a Will and Spirit moving behind the veil of matter, in a way and manner in which the works of nature are not. The tendency of a religion founded on nature, or Deism, is to establish as the world of God and man nature alone, the religious principle being adopted but made to coincide with the sphere of this world. Such a religion is weak in influence. The voice of God must come out of another world to command with authority ; such a voice spake to Abraham, Isaac, and Jacob ; their religion had its root in the Invisible ; but a God in nature only does not strike awe. One single real miracle is another ground in religion ; if the walls of nature have been broken through but once, we are divided by a whole world from a mere physical basis of religion. Do we in imagination assign a certain extraordinary depth and seriousness to those who have seen supernatural facts ? The language of the Apostles embodies our idea and type of the effect of so unearthly an experience upon the recipients.

But the remarkable change which Christianity made in the world was owing mainly not to the miracles, but to the doctrines of which they were the proof.

Undoubtedly the principal portion of the Gospel

miracles were, besides being proofs of doctrine, also acts of mercy, sympathy, and beneficence ; and attention has been properly directed to the philanthropical character of them—that they were not mere acts of power but acts of love. Indeed, the philanthropical purpose was the primary and principal purpose of each of these miracles as a single act, and with reference to the occasion on which it was wrought : while the evidential object belongs to them only as a body and a whole. The evidential object of miracles, indeed, was naturally achieved by the medium of the philanthropical object ; the general purpose was fulfilled by the very same acts which also served the special, particular, and occasional purposes. The one object adapted itself to the times and opportunities of the other, followed, waited upon, and linked itself on to them ; the proof of a dispensation was communicated in the form of miracles for the temporary relief and benefit of individuals. The evidential object of miracles was not executed in a forced and unnatural way, by set feats of thaumaturgy, and exhibitions of miraculous power as such, challenging the astonishment of beholders : it was accomplished in correspondence with the whole scale of the Divine character ; the acts of power were performed for those purposes which love pointed out, were elicited naturally by the several occasions, and fitted on to the course of events, the incidents of the hour, and the cases of infirmity which came in the way. Still, however naturally and in whatever connexion with other objects the evidential function of

miracles was introduced, that function was not the
less the principal object of mircles; that on which
they depended for any advantage ensuing from them
extending beyond the original and local occasions
themselves which elicited them, any permanent advantage to the world at large, any result affecting
the interests of mankind. Will it be said that these
philanthropical miraculous acts were a revelation of
the character of God to man as a God of mercy and
love? They could not be *that*, however, except by
the medium of the evidential function. For they
could only be a revelation in act of the Divine character, on the supposition that the Person who
wrought them was "God manifested in the flesh"—
a result for which the doctrine of the Incarnation,
to prove which this evidential function is necessary,
is assumed.

That the Gospel miracles, then, founded a system
of doctrine which was lasting, and did not pass
away like a creature of the day, is justly noticed
by writers on evidence as an important note in
favour of them; but what I remark now is not
the permanent doctrine which was the effect of the
miracles, but the great permanent change which was
the effect of the doctrine; that this doctrine did not
leave mankind as it found them, but was a fresh
starting-point—(ἀφορμή)—of moral practice, whence
we date, not certainly the complete regeneration of
the world, but such an alteration in it as divides
the world after the Christian era from the world
before it.

The Epistle to the Romans is in substance a declaration of this power and effect of Christian doctrine, a prophecy, if we may call it so, of the actual result which has followed it. This Epistle is distinguished as the great doctrinal Epistle, and truly ; but this is not an adequate description of it, because the writer sets forth there Christian doctrine, not in itself as truth merely, but as that great new motive to *action* which was the prominent and conspicuous want and need of mankind. The Epistle to the Romans is one long assertion of this power of doctrine as a motive to action. First comes the statement that the world up to that moment had been, morally speaking, a failure, and had utterly disappointed the design for which it was made ; not because man was without the knowledge of his duty, but because, the knowledge existing, there was between knowledge and action a total chasm, which nothing yet had been able to fill up. The Apostle looks upon that as yet unbridged gulf, this incredible inability of man to do what was right, with profound wonder ; yet such was the fact. The sublime moral maxims of Oriental nations strike us now ; it is impossible to deny the light, the height of pure knowledge which they shew ; but can the transcendent code of duty get itself acted on ? Is it looked upon even in that point of view ? Has it even a practical intention that deserves to be called so ? No ; it is a beautiful erection of moral sentiment, but there it ends. Man possesses a moral nature, and, if he has in-

tellect enough, he can put his moral ideas into
words, just as he can put metaphysical ideas; nor
is his doing so any test of his moral condition.
Take any careless person of corrupt habits out of
the thick of his ordinary life, and ask him to
state in words what is his moral creed? Has
he any doubt about it? None: he immediately
puts down a list of the most sublime moral truths
and principles. But as regards their being a law
to himself, he feels that he has no more to do with
them than with anything else which is impossible.
Between them and action there exists in his eyes
an impassable interval; and so far as relates to
himself, as soon as ever these truths are formally
and properly enunciated, their whole design and
purpose is fulfilled.

Such was the contrast which met St. Paul in
the condition of the whole world Jew and Gentile
—knowledge without action. What was there to
fill up this void, and effect a junction between
these two? Now when a man feels something to
be wholly out of his reach, and that he has nothing to do with it, because he *cannot* do it;
the first notion of a remedy for this sense of utter
impotence is an appeal to his will—Believe that
you can do it, and you can do it. But how can
a man believe simply because he is told to do
so? Believe upon no foundation? On the other
hand, if you can tell him anything new about
himself, any actual fresh source of strength from
which he has not drawn but now may draw, this

is a ground for a new belief about himself and what he can do. And this ground for a new belief about himself is what St. Paul proceeds to lay before impotent and despairing man, whose cry was, "To will is present with me, but how to perform that which is good I find not. For the good which I would I do not, but the evil which I would not that I do. Who shall deliver me from the body of this death?" Nothing but some wholly new agency, some effective and powerful motive not yet known to the world, could set this nature in action; but that motive St. Paul could supply.

The force, then, which Christianity applied to human nature, according to St. Paul, and by which it was to produce this change in the moral state of man, was a new doctrine. This new impulse and inspiration to goodness, able to lift him above the power of sin, the love of the world, and the lusts of the flesh, was contained in the great truth of the Incarnation and Death of the Son of God. God was by this transcendent act of mediation reconciled to man, pardoned him, and sent him forth anew on his course, with the gift of the Holy Spirit in his heart. This new foundation, then, upon which human life is raised is an actual event which has taken place in the invisible world, but inasmuch as God communicates the advantage of that event to man by the medium of man's own knowledge of and belief in it, this event necessarily becomes a doctrine; and that doctrine is the new impulse to human nature. " The righteousness of God is manifested unto all and upon all them that *believe*." The knowledge of and faith in the new supernatural relation in which he stands to God, is henceforth the moral strength of man, that which enables him to obey the Divine law. That new relation does not produce its effect without his own convictions, but knowing it and believing it, he experiences a movement from it so forcible, so elevating, and so kindling, that he is raised above himself by it. " Sin has not dominion over him." " The law of the Spirit of life hath made him free from the law of sin and death. For what the law could not do, in that it was weak through the flesh, God sending His own Son in the likeness of sinful flesh, and for sin, condemned sin in the flesh : that the righteousness of the law might be fulfilled in us." " He that raised up Christ from the dead shall quicken our mortal bodies, by His Spirit that dwelleth in us." " He that spared not His own Son, but delivered Him up for us all, how shall He not with Him also freely give us all things[a] ?" He appeals to men's belief in the great facts and doctrines of the Gospel, as that which is henceforth to constitute the motive power to urge them to and fix them in moral practice. The prefaces, " How shall we," " Know ye not," " Reckon yourselves," " Ye are debtors to," " Ye are servants to,"

---

[a] Rom. viii. 2, 3, 11, 32.

express the sense of an impossibility of acting against such a belief if it is genuine.

If we examine the mode in which the doctrine of the Incarnation and Death of the Son of God is adapted to act upon moral conduct, first comes the influence and the motive contained in the character of the Divine Being, of which this is a new and striking revelation. The Atonement stamps upon the mind with a power, with which no other fact could, the righteousness of God. To trifle with a Being who has demanded this Sacrifice is madness; and hence arises awe: but from the acceptance of the Atonement arises the love of God. A strict master is a stimulus to service if he is just; servants wish to please him: his pardon, again, is the greater stimulus, on account of his very strictness, because it is the greater prize. Thus the belief in the Atonement becomes that inspiring motive to action which St. Paul represents it as being. Man appears in his Epistles as a pardoned being,—pardoned by that very God of whom he thus stands in awe,—and as a pardoned being a rejoicing being; rejoicing, not because he has nothing to do, but because having much to do, he feels himself possessed of a high spirit, and strength enough to do it. The sense of pardon is the inspiriting thing. "For if when we were enemies we were reconciled to God by the death of His Son, much more being reconciled we shall be saved by His life[b]." From that event man

---

[b] Rom. v. 10.

dates his adoption, his glorious liberty, the law of
the Spirit of life, the witness of that Spirit in
his own heart, the expectation of that glory which
shall be revealed in him, and the gift of eternal
life.

We thus observe it as a remarkable characteristic
of Scripture, and specially of St. Paul's language,
that it takes what may be called the high view of
human nature ; i. e. of what human nature is capable
of when the proper motive and impulse is applied to
it. In this sense St. Paul, if I may use the expression, *believes* in human nature ; he thinks it capable
of rising to great heights even in this life, he sees
that in man which really can triumph over the world,
the flesh, and the devil ; which can struggle, and
which can conquer in the struggle. His is what
may be called the enthusiastic view of human nature,
though tempered by the wisdom of inspiration. He
sees in Christian doctrine that strong force which
is to break down the *vis inertiæ* of man, to kindle
into life the dormant elements of goodness in him,
to set human nature going, and to touch the spring
of man's heart. Hence it is that the writer is borne
along at times breathless with vehemence and with
rapture, as the visions of hope rise up before him,
and man is seen in the prospect over all the face
of the earth, ascending in mind to heaven. Hence
it is that the flood of thought becoming too rapid
for the medium which conveys it, struggles with and
interrupts itself. Though at the same time he is
equally arrested by the mystery of limitation which

adheres to Divine grace, and sees the true Church of God as separate from the world.

How marked the contrast, when from this high estimate of, this ardent faith in, the capabilities of human nature which a doctrinal foundation imparts, we turn to the idea of man presented to us in a religion of pure Deism. The religion of Mahomet is not a doctrinal religion; it is without an Incarnation, without an Atonement; no sacrifice for sin reveals the awful justice of God, no pardon upon a sacrifice His awful mercy; in the high court of heaven the Deity sits enthroned in the majesty of omnipotence and omniscience, but without the great symbol of His Infinite Righteousness by His side— the Lamb that was slain. And now observe the effect of this doctrinal void upon the idea of God and the idea of man in that religion. If one had to express in a short compass the character of its remarkable founder as a teacher, it would be that that great man had no faith in human nature. There were two things which he thought man could do and would do for the glory of God—transact religious forms, and fight; and upon those two points he was severe; but within the sphere of common practical life, where man's great trial lies, his code exhibits the disdainful laxity of a legislator, who accommodates his rule to the recipient, and shews his estimate of the recipient by the accommodation which he adopts. Did we search history for a contrast, we could hardly discover a deeper one than that between St. Paul's overflowing standard of the capa-

bilities of human nature and the oracular cynicism of
the great false Prophet. The writer of the Koran does
indeed, if any discerner of hearts ever did, take the
measure of mankind ; and his measure is the same
that Satire has taken, only expressed with the majestic brevity of one who had once lived in the realm
of Silence. " Man is weak," says Mahomet. And
upon that maxim he legislates. " God is minded to
make his religion light unto you, for man was
created weak "—" God would make his religion an
ease unto you "—a suitable foundation of the code
which followed, and fit parent of that numerous
offspring of accommodations, neutralizing qualifications, and thinly-disguised loopholes to the fraud
and rapacity of the Oriental, which appear in the
Koran, and shew, where they do appear, the author's
deep acquaintance with the besetting sins of his devoted followers. The keenness of Mahomet's insight
into human nature, a wide knowledge of its temptations, persuasives, influences under which it acts,
a vast immense capacity of forbearance for it, half
grave half genial, half sympathy half scorn, issue
in a somewhat Horatian model, the character of
the man of experience who despairs of any change
in man, and lays down the maxim that we must take
him as we find him. It was indeed his supremacy
in both faculties, the largeness of the passive nature,
and the splendour of action, that constituted the secret
of his success. The breadth and flexibility of mind
that could negotiate with every motive of interest,
passion, and pride in man is surprising ; there is bound-

less sagacity; what is wanting is hope, a belief in the capabilities of human nature. There is no upward flight in the teacher's idea of man. Instead of which, the notion of the power of earth, and the impossibility of resisting it, depresses his whole aim, and the shadow of the tomb falls upon the work of the great false Prophet. (Note I.)

The idea of God is akin to the idea of man. "He knows us," says Mahomet. God's *knowledge*, the vast *experience*, so to speak, of the Divine Being, His infinite acquaintance with man's frailties and temptations, is appealed to as the ground of confidence. "He is the Wise, the Knowing One," "He is the Knowing, the Wise," "He is easy to be reconciled." Thus is raised a notion of the Supreme Being which is rather an extension of the character of the large-minded and sagacious man of the world, than an extension of man's virtue and holiness. He forgives because He knows too much to be rigid, because sin universal ceases to be sin, and must be given way to. Take a man who has had large opportunity of studying mankind, and has come into contact with every form of human weakness and corruption ; such a man is indulgent as a simple consequence of his knowledge, because nothing surprises him. So the God of Mahomet forgives by reason of His vast knowledge. The absence of the doctrine of the Atonement makes itself felt in the character of that Being who forgives without a Sacrifice for sin ; shewing that without that doctrine there cannot even be high Deism. So knit together is the whole fabric of truth ; with-

out a sacrifice, a pardoning God becomes an easy
God : and an easy God makes a low human nature.
No longer awful in His justice, the Wise, " the
Knowing One," degrades His own act of forgiveness
by converting it into connivance ; and man takes full
advantage of so tolerant and convenient a master.
" Man is weak," and " God knows him,"—these two
maxims taken together constitute an ample charter
of freedom for human conduct. " God knows us,"
says man ; He knows that we are not adapted to
a very rigid rule, He does not look upon us in that
light, He does not expect any great things from us ;
not an inflexible justice, not a searching self-denial,
not a punctilious love of our neighbour ; He is considerate, He is wise, He knows what we can do, and
what we cannot do ; He does not condemn us, He
makes allowance for us, " He knows us." So true is
the saying of Pascal that " without the knowledge
of Jesus Christ we see nothing but confusion in the
nature of God and in our own nature c."

The force which Christianity has applied to the
world, and by which it has produced that change in
the world which it has, is, in a word, the doctrine of
grace. There has been a new power actually working in the system, and that power has worked by
other means besides doctrine ; but still it is the law
of God's dealings with us to apply His power to us
by means of our faith and belief in that power ; i. e.
by doctrine. Faith in his own position, the belief

---

c Pensées, vol. ii. p. 317.

at the bottom of every Christian's heart that he
stands in a different relation to God from a heathen,
and has a supernatural source of strength—this it is
which has made him *act*, has been the rousing and
elevating motive to the Christian body, and raised
its moral practice.

If we go into particulars, the force of the great
Example of the Incarnation, which we include in
the effect of the doctrine of the Incarnation, has
founded the great order of Christian, as distinguished
from heathen virtues. It is evident what power the
great act of forgiveness in the Atonement has had
in stamping the great law of forgiveness upon human
hearts ; what power the Incarnation, as a great act
of humiliation, has had in creating another estimate
of human rank and glory ; what effect again the
same great doctrine has had in producing that interest in the poor and whole difference of relations
to them which has characterized Christian society.
For whence has that idea of the poor and their
claims come, but from the idea of man's brotherhood to man which the Incarnation has founded,
and the recommendation of a low estate contained
in the Humiliation of the Incarnation. There has
been deep in men's minds the notion that they
were uniting themselves to that Act, and attaching to
themselves the benefit of it, by copying it ; by trans-
ferring it to Christian life, and reproducing it, so to
speak, in an act of their own,—the descent from their
own position to that of a lower fellow-creature. The
doctrine of the Holy Spirit, again, has enlightened

man with respect to his body, and the respect due
to it as the temple of that Divine Spirit; and has
thus produced that different estimate of sins of the
body which so distinguishes the Christian from the
heathen world. The doctrine of a future life, as
attested by the miracle of the Resurrection, was
practically a new doctrine in the world : it has inspired a belief and a conviction of a world to come,
altogether distinct from any notion entertained by
the heathen; and it has acted as the most powerful
motive to moral practice.

It must be observed that the great public causes,
which have produced the moral movements of communities and of society in the modern world, have
leaned upon *doctrine;* and relied upon that power
for the propagating energy necessary for them.
Hence has arisen the inoculation of hearts, the excitement of genuine interest. The cause of the
poorer classes, as just stated, has had a doctrinal foundation. The cause of the slave has had
the same. The doctrine of the Incarnation has
through the idea of man's brotherhood to man,
also founded the rights of man. Christianity tole-
rated slavery in the days of the Apostles, and it
does so now because it tolerates all conditions of life
which admit of Christian devotion and practice being
conducted in them. But Christianity has always
opposed this abuse : the Church was the great manu-
mitter and improver of the condition of the serf in
the middle ages; and in the present age religious
feeling has been at the bottom of the great move-

ment against slavery. For was that being to be bought and sold whose nature Christ assumed, and for whom Christ died ? Thus the public effort which ended in relieving this country from the stigma of the capture and ownership of slaves, received its impulse from doctrine, and the great leader of it was himself the leader of a doctrinal revival. Public education has been partly a movement of charity and benevolence to man, and partly a movement for the advance of science. As a movement of charity to impart knowledge to and elevate the minds of the poor, it has been indebted principally and primarily to a religious motive ; for George III caught the *animus* of society and represented it correctly in his well-known prophecy of the day " when every man in England would be able to read his Bible." And whence has the relief of sickness obtained its dignity and loftiness as a duty under Christianity ? Whence but from the same great doctrine which makes mankind one body, as members of " Him who filleth all in all ?" Hence every individual member partakes of the dignity of the whole ; and the act of ministering to him becomes a noble service, paid to the whole body, and to its Head. " I was sick and ye visited Me, I was in prison and ye came unto Me." The idea of the dignity of man as such, the equality of man with man in the sight of God, the nobility of ministry and service to him, for the relief of his wants and diseases, did not exist in the world before the Gospel ; the heathens had no value for man as such, but only for man under certain flattering circum-

stances, as developed by knowledge, or greatness.
Reduced to his own nature, he was nothing in their
eyes : the slave was another being from his master.
The light of truth first broke through this blindness
and stupor in the doctrine of the Incarnation, and
that doctrine is the historical date of the modern
idea of man. To say that the inspiration of the
missionary cause has been the belief in Christian
doctrine is almost superfluous; because we can
hardly in imagination conceive missionary enterprise without it. Zeal in this cause is essentially
the child of faith ; and without the conviction in the
Church of a supernatural truth to communicate, and
a supernatural dispensation to spread, Christianity
must give up the very pretension of propagating
itself in the world. The great public causes which
are part of modern history and distinguish modern
society from ancient, thus witness to the power of
doctrine ; but public causes are but one channel in
which Christian action has flowed ; they do but
exhibit in aggregate forms that Christian disposition
and practice which goes on principally in private.

Christianity simply regarded as a code of morals
will not account for this moral change in the world ;
for men do not do right things because they are told
to do them. Mere moral instruction does not effect its
purpose unless it is seconded by some powerful force
and motive besides the lesson itself. Nor is this
change in the world accounted for by the natural
law of example, by saying that a body of men of
high moral character and aims, under a remarkable

leader, set up a high model, which model spread originally and transmitted itself age after age by its own power and influence as a model and pattern. The force of example has a natural tendency to wear out. We see this in institutions and in states. Particular societies have in different ages been set going by earnest men, who infused at first their own spirit and put men of their own type into them ; but the force of example became gradually weaker in the process of transmission ; at every stage of the succession something of it was lost, till at last the body wholly degenerated. So a great example set by founders and their associates has imparted a mould and character to political communities, which has lasted some time ; but this mould has altered as the original influence by little and little died away ; and the state has become corrupt. Thus the pattern of public spirit and devotion to the public good which was originally stamped upon Sparta, Rome, and Venice, gradually lost its hold, and those states degenerated. The force of example, then, is not self-sustaining ; and therefore when a moral change in society is made for a perpetuity, and is a permanent characteristic, lasting through and surviving all other changes or transitions, this effect must be owing to some other principle than that of example, some permanent force from another root, by which example itself is kept up. I may add that the source of Christian practice in Christian truth does not agree with any settled principle of decay in Christian practice, and with extreme statements of the inferiority of modern Christians to ancient. For though doubtless, with the same truth to move the human heart, its energies may be brought out in one age more than in another, still the idea of a regular tendency of Christian practice to degenerate with time, combines with the explanation of example as its cause, rather than with the operation of a constant cause in revealed truth.

What I remark, then, is that the prophecy in the Epistle to the Romans has been fulfilled, and that doctrine has been historically at the bottom of a great change of moral practice in mankind. By a prophecy I mean that St. Paul assigns a certain property and effect to doctrine, viz. that of eliciting the good element in man, setting man's moral nature in action ; and that this property has been realized. The world, he says, has been hitherto a failure, everything has gone wrong, because man has not been able to act ; he could not do the thing that he would ; he has laboured under an insurmountable weakness, and defect of some motive power adequate to tell upon him. But this is what is to change man ; this is what is to touch the seat of action in his heart, the truth which is now revealed from heaven—the doctrine of the Incarnation and Death of Christ. This doctrine will rouse and awaken human nature, and give it what it now wants—the great practical impulse. This account, I say, of the power of doctrine in St. Paul has been fulfilled by the fact. The history of man coincides with this assertion of St. Paul's of the property of doctrine.

Not that the result has been by any means a complete one, or that St. Paul expected it to be ; far otherwise. His doctrine of election shews that ; that doctrine evidently represents the body of really good and holy men in the world, the spiritual Church, as always insulated in the world, always a small number in comparison with the great mass of mankind ; and a dark shadow rests upon one portion of the field of prophecy, contrasting remarkably with the light and glory of the other. But the issue of the Gospel, though not a complete result, has still been a great result ; such a result as divides the world after the Christian era morally from the world before it. A stimulus has been given to human nature, which has extracted an amount of action from it which no Greek or Roman could have believed possible, but which, had it been placed in idea before him, he would have set aside as the dream of an enthusiast.

Undoubtedly the doctrines of false religions have extracted remarkable action out of human nature ; especially the doctrines of Oriental religions. The Hindoo doctrine of Absorption, e.g. has produced a great deal of extraordinary action. But what sort of action is it ? Is it action upon the scale of our whole moral nature, worthy *of* that nature, or the fulfilment of the law as the Scripture calls it ? No, it is such wild, eccentric, one-sided energy of the erratic will as is more allied to phrenzy than morals. The fruits of the doctrine of Absorption are gigantic feats of self-torture and self-stupefaction, ending in themselves, and unconnected with charity to man : a fruit worthy of its source. For the doctrine of Absorption is itself a falsehood : no man can wish for the loss of his own personality, i.e. his own annihilation : no man ever *did* wish for it, whatever length of torture he may have undergone to obtain it. The conception is a counterfeit ; it wants truth, and "the tree is known by its fruits." Do men gather grapes of thorns, or figs of thistles ? So neither can moral practice issue out of the doctrine of Absorption ; but a fiction produces the wild and poor fruit of extravagance. (Note 2.)

In attributing this effect to Christian doctrine, we must at the same time remember that the old Law foreshadowed that doctrine. The religion of the Jew was not Deism. In the first place it was founded on miracles, and on that higher revelation of the personality of the Deity which miracles are. In the next place it was accompanied by the institution of sacrifice, which was a peculiar revelation of the righteous character of God, as a *rite;* and an intimation of the real Atonement as a *type.* From these sources was derived the deep doctrine of repentance and forgiveness, which penetrates the Psalms and Prophecy ; the sense of the necessity of an act of pardon on God's part, in order to allay the trouble in man's heart, and reinstate him in peace of mind ; the intimate communion with God *upon* this sense of the necessity of His favour and acceptance ; the language of tender complaint and remonstrance with Him founded upon what we may

call the devotional fiction of His hardness and in-
flexibility—the affectionate irony of prayer. In this
whole relation to God lay the motive power of the
old Law, the stimulus to goodness in it; to the
force of which the Jew was indebted for raising him
above the pagan in morals; and which actually
issued in producing *a body or class* of holy men in
every generation of the people. Whereas paganism
had high individual examples, but not a class. But
this relation under the old Law was an anticipation of
Christian light. The Law as such could not "give
life," nor "could righteousness come by the Law," as a
law; but so far as the old Law contained the germ
of Gospel truth, so far it gave life; so far it supplied
an effective motive to rouse the heart of man to
exertion. (Note 3.)

The relation of religion to morals has indeed been
exemplified most conspicuously under Christianity.
Morality may in the abstract exist without religion,
and is not identical with it; but religion has been
the practical producer of it; the practical motive
to morals in the world. Our moral nature is not
its own moving principle; it is so at least very
inadequately; and so we find that in point of fact
doctrine has been the impulse which has set it in
action. It is not in human nature to set about its
work wholly in the dark; it wants a vision of
the invisible world, a revelation of God and of
its own prospects and destiny, to set it to work.
The revelation of God in Jesus Christ, and of life
eternal in the same Jesus Christ, is this vision or

supernatural truth which has produced action. The strong need of the sense of favour with God, which the Gospel manifestation of Him has created ; the overpowering disclosure of man's destiny, that he was made for a state of endless glory and happiness, has forced men, in spite of themselves, to do good acts. And therefore doctrine has been a part of human progress, a fresh groundwork, a higher level gained ; analogous in morals to civilization in social and political life. And to give up doctrine would be a retrograde movement for the human race, the surrender of ground made, a relapse from a later to an earlier stage of humanity ; the abandonment of a superior motive power which commands the spring of action in the human heart, for an inferior one which did not touch it.

But still it will be asked—Would not all this result of Christianity have been just the same without the peculiar doctrines ? are not these merely the accidental appendages of a spirit which rose up in man, which has been the energizing power throughout ? But though it is always open to men, when great results have taken place in connexion with certain apparent causes, to say that they would have taken place all the same *without* those causes, this cannot in the nature of the case be more than a conjecture. We have an obvious and matter-of-fact coincidence of a higher state of mankind with doctrine ; which coincidence is of itself a strong argument. And we have, moreover, man's own witness to doctrine, as being the cause which has produced this effect. If we are to take men's own account of their own action, and their own power of action, this has been the impulse to them : the call which has awakened them to moral life has been a doctrinal one ; what has enabled them to maintain this action has been the support of certain truths, in the absence of which they would not have been able to do what they did. In this state of the case, to say that all this change would have gone on without doctrine, is unsatisfactory, and suppositional only. Let us conceive for a moment Christian doctrine obliterated, and mankind starting afresh without it, with only the belief in a Benevolent Deity, and a high moral code. With the fact before us of what has been the working power of doctrine upon man's heart, and what has been the weakness of our moral nature without doctrine, could we commit mankind to a moral Deism without trembling for the result ? Could we deprive human nature of this powerful aid and inspiring motive, and expect it to act as if it had it ? Could we look forward without dismay to the loss of this practical force which has been acting upon human nature for eighteen centuries ? Would any one in his heart expect that Christianity deprived of its revealed truths would retain its old strength, would produce equal fruits, the same self-sacrificing spirit, zeal, warmth, earnestness ? that it would give the same power of living above the world ? that its effects on the heart, its spiritualizing influence, would be the same without its doctrines ?

No! When men speculate they want to get rid of doctrine ; but when they want practical results to be produced, then they fall back upon doctrine, as that alone which can produce them, which can awaken man from his lethargy, and supply a constraining motive to him. I do not mean to say that many have not taken an active part in the great objects and movements of Christian society who have not accepted Christian doctrine ; but such men have acted upon an idea obtained from revelation, although they have ceased to believe the revelation from which it came. Example is not the full account of the origin of Christian practice, but still that practice existing, its example tells, and inoculates many who reject the creed. A moral standard is imbibed with the atmosphere of life. Such men are the production of Christian doctrine, however they may disclaim it :—so far at least as concerns this practical zeal.

What is offered as a substitute for the doctrine of the Incarnation, to set man's moral nature in action, is the enthusiastic philosophical sentiment of the divinity of human nature. But though I would not say that this, like other ideas which have an element of truth in them, has not given a high impulse to some minds ; that it has been a forcible engine for impelling mankind to the practice of duty would be plainly overrating its results. And there is a reason for its weakness and want of power, viz. that the idea does not stand the test of observation. For let us suppose a sagacious man of great experience and knowledge of the world, who had had opportunity of observing human nature upon a large scale—its expressions and its disguises, the corruption of men's motives, and all those well-known traits and characteristics of mankind which acute men have embodied in various sayings—let us suppose such a person having laid before him for his acceptance the above idea of the divinity of human nature. He would treat it with derision and ridicule; representing that though men of the profoundest sagacity have in all ages believed in mysteries, it is another thing to ask them to believe that facts themselves are different from what they are seen to be. But let us suppose again, the same penetrating observer not wholly satisfied with the low estimate of man as the full account of him, but catching also obscure signs of a different element in the being, working its way under great disadvantages, and not to be left out of the calculation, though he cannot tell what it may turn out to be, and what it may shadow and prognosticate in the destiny of this creature. Were then, at this stage, the idea of a design that this creature should be partaker of the Divine nature to be offered to him, whatever astonishment the thought might excite, conscious that he had no solution of his own of the enigma before him, he would not wholly reject it; but one condition he would think indispensable—he would not listen to the notion of this creature's exaltation except through the passage of some deep confession first, by which

o

he would condemn himself utterly, and in condemning cast off his old vileness. Without this tribute, this sacrifice to truth, such an idea would appear a mockery.

Such a distinction as this divides one doctrine of exalted humanity from another. A deification of humanity upon its own grounds, an exaltation which is all height and no depth, wants power because it wants truth. It is not founded upon the facts of human nature, and therefore issues in vain and vapid aspiration, and injures the solidity of man's character. That serious doctrine of man's greatness, which lays hold on man's moral nature, and brings it out, is one which lays its foundation first in his guilt and misery ; his exaltation is remedial, a restoration from a fall. Thus the school of experience accepts man's vileness in the Gospel portrait, the sanguine school his loftiness ; the one depresses man, the other inflates him ; the Gospel doctrine of the Incarnation and its effects alone unites the sagacious view of human nature with the enthusiastic. It is the only doctrine of man's exaltation which the observer of mankind can accept ; while also it is only as a mystery transacted in the highest heaven that man's exaltation has ever been cared for by himself, ever commanded his serious energies. (Note 4.)

But if, as the source and inspiration of practice, doctrine has been the foundation of a new state of the world, and of that change which distinguishes the world under Christianity from the world before it; miracles, as the proof of that doctrine, stand before us in a very remarkable and peculiar light. Far from being mere idle feats of power to gratify the love of the marvellous; far even from being mere particular and occasional rescues from the operation of general laws; they come before us as means for accomplishing the largest and most important practical object that has ever been accomplished in the history of mankind. They lie at the bottom of the difference of the modern from the ancient world; so far, i.e. as that difference is moral. We see as a fact a change in the moral condition of mankind, which marks ancient and modern society as two different states of mankind. What has produced this change, and elicited this new power of action? Doctrine. And what was the proof of that doctrine, or essential to the proof of it? Miracles. The greatness of the result thus throws light upon the propriety of the means; and shews the fitting object which was presented for the introduction of such means; the fitting occasion which had arisen for the use of them; for indeed no more weighty, grand, or solemn occasion can be conceived, than the foundation of such a new order of things in the world. Extraordinary action of Divine power for such an end has the benefit of a justifying object of incalculable weight; which though not of itself indeed proof of the fact, comes with striking force upon the mind in connexion with the proper proof. It is reasonable, it is inevitable that we should be impressed by such a result; for it shews that the miraculous system has been a practical one ; that it has been a step in the ladder of man's ascent, the means of introducing those powerful truths which have set his moral nature in action.

Nor, must it be observed, can professed subsequent miracles for the conversion of particular populations, *after* the original miraculous proof and propagation of the Gospel, avail themselves of the argument which applies to those original miracles themselves. Because the argument for these miracles, which is thus extracted from the great result of them, is based upon the *necessity* of those miracles for this result. But though the original miracles are necessary for the proof of doctrine, subsequent miracles cannot plead the same necessity ; because when that doctrine has been once attested, those original credentials, transmitted by the natural channels of evidence, are the permanent and perpetual proof of that doctrine, not wanting reinforcements from additional and posterior miracles ; which are therefore without the particular recommendation to our belief, of being necessary for the great result before us. The Anglo-Saxon nation was doubtless as important a nation to convert as the Jewish or Greek ; but the miracles of our Lord and His Apostles were necessary to convert the Jews and the Greeks ; St. Augustine's reputed miracles were not necessary to convert the Anglo-Saxons. First miracles in proof of a new dispensation, and miracles in a subsequent age for the spread of it, stand upon different grounds in this respect ; the latter are without that particular note of truth which consists in a *necessary* connexion with great permanent ends. First credentials cannot be dispensed with, second ones can be. It may be said that second ones are useful for facilitating and expediting conversion ; but we are no judges of the Divine intentions with reference to the speed or gradualness of the conversion of mankind to the Gospel ; which considerations therefore stand on a different ground from the fundamental needs of a dispensation. The saying of our Lord, " Blessed are they that have not seen and yet have believed," evidently contemplates the future growth of the Christian faith by means of testimony to, as distinguished from the actual sight of, the miraculous evidences of the Gospel.

This view of miracles, as the indispensable means for producing that great result which we have before us, and that new moral era of the world under which we are living, meets again another objection which is sometimes raised against the truth of miracles. ' The general sense of society,' it is stated, rejects the notion of miracles taking place now-a-days ; these extraordinary actions of Omnipotence are conveniently located in the past. But why this sort of general consent that a supernatural event is impossible now, if it was really possible *then ?* It is evident that the imagination is only less scandalized by a miracle now than by a miracle then, because it realizes present time, and does not realize past. But if so, the modern acceptance of miracles is con-

victed of being unreal : and therefore whatever speculative arguments may be urged for the possibility of
such events, the matter-of-fact test of human educated belief rejects them.' (Note 5.)

It is, then, to be admitted that the mind of society
now is adverse to the notion of an hodiernal supernatural event.   But I remark in the first place
that this position is taken with a reserve.   For,
not to mention the undoubting belief in special Providences now, let a reported instance of a
communication in later times between the world of
departed spirits and the visible world be discussed;
a fair representative of the established standard
of belief does not commit himself to any absolute
position against the possibility of such an occurrence.
The relations between the seen and the unseen
worlds, the state of the dead, and what channels
are capable of being opened between unclothed
spirit and the mind which still tenants the frame
of the flesh—all this lies so completely out of our
knowledge, that to decline to lay down the principle
of an impassable boundary between one portion of
the Divine dominion and another, is felt to be not
superstition, but caution.

Of the weight, importance, and significance of a
reserve, indeed, different estimates will be formed.
To some a reserved ground appears but a light
appendage to a dominant decision, a formality, a
piece of argumentative etiquette, not to be taken
into account in the general calculation ; but to
others, a reserved ground is a weighty thing : it

represents some claim which is only weak in the
scale at present because it happens to be distant,
but which is strong in its own place, and which we
may have some day to meet in that place.   An
argumentative reserve speaks to them with the
force of silent prophecy ; it points to some truth
whose turn will come some day, perhaps when we
least expect it, and remind us of our proviso.   All
minds that require to be individually satisfied about
the matter of their belief, must hold some truth or
other under the form of a *reserve*.   All truths do
not come equally beneath our focus ; but if in
this state of the case a mind ignores whatever
hovers about the dim region of the circumference
and meets the vision imperfectly, it condemns itself
to that barrenness which results from seeing a very
little clearly, and seeing nothing else at all.   A
thoughtful mind sees in these distant reserves of the
reason the skirts of great arguments, the borders of
large regions of truth ; and the shadowy and imperfect
vision supports the clear, enriching it with additional
significance and important bearings.   Thus in the
wider circuit of religious doctrine we may see
enough in one or other particular matter of belief
to think that there may be more which we do not
see ; and a theological mind will make allowance
for its own defect of scope, admit such matter partially into its system, and give the benefit of a
reserve to truths which lie in the distance and in
the shadow.

   When, then, it is said that society neutralizes its

belief in past miracles by a practical disbelief in the possibility of present, we reply that society does not reject the idea of the hodiernal supernatural, but expresses its judgment on that subject with a reserve. But we next observe, that if the mind of Christian society at the present day is adverse to the notion of hodiernal miracles, and scrutinizes with great rigour all pretensions of that kind, there is a sound and sufficient reason which may be assigned for this fact; viz. that the great end for which miracles were designed is now accomplished; and that we are now living under that later providential era, and amidst those results, to which miracles were the first step and introduction. If we do not expect miracles now, there is a natural reason for it, viz. that the great purpose of them is past. Of our different attitude to past and present time upon this point, one account is, that our belief in the miraculous does not stand the touchstone of the actual present; but there is another explanation of it which is just as obvious, and which a believer can give, viz. that any set of means whatever unavoidably becomes retrospective and a thing of the past when the end is achieved. So far as miraculous agency *is* regarded as a *past* agency by us, there is a reason to give for this view of it, arising from the facts of the case. We are living amid mighty and deep influences, which were originally set going by that agency; but which having been set going, no longer want it; and at such a stage it is natural to us to look upon the irregular and extraordinary expedients employed in laying the foundation as superseded ; just as we remove the scaffolding when the edifice is raised, and take away the support of the arch when the keystone has been inserted.

The preparatory and introductory period to a final dispensation *is* a natural period of miracles ; while the period subsequent to that final gift is not. In the antecedent state there was a great want felt, a void which the existing dispensation did not satisfy ; and the religious thought of the day was cast forward into a mysterious future, not as Christian thought is now, but toward a final communication from God to man here below. The ancient Jew saw in his own dispensation an imperfect structure, the head of which was still wanting—the Messiah : all pointed to Him ; its ceremonial was typical ; and the whole system was an adumbration of a great approaching Divine kingdom, and a great crowning Divine act. The very heart of the nation was thus the seat of a great standing prophecy ; all was anticipation and expectation ; prophets kept alive the sacred longing ; miracles confirmed the prophetical office ; and the miraculous outbreak of Divine power in the great consummation itself closed the prospect. But this whole expectant attitude is in our case reversed. Ours is not a state of expectancy, and a day of forecastings and foreshadowings : we feel no void, throwing us on the future. On the contrary, we repose in Christian doctrine as the final stay of the human soul, and we are conscious that in this doctrine is contained all that can develop man; we know that it *has* developed man, and that Christianity has made a moral change in the state of the world. With us, then, miracles are passed so far as they are connected with the principal object with which miracles are concerned—revelation. It would be wholly unnatural, it would be contrary to the very account which we give of our own position, for us at this day to simulate the expectant state of the old Law, and throw ourselves back into the prospective stage. This would be doing violence to our whole knowledge and sense of reality. Though we cannot restrict the scope of miracles to one object, still, to cease to expect them when their chief end is gained, is only to do justice to the greatness of that end, to appreciate the truth and power of the Christian dispensation, and to observe what Christian doctrine has done for man.

LECTURE VIII.

MATT. VII. 22.

*Many will say to Me in that day, Lord, Lord, have we not
prophesied in Thy name ? and in Thy name have cast out
devils ? and in Thy name done many wonderful works ?*

A LARGE class of miraculous pretensions is not
confined to one religion, or even to religion altogether,
but belongs to human nature. Does man desire a
miracle as a proof that a revelation is true ? That
is a legitimate want. Does he desire one merely
to gratify his curiosity and love of the marvellous,
for excitement and not for use ? That is a morbid
want. For though the innate love of the supernatural in man's heart is legitimately gratified by
a miracle, man has no right to ask for miracles in
order to gratify this affection, any more than he
has to ask for them even as *evidence*, idly and trea-
cherously, when he does not intend to accept them
as such even when done. On both accounts "an
adulterous generation" which "sought after signs"
was once rebuked. This morbid want, however,

joined to the eager expectation that God would constantly interpose to prevent the injurious effects of
His general laws, has produced a constant stream
of miraculous pretension in the world, which accompanies man wherever he is found, and is a part of
his mental and physical history. Curiosity, imagination, misery, helplessness, and indolence, have all
conspired to throw him upon this support, which he
has sought in order to penetrate into the secrets
of the future, to lift up the veil of the invisible world,
and to obtain under calamity and disease that relief
which God either did not design to give at all, or
only to give through the instrumentality of human
skill and industry.

This perpetual phenomenon of miraculous pretension, this running accompaniment of human nature,
takes indeed different forms, according to the religious belief, or the prevailing notions and movements
of different ages; to which it joins itself on, and which
supply it with a handle. The affection for the marvellous has been successively heathen, Christian, and
philosophical or scientific. Heathenism had its running stream of supernatural pretensions in the shape
of prophecy, exorcism, and the miraculous cures of
diseases which the temples of Esculapius recorded
with pompous display. The Christian Church inhe-
rited the common features and characteristic impulses
of human nature, for Christians were men, and became
a scene of the same kind of display :—I speak of
the miracles of the early and later Church *so far as*
they come under the head of this standing result

of human nature, without inquiring at present which of them have evidence of a peculiar and distinguishable kind. The doctrine of the Incarnation was the instrument of this human affection under Christianity ; it joined itself on to that doctrine, and used the virtues of the saints, or the fruits of man's participation through the Incarnation of the Divine nature, for its own purpose. The same affection in our own day, abandoning its connexion with doctrine, and even with religion, adopts philosophical ground, and avails itself of a scientific handle ; and, the trace of an occult law of our sentient being having been discovered, which resulted in some extraordinary bodily conditions and affections, has raised upon this basis a wild superstructure of Supernaturalism, extending at last to a systematic intercourse with the invisible world. This strong human affection has thus flourished successively upon heathen, upon Christian, and upon scientific material ; because in truth it is neither heathen, nor Christian, nor scientific, but human. Springing out of the common stock of humanity, which is the same in all ages, it adapts itself to the belief, the speculations, and the knowledge of its own day. It avails itself of every opening which religious truth or obscure laws of nature may afford, and every fresh growth of supernaturalism borrows the type of the age. And thus is produced that constant succession of miraculous pretensions, which, varying in shade and form, and taking its colour from heathen mythology, or Christian truth, or Gothic or Celtic fancy, or

scientific mystery, is a perpetual and standing phenomenon of human nature ; its evidences being of
one homogeneous type and one uniform level, which
lies below a rational standard of proof.

The criterion, therefore, which *evidential* miracles,
or miracles which serve as evidence of a revelation,
must come up to, if they are to accomplish the object
for which they are designed, involves at the very
outset this condition,—that the evidence of such
miracles must be distinguishable from the evidences
of this permanent stream of miraculous pretension
in the world ; that such miracles must be separated
by an interval not only from the facts of the order
of nature, but also from the common running miraculous, which is the simple offshoot of human nature.
Can evidential miracles be inserted in this promiscuous mass, so as not to be confounded with it,
but to assert their own truth and distinctive source ?
If they cannot, there is an end to the proof of a
revelation by miracles : if they can, it remains to
see whether the Christian miracles are thus distinguishable, and whether their nature, their object,
and their evidence vindicate their claim to this
distinctive truth and Divine source.

1. The first great point, then, in the comparison
of one set of miracles with another, is the nature
and character of the facts themselves. Supposing
both sets of facts to be true, are we equally certain
that both of them are miracles ? Now on this head
we have to notice first a spontaneous admission and
confession on the part of the running miraculous,

viz. that the believers in it appear, in the case of
a clear and undoubted miracle, i. e. a fact which
if it is a true occurrence is such, to see almost as
strong a distinction between such a miracle and
their own supernaturalism as they do between that
miracle and the order of nature. When the heathens
of the patristic age were confronted by the assertion
of Christ's Resurrection, they answered at once that
it was impossible that a dead man should come to
life again, although they had their own current
supernaturalism going on. But this was to admit
a broad interval between the latter and the genuine
miraculous. Jewish supernaturalism was indeed
going on side by side with our Lord's miracles ;
and thence the inference has been drawn that His
miracles could not in the very nature of the case
be evidences of His distinctive teaching and mission,
inasmuch as miracles were common to Himself and
His opponents. But the same record which refers
to Jewish thaumaturgy, also reveals the enormous
distinction which those who practised or believed
that thaumaturgy themselves made between it and
our Lord's miracles. The restoration of sight to
the man born blind was obviously regarded as a
miracle in a sense quite distinguished from that
in which they would have applied the term to a
Jewish exorcism : it excited much the same resistance
in their minds as if they had not had their own
standing supernaturalism as a rival at all. And
when our Lord's prophecy of His own resurrection
was reported to the Roman governor, the statement

was—" Sir, this *deceiver* said." Why "deceiver?"
Why was this reported as a pretended miracle and
an imposture, if the real miracle would have made
no difference to them, being neutralized and reduced
to the measure of an ordinary current instance of
supernaturalism by their own thaumaturgy? Why
instead of involving themselves in difficulties by
resisting testimony to the facts of our Lord's miracles, did the Jews not accept the facts, and only
deny the argument from them? What reason could
there be but one, viz. that they recognized a true
miraculous character in our Lord's miracles which
was wanting in their own? And so when we come
to the current miracles of the early Church, we
meet with the same admission and confession of
the broad distinction between them and the Gospel
miracles, only not extracted unwittingly from Christian writers, but volunteered with full knowledge.
The Fathers, while they refer to extraordinary Divine
agency going on in their own day, also with one
consent represent miracles as having ceased since
the Apostolic era. But what was this but to confess
that though events which pointed to the special
hand of God, and so approximated to the nature
of the miraculous, were still of frequent occurrence
in the Church ; miracles of that decisive and positive
character that they declared themselves certainly to
be miracles no longer took place? (Note i.)

But this spontaneous admission on the part of
the running miraculous having been noticed, we
next see that the very nature and type of the facts

themselves account for and explain the admission. A deep latent scepticism accompanies the current supernaturalism of mankind, which betrays itself in the very quality and rank of the reputed marvels themselves,—that they never rise above a low level, and repeat again and again the same ambiguous types. There is a confinement to certain classes of occurrences, which, even if true, are very ambiguous miracles. The adhesion to this neutral, doubtful, and indecisive type, evinces a want of belief at the bottom in the existence of a real right in the system to assert a true dominion over nature. The system knows what it can do, and keeps within a safe line. Miraculous cures, vaticinations, visions, exorcisms, compose the current miracles of human history; but these are just the class which is most susceptible of exaggerating colour and interpretation, and most apt to owe its supernatural character to the imaginations of the reporters. Hence the confession of inferiority, when this running supernaturalism was confronted by real miracles; the admission of the distinction which existed between itself and the latter. The heathen saw that a resurrection from the dead was a fact about which, if it was true, there could be no mistake that it was a miracle; whereas that some out of the crowds of sick that were carried to the temple of Esculapius afterwards recovered, was, notwithstanding the insertion of their cures in the register of the temple, no proof of miraculous agency to any reasonable man. Exorcism, which is the contemporary Jewish miracle referred to in the Gospels, is evidently, if it stands by itself and is not confirmed by other and more decided marks of Divine power, a miracle of a most doubtful and ambiguous character. However we may explain demoniacal possession, whether we stop at the natural disorder itself, or carry it on to a supernatural cause, in either case a sudden strong impression made upon the patient's mind, such as would awaken his dormant energy and enable him to recollect the scattered powers of his reason, would tend to cast off the disorder. The disease being an obstruction of the rational faculties, whatever resuscitated the faculties thoroughly would expel the disease ; and an agency which was not miraculous but only moral, might be equal in certain cases to thus reawakening the faculties : a moral power might dismiss the demon that brooded upon the understanding, as it does the demon that tempts to sin. Exorcism therefore, even the legitimate practice, did not necessarily involve miraculous power ; and the Jewish practice was replete with imposture.

When we come to the miracles of the early Church we have to deal with a body of statement which demands our respect, on account of the piety and faith of those from whom we receive it ; but it is still open to us to consider the rank and pretension of these miracles,—whether the very type and character of them does not, upon the very point of the claim to be miraculous, radically distinguish them from the Gospel miracles ; as the very confession of the Fathers, just noticed, implies. The current miracles of the patristic age are cures of diseases, visions, exorcisms : the higher sort of miracle being alluded to only in isolated cases, and then with such vagueness that it leaves a doubt as to the fact itself intended. But these are of the ambiguous type which has been noticed. Take one large class—cures of diseases in answer to prayer. A miracle and a special providence, as I remarked in a previous Lecture [a], differ not in kind but in degree ; the one being an interference of the Deity with natural causes at a point removed from our observation ; the other being the same brought directly home to the senses. When, then, the Fathers speak of sudden recoveries, in answer to prayers of the Church or of eminent saints, as miracles, they appear to mean by that term special providences rather than clear and sensible miracles. And re- markable visions would come under the same head.

The very type, then, of the facts themselves which compose the current miracles of human history, the uniform low level which they maintain, stamps the impress of uncertainty upon them, in striking con- trast with the freedom and range of the Gospel miracles. About the latter, supposing them to be true, there can be no doubt,—that they are a clear outbreak of miraculous energy, of a mastery over nature ; but we cannot be equally assured upon this point in the case of the current miracles of the

a page 8.

first ages of the Church, even supposing the truth of the facts.

It will be urged perhaps that a large portion even of the Gospel miracles are of the class here mentioned as ambiguous: cures, visions, expulsions of evil spirits : but this observation does not affect the character of the Gospel miracles as a body, because we judge of the body or whole from its highest specimens, not from its lowest. The question is, what power is it which is at work in this whole field of extraordinary action? what is its nature, what is its extent? But the nature and magnitude of this power is obviously decided by its greatest achievements, not by its least. The greater miracles are not cancelled by the lesser ones; more than this, they interpret the lesser ones. It is evident that this whole miraculous structure hangs together, and that the same power which produces the highest, produces also the lowest type of miracle. The lower, therefore, receives an interpretation from its connexion with the higher which it would not receive by itself. If we admit, e. g. our Lord's Resurrection and Ascension, what could be gained by struggling in detail for the interpretation of minor miracles; as if these *could* be judged of apart from that great one?

The difference, again, in the very *form* of the wonder-working power in the case of the Gospel miracles, as compared with later ones, makes a difference in the character of the miracles themselves. A standing miraculous power lodged in a

Person, and through Him in other persons expressly admitted to the possession of it ; not making trials, in some of which it succeeds in others not, but always accomplishing a miracle upon the will to do so,—this, which is the Gospel fact or phenomenon asserted, is undoubtedly, if true, miraculous. But when the wonder-working power comes before us as a gift residing in the whole Christian multitude and sown broad-cast over the Church at large, the miracles which issue out of this popular mass are only a certain number of attempts which have succeeded out of a vastly greater number which have failed. But such tentative miracles are defective in the miraculous character from the very nature of the facts ; because chance accounts for a certain proportion of coincidences happening out of many which did not happen.

When the running miraculous is raised above the low level, which betrays its own want of confidence in itself and its professed command over nature, it is by a peculiarity which convicts it upon another count. There is a wildness, a puerile extravagance, a grotesqueness, and absurdity in the type of it such as to disqualify it for being a subject of evidence. The sense of what is absurd, ridiculous, and therefore impossible as an act of God, is part of our moral nature : and if a miracle even seen with our own eyes, cannot force us to accept anything contrary to morality or a fundamental truth of religion, still less can professed evidence force us to believe in Divine acts, which are upon the face of them un-

worthy of the Divine authorship[b]. It is true that of
this discrediting feature there is no definite standard
or criterion, and that when we refuse to believe in
a miracle on account of the absurdity and puerility
in the type of it, we do so upon the responsibility
of our own sense and perceptions ; but many important questions are determined in no other way than
this ; indeed all morality is ultimately determined
by an inward sense.

A fact, however, is not in itself ridiculous, because
a ridiculous aspect can be put upon it. The dumb
brute speaking with man's voice to forbid the madness of the prophet, the dismissal of a legion of
foul spirits out of their usurped abode in man into

---

[b] We observe indeed in the region of God's animate creation,
various animal natures produced of a grotesque and wild type ;
but to argue from this that we are to expect the same type in
bodies and classes of miracles, is to apply the argument of analogy
without possessing that condition which is necessary for it—a
parallel case (see p. 47). We can argue from one Divine act to
the probability or not improbability of another like it, provided the
cases with which the two are concerned are parallel cases ; but the
creation of an animal is no parallel case to the Divine act in a
miracle ; nor therefore can wildness, enormity, and absurdity in
a miracle plead the precedent of the singular types which occur
in the animal kingdom. The latter has been diversified for reasons
and for ends included within the design of creation : but a miracle
is not an act done by God *as Creator ;* it is a communication to
man, it is addressed to him, and therefore it must be suited to him
to whom it is addressed, and be consistent with that character
which our moral sense and revelation attribute to the Divine Being.
Upon this ground a solemn, a high stamp must always recommend
a miracle, while a ridiculous type is inconsistent with the intrinsic dignity of a Divine interposition.

a herd of swine,—whatever be the peculiarity in
these two miracles which distinguishes them from
the usual scriptural model, it is no mean, trivial,
or vulgar character. Did we meet with these two
simply as poetical facts or images in the great religious poem of the middle ages, they would strike
us as full of force and solemnity, and akin to a grand
eccentric type which occurs not rarely in portions
of that majestic work, and serves as a powerful
and deep instrument of expression in the hands of
the poet. Looking then simply to their type, these
miracles stand their ground. While it must also
be observed that in the case of miracles of an eccentric type, the quantity of them and the proportion
which they bear to the rest is an important consideration. The same type which in unlimited pro-
fusion and exuberance marks a source in human
fancy and delusion is not extravagant as a rare and
exceptional feature of a dispensation of miracles, just
emerging and then disappearing again, as a fragmentary deviation from a usual limit and pattern,
to which it is in complete subordination. One or
two miracles of a certain form in Scripture have
indeed been taken full advantage of, as if they supplied an ample justification of any number and
quantity of the most extravagant later miracles ;
but, supposing in our estimate we even reduced the
eccentricity of the latter to this exceptional Scripture
type, quantity and degree make all the difference
between what is impressive and what is puerile,
what is weighty and what is absurd. The miraculous

providence of Scripture, it must be remembered, covers the whole period from the creation of the world to the Christian era. The very rare occurrence of a type in a long reach of Providential operations, is no precedent for it as the prevailing feature of whole bodies and classes of miracles. The temper of the course and system of supernatural action is shewn by the proportion preserved in it, and by the check and limit under which such a type appears.

2. In comparing two different bodies of miracles their respective objects and results necessarily come into consideration. I have, however, in a previous lecture considered the great moral result of the Gospel miracles, exhibited in that new era of the world and condition of human society which they were the means of founding. Any comparison of this great result with the objects of current supernaturalism can only reveal the immense inferiority of the latter; —even when these objects are not volatile, morbid, or mean. But in how large a proportion do motives of the latter kind prevail! Motives of mere curiosity and idle amusement! Motives even worse than these —impatience and rebellion against the boundaries which separate the visible and invisible worlds! What is the chief avowed object, e.g. of the supernaturalism of this day? To open a regular systematic intercourse between the living and the dead! But how does such a fantastic and extravagant object, as that of breaking down the barriers of our present state of existence, at once convict and

condemn such pretensions themselves as fallacious ! As much so as, on the other hand, their grand and serious moral result recommends and is an argument for the Gospel miracles.

3. When from the type and character of the professed miracles of subsequent ages, and their objects, as compared with the miracles of Scripture, we turn to the evidence on which they respectively rest, we meet with various distinctions which have been very ably brought out and commented on by writers on evidence. And in the first place, a very large proportion of the miracles of subsequent ages stop short of the very first introduction to valid evidence, that preliminary condition which is necessary to qualify them even to be examined ;—viz. contemporary testimony. That certain great and cardinal Gospel miracles—which if granted clear away all antecedent objection to the reception of the rest—possess contemporary testimony, must be admitted by everybody, at the peril of invalidating all historical evidence, and involving our whole knowledge of the events of the past in doubt. That the first promulgators of Christianity asserted as a fact which had come under the cognizance of their senses the Resurrection of our Lord from the dead, is as certain as anything in history. But the great mass of later miracles do not fulfil even this preliminary condition, or reach even this previous stage of evidence.

But the level of contemporary testimony gained, the character of the witnesses, and the extent to which their veracity is tested by pain and suffering, make an immense difference in the value of that testimony.

1. In estimating the strength of a witness we must begin by putting aside as irrelevant all those features of his character, however admirable, striking, and impressive, which do not bear upon the particular question whether his report of a fact is likely to be correct. We have only to do with character in one point of view, viz. as a guarantee to the truth of testimony; but a reference to this simple object at once puts on one side various traits and qualities in men which *in themselves* are of great interest and excite our admiration. We value an ardent zeal in itself, but not as a security for this further object, because men under the influence of enthusiasm are apt to misstate and exaggerate facts which favour their own side. So, again, an affectionate disposition is beautiful and admirable in itself, but it does not add weight to testimony; and the same may be said of other high and noble moral gifts and dispositions—generosity, courage, enterprising spirit, perseverance, loyalty to a cause and to persons. Even faith, only regarded as one specific gift and power, in which light it is sometimes spoken of in Scripture, the power, viz. of vividly embracing and realizing the idea of an unseen world, does not add to the strength of a witness, though in itself, even as thus limited, a high and excellent gift. And thus might be constructed a character which would be a striking and interesting form of the religious mind, would lead the way in high undertakings, would command the obedience of

devoted followers, and would be in itself an object of singular admiration ; but which would not be valuable as adding solid weight to testimony. Perfect goodness is undoubtedly goodness in all capacities and functions, and stands the test of relation to all purposes ; but, taking human nature as we find it, a good man and a good witness are not quite identical. For all this assemblage of high qualities may exist, and that particular characteristic may be absent upon which we depend when we rely upon testimony in extreme and crucial cases.

That characteristic is a strong perception of a regard to the claims of truth. Truth is a yoke. If we would wish facts to be so and so, and they are not, that is a trial ; there is a disposition to rebel against this trial ; and this disposition has always a ready instrument in the faculty of speech, to whose peculiar nature it belongs to state facts either as they are or as they are not, with equal facility. To submit then to the yoke of truth under the temptation of this singularly simple and ready agency for rejecting it, requires a stern and rigorous fidelity to fact in the mind, as part of our obedience to God. But where there are many excellent affections and powers, sometimes this solid and fixed estimate of truth is wanting ; while, on the other hand, there are characters not deficient in these affections and powers, into whose composition it deeply enters, and whose general moral conformation is a kind of guarantee that they possess it.

Such a character is that which lives in the pages

of the New Testament as the Apostolic character. If we compare that model with the model set up in later times, the popular pattern of Christian perfection which ruled in the middle ages, we find a great difference. There is undoubtedly deep enthusiasm, if we may call it so, in the character of the Apostles, an absorption in one great cause, a depth of wonder and emotion, high impulse, ardent longing and expectation ; and yet with all this what striking balance and moderation, which they are able too—a very strong test of their type—to maintain amid circumstances just the most calculated to upset these virtues ! At war with the whole world, lifted up above it, and trampling its affections beneath their feet ; living upon heavenly hopes, and caring for one thing alone, the spread of the Gospel,— theirs was indeed a grand and elevating situation ; but at the same time it was just one adapted to throw them off their balance, and narrow their standard. Mere enthusiastic men would have been carried away by their antagonism to the whole existing state of society to set up some visionary model of a Christian life, wholly separated from all connexion with the cares and business of earth. But although the Apostles certainly give scope to and assert the duty of an extraordinary and isolated course of life, under certain circumstances and with reference to particular ends, their standard is wholly free from contraction ; their view of life and its duties is as sensible and as judicious as the wisest and most prudent man's ; nor do they say—'You may be an inferior Christian if you live in the world, but if you want to be a higher Christian you must quit it;' but they recognize the highest Christian perfection as consistent with the most common and ordinary form of life. Their great lessons are, that goodness lies in the heart, and that the greatest sacrifices which a man makes in life are his internal conquests over vain, desires, aspirations, and dreams of this world; which deepest mortifications consist with the most common outward circumstances. This plain, solid, unpretending view of human life in conjunction with the pursuit of an ideal, the aim at perfection, is indeed most remarkable,—if it was not a new combination in the world. What I would observe, however, now is that such men are weighty witnesses; that their testimony has the force of statements of fact from men of grave and solid temperament, who could stand firm, and maintain a moderate and adjusted ground against the strong tendencies to extravagance inherent in their whole situation and aim.

On the other hand, when I come to a later type of character which rose up in the Christian Church, I see in it much which is splendid and striking— high aim and enterprise, courageous self-denial, aspiring faith, but not the same guarantee to the truth of testimony. Ambition or exaggeration in character is in its own nature a divergence from strict moral truth; which, though it is more effective in challenging the eye, and strikes more instantaneously as an image, detracts from the authority of the character, and the dependence we place upon it for the purpose now mentioned.

The remark may be made, again, that the original promulgation of Christianity was one of those great undertakings which react upon the minds of those engaged in it, and tend to raise them above insincerity and delusion. The cause itself was, so far as any cause can be, a guarantee for the truthfulness of its champions ; its aim was to renovate the human race sunk in corruption ; it proclaimed a revelation indeed from heaven, but that revelation was still in connexion with the most practical of all aims. But this cannot be said of most of the later causes in behalf of which the professed evidence of miracles was enlisted : spurious and corrupt developments of Christian doctrine do not give the same security for the truthfulness of their propagators. The quality of the *cause*, the nature of the object, is not in fact wholly separable from the *character* of the witness ; and one of these heads runs into the other. But this consideration of itself goes far to dispose of whole bodies of later miracles; for if we hold certain later doctrines, the deification of the Virgin Mother, Transubstantiation, and others to be corruptions of Christianity, we are justified in depreciating the testimony of the teachers and spreaders of these doctrines to the alleged miracles in support of them. The nature of the cause affects our estimate of the propagators. Indeed, let the human intellect once begin to busy itself not only about false deductions from Christian doctrine, but even about doubtful ones, nay even about true but minute and remote ones, and the spirit and temper of the first promulgators of Christianity is soon exchanged for another. Propagandism has not a reputation for truthfulness. As doctrine diverges from the largeness of the Scripture type into narrow points, the active dissemination of it interests, excites, and elates as a speculative triumph.

When from the character of the witnesses to the Gospel miracles we turn to the ordeal which they underwent, we find another remarkable peculiarity attaching to their testimony, viz. that it was *tested* in a manner and to an extent which is without parallel : because, in truth, the whole life of sacrifice and suffering which the Apostles led was from beginning to end the consequence of their belief in certain miraculous facts which they asserted themselves to have witnessed ; upon which facts their whole preaching and testimony was based, and without which they would have had no Gospel to preach. In all ages, indeed, different sects have been persecuted for their opinions, and given the testimony of their suffering to the sincerity of those opinions ; but here are whole lives and long lives of suffering in testimony to the truth of particular facts ; the Resurrection and Ascension being the warrant to which the Apostles appeal for the authority and proof of their whole ministry and doctrine.

On the other hand, those mere current assertions of supernatural effects produced, which prevail in all days, and in our own not least, but which are made irresponsibly by any persons who choose to make them, without any penalty or risk to the assertors to act as a test of their truthfulness, have hardly, in strict right, a claim even upon our grave consideration ; because in truth upon such subjects untested evidence is worthless evidence.   We can conceive a certain height of character which would of itself command the assent of individuals, but the world at large cannot reasonably be satisfied without some ordeal of the witnesses.   We apply an ordeal to testimony even to ordinary facts, when the life or liberty of another depends upon it, and in this case cross-examination in a court is the form of ordeal ; but pain and sacrifice on the part of the witnesses is also intrinsically an ordeal and probation of testimony ; which condition current supernaturalism does not fulfil, but which the Gospel miracles do.   The testimony to the latter is tested evidence of a very strong kind ; because the trials which the Apostles endured were both lasting, and also owing directly to their belief in certain facts, to which they bore witness; thus going straight to the point as guarantees for the truth of that attestation.   But it would be difficult to discover any set of later miracles which stand upon evidence thus tested ; which can appeal to lives of trial and suffering undergone by the witnesses as the direct result of their belief in and witness to such miracles. (Note 2.)

One consideration, however, of some force remains to be added.   It is confessed that the mediæval record contains a vast mass of false and spurious miracles,—so vast indeed that those who wish to claim credence for some particular ones, or who, without mentioning particular ones, argue that some or other out of the whole body may have been true, still virtually abandon the great body as indefensible. The mediæval record therefore comes before us at the very outset as a maimed and discredited authority—discredited because it has adopted and thrown its shield over an immense quantity of material admitted to be untrue and counterfeit, and so identified itself with falsehood. So far as any informant takes up and commits himself to false intelligence, so far he destroys his own credit. An immense mass of admitted spurious miracles therefore adopted by the mediæval record throws doubt upon *all* the accounts of such facts transmitted to us through the same channel; because to that extent it affects the general character of the record as an informant, and invalidates its authority. The Scripture record, on the other hand, does not at any rate come before us with this admitted blot upon its credit in the first instance. The information it contains has doubtless to be examined with reference to the evidence upon which it rests; that is to say, the authority of the record has to be investigated; but it does not present itself with any admitted discrediting stain in the first instance; whereas such an admitted stain does *in limine* attach to the mediæval record. But this consideration receives additional force when we take into account two great causes of miraculous pretensions which were deeply

Q

rooted in the character of the middle ages, but from which Christianity at its original promulgation was free.

1. It is but too plain that in later ages, as the Church advanced in worldly power and position, besides the mistakes of imagination and impression, a temper of deliberate and audacious fraud rose up within the Christian body, and set itself in action for the spread of certain doctrines, as well as for the great object of the concentration of Church power in one absolute monarchy. Christianity started with the sad and ominous prophecy that out of the very bosom of the religion of humility should arise the greatest form of pride that the world should ever know —one, " as God, sitting in the temple of God, shewing himself that he is God[c] ;" the complete fulfilment of which, if yet in store, has certainly not been without its broad foreshadowings; for indeed Christian pride has transcended heathen by how much Christianity is a more powerful stimulus to man than heathenism, giving a depth to his whole nature, which imparts itself even to his passions, to his ambition and love of dominion, and to his propagation of opinion. But this formidable spirit once arisen in the Church, falsehood, which is the tool of the strong even more than of the weak, is its natural instrument. Hence the bold forgeries of the middle ages, which were the acts of a proud will, determined that nothing should stand in the way between it and certain objects, and that if facts

[c] 2 Thess. ii. 4.

did not exist on its side, they should be made. And
hence also counterfeit miracles. But mere historical
criticism must admit that this spirit of daring, determined, and presumptuous fraud, which compiled false
authorities, and constructed false marvels simply because they were wanted, was the manifestation of a
later age, and that the temper of the first promulgators of the Gospel was wholly free from such a
stain. (Note 3.)

2. Another great cause of miraculous pretensions
in later ages was the adoption of miracles as the
criterion and test of high goodness ; as if extraordinary sanctity naturally issued in a kind of
dominion over nature. This popular idea dictated
that rule of canonization which required that before
a saint was inserted in the Calendar, proof should be
given of miracles either performed by him in his
lifetime or produced by the virtue of his remains.
Such a criterion of sanctity is intrinsically irrelevant ;
for in forming a judgment of a man's character, motives, and dispositions, the extent of his charity and
self-denial and the like, what can be more beside the
question than to inquire whether or not these moral
manifestations of him were accompanied by suspensions of the laws of nature. The natural test of
character is conduct ; or, which is the same thing,
moral goodness is its own proof and evidence. The
man is before us ; he reveals himself to us not only
by his formal outward acts, but by that whole mani-
fold expression of himself, conscious and unconscious,
in act, word and look, which is synonymous with life.

The very highest form of goodness is thus a disclosure to us which attests itself, and to which
miracles are wholly extrinsic. But what I remark
now is that the adoption of such a test as this
must in the nature of the case produce a very large
crop of false miracles. The criterion having been
adopted must be fulfilled ; providence does not fulfil
it because providence is not responsible for it, and
therefore man must ; he who instituted the test must
look to its verification. But this whole notion of
miracles as a test of sanctity was a complete inno-
vation upon the Scripture idea. The Bible never
represents miracles as a tribute to character, but as
following a principle of use, as means to certain ends.
One saint possesses the gift because it is wanted for
an object ; as great a saint does not because it is
not wanted. The fruits of the Spirit always figure
as their own witnesses in Scripture, superior to all
extraordinary gifts, and not requiring their attestation. The Christian is described as gifted with discernment. There needs no miracle to tell *him* who
is a good man and who is not ; he knows him by
sure signs, knows him from the hypocrite and pre-
tender ; "he that is spiritual judgeth all things,"
is a scrutinizer of hearts, and is not deceived by
appearances. (Note 4.)

Between the evidence, then, upon which the Gospel miracles stand and that for later miracles we
see a broad distinction, arising—not to mention
again the nature and type of the Gospel miracles
themselves—from the contemporaneous date of the

testimony to them, the character of the witnesses, the probation of the testimony; especially when we contrast with these points the false doctrine and audacious fraud which rose up in later ages, and in connexion with which so large a portion of the later miracles of Christianity made their appearance. But now to carry the argument into another stage. What if—to make the supposition—it was discovered, when we came to a close examination of particulars, that for one or two, or even several, of the later miracles of Christianity there was evidence forthcoming approximating in strength to the evidence for the Gospel miracles—what would be the result? Would any disadvantage ensue to the Gospel miracles, any doubtfulness accrue to their position as a consequence of this discovery, and additional to any previous intrinsic ground of difficulty? None: all the result would be that we should admit these miracles over and above the Gospel ones: but the position of the latter would not be at all affected by this conclusion: they would remain, and their evidence would remain, just what they were before. We reject the mass of later miracles because they want evidence; not because our argument obliges us to reject all later miracles whether they have evidence or not. The acceptance of the Gospel miracles does not commit us to the denial of all other; nor therefore would the discovery of strong evidence for some other miracles at all imperil the ground and the use of the Gospel ones. Many of our own divines have admitted the truth of later miracles, only raising the question of the date up to which the continuance of miraculous powers in the Church lasted, some fixing this earlier, and some later. But were our divines therefore precluded from using the Gospel miracles as evidences of Christianity? Do our brethren even of the Roman communion, because they accept a much larger number of later miracles than our divines do, thereby cut themselves off from the appeal to the miraculous evidences of Christianity? Pascal accepted a miracle of his own day, of which he·wrote a defence; and yet he prepared the foundation of a treatise on the Evidences of Christianity, and the evidences of miracles with the rest: nor was he guilty of any error of logic in so doing. It is true our divines may have been under a mistake in accepting some miracles which they did; and certainly our Roman Catholic brethren are in our judgment very much mistaken in a great number of miracles which they accept: but a mistake as to the particular later miracles accepted does not affect the general question of the consistency of belief in and use of the Gospel miracles *with* the belief in later ones. (Note 5.)

The application of the fact of the crowd of later and mediæval miracles to neutralize the evidences of the Gospel miracles proceeds upon one or other of two assumptions. One assumption is, that the rejected later miracles do in reality rest upon evidence as strong as that of the Gospel miracles: the other assumption is that we are obliged to reject all later

miracles. The argumentative effect of the former
is direct, and has been met in the body of the remarks offered in this Lecture. But the latter assumption, that we are obliged to reject all later miracles
upon whatever evidence resting, has also a hostile
bearing upon the position of the Gospel miracles ;
because, should upon examination any later miracles
be discovered to have a certain amount of real evidence, in proportion as that evidence approaches
to the evidence of the Gospel miracles, in that proportion by rejecting the one we imperil the credit
of the other too. This latter assumption, however,
is without authority. We assert indeed that none
of the later miracles have *equal* evidence with the
miracles on which the Gospel is based ; that the
great mass have not even contemporary testimony,
and that in the case of those which have, neither
the character of the witnesses nor their probation
is equal to that of the Apostolic witnesses. But a
witness may not be equal to an Apostle, and yet his
testimony may go for something ; nor therefore are
we prepared to say that there may not be particular
later miracles the evidence of which is substantial
in its character and approximates to the evidence of
the Gospel miracles. But such an admission does
not tend in the slightest degree to endanger the
position of the latter, for one set of miracles is
not false because other miracles are true. Could it
even be shewn that one or other of the later
miracles had evidence fully *equal* to that of the
Gospel ones, no consequence unfavourable to the

latter would ensue. The result in that case would
be not that we should *reject* the later miracle, and
so in consistency be obliged to reject the Gospel
miracles, but that we should *accept* the later miracle;
which would entail no consequence whatever unfavourable to the Gospel miracles.

One conclusion, however, there is which is a tempt-
ing one to deduce from the multitude of spurious
miracles, viz. the impossibility of distinguishing the
true ones. 'We cannot,' it may be said, 'go into
particulars or draw minute distinctions. Here is
a vast crowd of miraculous pretensions, the product
of every age of Christianity, including that of its very
birth. Of this an overwhelming proportion is confessed to be false. But how can we distinguish between what is false and what is true of this promiscuous mass ? Miraculous evidence in such a condition defeats itself and is unavailable for use ; and
practically we must treat Christianity as if it stood
without it.'

Nothing then can be more certain than that,
granted true miracles, so long as man is man, these
true miracles must encounter the rivalry of a growth
of false ones, and the evidential disadvantage, whatever it be, thence ensuing. And therefore this position amounts to saying that permanent miraculous
evidence to any religion is an impossible contrivance.

But such a wholesale inference as this from the
existence of spurious miracles is contrary to all
principles of evidence, and to the whole method in

practice among mankind for ascertaining the truth of
facts.   Do we want to dispose of all cases of recorded
miracles by some summary rule which decides them
all in a heap, the rule that a sample is enough, that
one case settles the rest, and that the evidence of one
is the evidence of all ?   We have no such rule for
ordinary questions of moral evidence relating to
human actions and events.   If any one principle is
clear in this department, it is that every case which
comes under review is a special case.   In civil justice,
e.g. every case is determined upon its own merits,
and according to our estimate of the quality of the
testimony, the situation of the parties, and the connexion and coincidence of the facts in that particular case.   No two sets of witnesses, no two sets
of circumstances are exactly alike.   Inasmuch, then,
as these constitute in every case the grounds of
decision, every case of evidence in our courts is a
special case.   Two successive causes or trials might
be pronounced upon a *prima facie* view to be
exactly alike as cases of evidence ; they look the
same precise mixtures of evidence and counter
evidence, probabilities and counter probabilities ;
and a person would be tempted to say that one
decided the other.   Yet upon a close examination
the greatest possible difference is discovered in the
two fabrics of evidence, and consequently the judgment is different.   In proportion as the examination
penetrates into each case and comes into close quarters with the witnesses, the circumstances, the connexion of facts in it, the common type of the two is

cast off, the special characteristics of each come out into stronger and stronger light, the different weight of the testimony, the different force of the facts. There are universal rules relating to the punishment when the crime is proved, and to the right when the conditions are proved, but of what constitutes proof there is no rule. This is a special conclusion, according to the best judgment, from the special premisses. There is no royal road to truth in the evidence of facts; every case is a special case. It is true that main features of fact, as well as types of testimony, repeat themselves often; but in every case they demand and we give them a fresh inspection.

It only requires the advantage of this principle to bring out the strong points, the significant features, and the effective weight of the evidence for the Gospel miracles. Upon the summary supposition indeed that the evidence of miracles is a *class* of evidence, which, after the sight of some samples, dispenses with the examination of the rest, those miracles would stand little chance; but we have no right to this summary supposition; the evidence of the Gospel miracles is a special case which must be decided on its own grounds. Were the annals of mankind crowded even much more than they are with spurious cases, we should still have to take the case of the Gospel miracles by itself. The general phrase in use, "the value of testimony," conceals degrees of strength; the term "competent witness" hides all the interval which lies between an average witness who appears in court, and the sublimest impersonation of the grave, the holy, the simple and truthful character. The phrase " ordeal of testimony" covers all the degrees in severity and duration of such ordeal. This *degree* in the strength of testimony is, however, in truth the critical and turning-point in the evidence of miracles ; for miracles are a weight resting upon the support of that evidence ; but whether a support can bear a particular weight must depend on the degree of strength residing in that support. To ascertain the degree of strength then which belongs to the evidence for the Gospel miracles, we must go into the special case of that evidence ; and what we maintain is, that when we *do* go specially into the evidence for those miracles, we find this high degree of strength in it : that its foundation lies so deep in the wonderful character and extraordinary probation of the witnesses, and in the unique character and result of the revelation, that it sustains the weight which it is required to sustain.

The truth of the miraculous credentials of Christianity rests upon various arguments, the mutual coherence and union of which forms the evidence of them. Nor in a case of evidence must we narrow the term 'argument;' anything is an argument which naturally and legitimately produces an effect upon our minds, and tends to make us think one way rather than another. Nor in judging upon the force and weight of these arguments, can we dispense with a proper state of the affections. It is no condition of a sound judgment that there should be an absence of feeling in it; our affections are a part of our judgment; an argument only sinks into us properly, and takes proper hold of our minds, by means of the feelings which take it up and carry it into the understanding. One man thinks nothing of an argument, another a great deal of it, because feeling enables the one to *see* the argument, the other wants this light by which to see it. It is thus a great mistake to suppose that those who are absorbed in the pleasurable exertion of the intellect and are without the religious emotions, who do not hope, who do not fear as spiritual beings, are the best judges of religious evidences. For the truth is, in such a state a man is not possessed of his whole nature; a man is only half himself; nay, he is but a miserable fragment of himself. Hope and fear are strong impulses to and enliveners of the understanding; they quicken the perceptions; under their purifying and sharpening influence we see the force of truths and arguments which otherwise we are too dull to see. Thus half of a man's nature *may* reject the Christian evidence, but the whole accepts it. When every part of us is represented in our state of mind, when the religious affections as well as the intellect are strong and lively, then only is our state of mind a reasonable one, then only are we our proper selves; but the issue of this collective whole is Christian belief.

NOTES.

NOTES.

LECTURE I.

NOTE 1, p. 18.

THE necessity of miracles to prove a revelation is assumed in the general language of divines. Thus Butler: "The notion of a miracle, considered as a proof of a Divine mission, has been stated with great exactness by divines; and is, I think, sufficiently understood by every one. There are also invisible miracles, the Incarnation of Christ, for instance, which, being secret, cannot be alleged as a proof of such a mission, but *require themselves to be proved by visible miracles. Revelation itself too is miraculous, and miracles are the proof of it.*" (*Analogy*, pt. ii. ch. ii.) The writer assumes here that for the revelation of things supernatural and undiscoverable by human reason, miraculous evidence is necessary to attest its truth. The "invisible miracle," i. e. the *doctrine* of the Incarnation, he says, "*requires* to be proved by visible miracles." "Miracles are *the* proof of revelation," because revelation is itself miraculous,—is an invisible miracle which needs the visible to serve as guarantee to it. Again: "Take in the consideration of religion, or the moral system of the world, and then we see distinct particular reasons for miracles; to afford mankind instruction additional to that of nature, and to attest the truth of it." (*Analogy*, pt. ii. ch. ii.) Again: "In the evidence of Christianity there seem to be several things of great weight, not reducible to the head either of miracles or the completion of prophecy, in the common acceptation of the words. But

these two are its direct and fundamental proofs: and those
other things, however considerable they are, yet ought never
to be urged apart from its direct proofs, but always to be
joined to them." (*Analogy*, pt. ii. ch. vii.) Leslie writes : " The
deists acknowledge a God, of an Almighty power, who made
all things. Yet they would put it out of His power to make
any revelation of His will to mankind. For if we cannot
be certain of any miracle, how should we know when God
sent anything extraordinary to us ?" (*Short and Easy Method
with Deists.*) Paley says : " Now in what way can a revelation be made but by miracles ? In none which we are
able to conceive. Consequently in whatever degree it is
possible, or not very improbable, that a revelation should
be communicated to mankind at all, in the same degree
it is probable or not very improbable, that miracles should
be wrought." (*Evidences of Christianity : Preparatory Considerations.*)

That the truth of the Christian miracles, however, is
necessary for the defence of Christianity is a point altogether
independent of the question of the necessity of miracles for
a revelation in the first instance, as Mr. Mansel observes :—

" Whether the doctrinal truths of Christianity could or
could not have been propagated among men by moral evidence
alone, without any miraculous accompaniments, it is at least
certain that such was not the manner in which they actually
were propagated, according to the narrative of Scripture. If
our Lord not only did works apparently surpassing human
power, but likewise expressly declared that He did those
works by the power of God, and in witness that the Father
had sent Him ;—if the Apostles not only wrought works of
a similar kind to those of their Master, but also expressly
declared that they did so in His name; the miracles, as thus
interpreted by those who wrought them, become part of the
moral as well as the sensible evidences of the religion which
they taught, and cannot be denied without destroying both
kinds of evidence alike. . . . . .

" The scientific question relates to the possibility of supernatural occurrences *at all;* and if this be once decided in
the negative, Christianity as a religion must necessarily be
denied along with it. Some moral precepts may indeed
remain, which may or may not have been first enunciated by

Christ, but which in themselves have no essential connexion
with one person more than with another; but all belief in
Christ as the great Example, as the teacher sent from God,
as the crucified and risen Saviour, is gone, never to return.
The perfect sinlessness of His life and conduct can no longer
be held before us as our type and pattern, if the works which
He professed to perform by Divine power were either not
performed at all or were performed by human science and
skill.   No mystery impenetrable by human reason, no doctrine incapable of natural proof, can be believed on His
authority; for if He professed to work miracles, and wrought
them not, what warrant have we for the trustworthiness of
other parts of His teaching?" (*Aids to Faith*, pp. 4, 5.)

The moral results of Christianity when they are appealed
to as evidence, appear more strongly in that light when
regarded in connexion with prophecy, in which connexion
Pascal views them :—

"Prophétie avec l'accomplissement.   Ce qui a precédé et
ce qui a suivi J. C.

"Les riches quittent leur bien, &c.   Qu'est-ce que tout
cela?   C'est ce qui a été prédit si longtemps auparavant.
Depuis 2,000 ans aucun païen n'avait adoré le Dieu des
Juifs, et dans le temps prédit la foule des païens adore
cet unique Dieu.   Les temples sont detruits, les rois même
se soumettent à la croix.   Qu'est-ce que tout cela?   C'est
l'esprit de Dieu qui est repandu sur la terre. . . . . *Effundam
spiritum meum*. (*Joel* ii. 28.)   Tous les peuples étaient dans
l'infidelité et dans la concupiscence ; toute la terre fut ar-
dente de charité: les princes quittent leurs grandeurs; les
filles souffrent le martyre.   D'où vient cette force?   C'est que
le Messie est arrivé.   Voilà l'effet et les marques de sa venue.

"Il est prédit qu'au temps du Messie il viendrait établir
une nouvelle alliance qui ferait oublier la sortie d'Egypte;
qui mettrait sa loi, non dans l'exterieur, mais dans les cœurs;
que J. C. mettrait sa crainte, qui n'avait été qu'au dehors,
dans le milieu du cœur.

"Qui ne voit la loi chretienne en tout cela?

"Qu'alors l'idolâtrie serait renversée; que ce Messie abat-
trait toutes les idoles, et ferait entrer les hommes dans le
culte du vrai Dieu.

"Que les temples des idoles seraient abattus, et que parmi
toutes les nations et en tous les lieux du monde on lui of-
frirait une hostie pure, non pas des animaux." (vol. ii. *ed.
Fougeres*, pp. 273, 277, 308.)

NOTE 2, p. 22.

GENERAL statements of the evidence of miracles are current
in the Fathers, who insist upon that argument in their con-
troversies with the heathen, as modern apologists do in their
defence of Christianity against the infidel. Tertullian, e.g.
after stating the Eternal Sonship and Immaculate Conception
of our Lord, says : " Recipite interim hanc fabulam, similis
est vestris, dum ostendimus *quomodo Christus probetur.* . . .
. . . . Quem igitur [Judæi] solummodo hominem præsump-
serant de humilitate, sequebatur uti magum estimarent de
potestate, cum ille verbo dæmonia de hominibus excuteret,
cæcos reluminaret, leprosos purgaret, paralyticos restringeret,
mortuos denique verbo redderet vitæ, elementa ipse famularet,
compescens procellas et freta ingrediens, ostendens se esse
Logon Dei, i.e. Verbum illud primordiale primogenitum."
At the moment of His death upon the cross,—" Dies,
medium orbem signante sole, subducta est. . . . . . . Eum
mundi casum relatum in arcanis vestris habetis." The
crowning miracles of the Resurrection and Ascension follow,
upon the strength of which Tertullian says: " Et Cæsares
credidissent super Christo, si aut Cæsares non essent seculo
necessarii, aut si et Christiani potuissent esse Cæsares."
(*Apologeticus,* c. 21.)

Arnobius appeals to the evidence of miracles : " Ergone
inquiet aliquis, Deus ille est Christus ? Deus respondebimus.
Postulabit, an se ita res habeat, quemadmodum dicimus, *com-
probari.* Nulla major est comprobatio, quam gestarum ab eo
fides rerum." He then enumerates the Gospel miracles :
" Ergo ille mortalis aut unus fuit e nobis cujus imperium,
cujus vocem, invaletudines morbi, febres, atque alia corporum
cruciamenta fugiebant ? Unus fuit e nobis qui redire in
corpora jamdudum animas præcipiebat inflatas ? . . . . Unus
fuit e nobis qui, deposito corpore innumeris se hominum
prompta in luce detexit ? qui sermonem dedit atque accepit,
docuit, castigavit, admonuit ? qui ne illi se falsos vanis
imaginationibus existimarent, semel, iterum, sæpius familiari
collocutione monstravit." (*Adversus Gentes,* lib. i. c. 42, et seq.)

For the truth of the miracles he refers to the evidence of testimony : "Sed non creditis gesta hæc. Sed qui ea conspicati sunt fieri, et sub oculis suis viderunt agi, testes optimi, certissimique auctores et crediderunt hæc ipsi et credenda posteris tradiderunt. . . . Sed ab indoctis hominibus et rudibus scripta sunt, et idcirco non sunt facili auditione credenda. Vide ne magis hæc fortior causa sit, cur illa sint nullis coinquinata mendaciis, mente simplici prodita, et ignara lenociniis ampliare." (cc. 54, 58.)

"Abfuit ergo ab his," says Lactantius, " fingendi voluntas et astutia, quoniam rudes fuerunt. Quis posset indoctus apta inter se et cohærentia fingere. Non enim quæstus et commodi gratia religionem istam commenti sunt, quippe qui et præceptis et reipsa eam vitam secuti sunt quæ et voluptatibus caret, et omnia quæ habentur in bonis spernit." (Divin. Inst. v. 3.)

Athanasius, in a passage in the "De Incarnatione Verbi," marshals the great miracles of our Lord's ministry and life into one long evidential array, the conclusion·being : οὕτως ἐκ τῶν ἔργων ἂν γνωσθείη ὅτι οὐκ ἄνθρωπος ἀλλὰ θεοῦ δύναμις καὶ λόγος ἐστὶν ὁ ταῦτα ἐργαζόμενος. . . . . τίς ἰδὼν αὐτὸν τὰς νόσους ἰώμενον, ἐν αἷς ὑπόκειται τὸ ἀνθρώπινον γένος, ἔτι ἄνθρωπον καὶ οὐ Θεὸν ἡγεῖτο. . . . . . τίς γὰρ ἰδὼν αὐτὸν ἀποδιδόντα τὸ λοῖπον, οἷς ἡ γένεσις ἐνέλειψε, καὶ τοῦ ἐκ γενετῆς τυφλοῦ τοὺς ὀφθαλμοὺς ἀνοίγοντα, οὐκ ἂν ἐνενόησε τὴν ἀνθρώπων ὑποκειμένην αὐτῷ γένεσιν, καὶ ταύτης εἶναι δημιουργὸν τοῦτον καὶ ποιητήν. (c. 18.) A modern writer would have stated the argument both of Athanasius and Tertullian more accurately, and said not that such miracles proved that the worker was the Word, the Son of God, mere men having been Divine agents in miraculous operations, but that they were a guarantee to the truth of the *declaration* of the worker, if He pronounced Himself to be the Son of God.

Augustine speaks of miraculous evidence as the evidence upon which the Apostles relied in commencing the conversion of the world : " Qui enim Christum in carne resurrexisse, et cum illa in cœlum ascendisse non viderant, id se vidisse narrantibus . . . . . credebant." (De Civit. Dei, xxii. 5.) And to

the objection why miracles were not continued, he answers that
miracles were necessary at first for the purpose of evidence,
but not afterwards : " Necessaria fuisse priusquam crederet
mundus, ad hoc ut crederet mundus." (*Ibid.* c. 8.)   Origen,
whose works present a striking mixture of obsolete fanciful
speculation and intellectual modern criticism, meets Celsus
with the argument of miracles.   " Celsus," he says, " unable
to deny the miracles of Jesus, calumniates them as works of
magic; and I have often had to combat him on this ground."
(*Contra Cels.* lib. ii. s. 48.)   He appeals in the spirit of a
modern writer on evidences to the deep and permanent
effects of our Lord's Resurrection upon the Apostles, and
the change which took place in their whole conduct after
this alleged event, as evidence of the truth of that event.
"The zeal with which they devoted themselves to the work
of conversion, encountering every danger, is a clear proof
of the truth of the Resurrection of Jesus; for they could
not have taught with this earnestness had they feigned such
an event; they could not have inculcated contempt of death
upon others, and exemplified it themselves." (*Ibid.* s. 56.)   He
observes how few the cases of persons raised from the dead
in the Gospels are, and that if such cases were spurious
there would have been more of them.   Ὅτι δὲ καὶ νεκροὺς
ἀνίστη, καὶ οὐκ ἔστι πλάσμα τῶν τὰ εὐαγγέλια γραψάντων, πα-
ρίσταται ἐκ τοῦ, εἰ μὲν πλάσμα ἦν, πολλοὺς ἀναγεγράφθαι τοὺς
ἀναστάντας. . . . . . ἐπεὶ δ' οὐκ ἔστι πλάσμα πάνυ εὐαριθμήτους
λελέχθαι. (*Ibid.* c. 48.)   Chrysostom uses Origen's argument : " Had Christ not really risen from the dead, how do
we account for the fact that the Apostles, who in their behaviour to Him living had shewn such weakness and cowardice
that they deserted and betrayed Him, after His death shewed
such zeal that they laid down their lives for Him?" (*In
S. Ignatium*, tom. ii. p. 599.)   The Resurrection of Christ, as
being His own act, not brought about by the instrumentality
of another agent, visibly acting in His behalf as the medium
of the operation of the miracle (which was the manner in
which the other resurrections mentioned in Scripture had
taken place), is regarded as in and of itself a proof of His

Divinity. " His body," says Athanasius, " as having a
common nature with our own, was mortal and died; but,
inasmuch as it was united with the Word, could not incur
corruption, but on account of the Word of God dwelling in
it was incorruptible. In the same Body were fulfilled two
apparent opposites, both that it underwent death, and that
death and corruption, *by reason of the indwelling Word, were*
abolished. . . . . . Inasmuch as the Word could not die, but
was immortal, He assumed a Body that was able to die, in
order that He might offer it up for the sake of all, and
that the same Word *by reason of His junction to that Body,*
might destroy him that hath the power of death." (*De Incarn.*
§ 20.) Chrysostom singles out the peculiarity of the miracle
of the Resurrection—τὸ ἑαυτόν τινα δύνασθαι ἀναστῆν. (*In*
Joan xxiv. tom. viii. p. 136.)

But while the Fathers appealed familiarly to the evidence
of miracles in behalf of the truth of Christianity, there were
particular kinds of belief strong in the minds of the Fathers,
and of their age, which prevented the argument of miracles
from assuming in their hands the compactness and stringency
which it has gained in the hands of modern writers on evidence. Of the kinds of belief to which I refer, the first was
their acceptance to a certain extent of the " dispensation of
Paganism," to use Dr. Newman's phrase (*Arians,* p. 89), and
with it of certain miraculous pretensions which Paganism had
put forth; the second was their belief in magic. A writer on
evidence in the present age, in urging the evidence of miracles
to the divine nature and mission of Christ, is not incom-
moded by any strong belief, existing either in his own mind
or in the age, in the reality of any supernatural demonstra-
tions outside of the course of miracles which constitute the
evidences of Revelation, and standing in a position of rivalry
to them. The Scripture miracles, if proved, thus stand alone
in his plan of defence as true and admitted miracles, and
the inference from the truth of the miracles to the truth of
the doctrines is an unimpeded step, there being no counteracting force in the confessed existence of supernatural action
under a false religion, or from a corrupt and evil power,

which has to be allowed and accounted for, in drawing the evidential conclusion. But the Fathers believed that supernatural powers had been bestowed by Providence on various occasions, under Paganism; and they had also a strong and undoubting belief in magic and a diabolical source of supernatural exhibitions. The argument of miracles in their hands therefore was an obstructed and qualified argument, maintained in conflict with various counter admissions; and the conclusion from it, though undoubting and full, was not given in the summary and rigorous form in which a popular school of writers on evidence has put it.

1. The general attitude of the early Church toward the heathen world somewhat differed from that of modern Christendom. The early Church admitted of a common ground to a certain extent between herself and Paganism, and saw in the latter system more than relics of the goodness of fallen man, viz. traces of a lower but in some sort *Divine dispensation.* "Earlier Christianity," as I have remarked elsewhere, " regarded the Gentile world more as a field of promise, and saw in it the future harvest rather than the present foe." The doctrine of the Logos under the treatment of the Alexandrian school imparted a systematic form and theological basis to this estimate of Paganism : for in the eye of that school " the dispensation of Paganism, so far as it contained truth, was but a lower part of one large dispensation, which our Lord, as the Divine Reason, had instituted and carried on for the enlightenment of the human race, and of which the Gospel was the consummation; heathens and Christians were, though in a different measure, still alike partakers of that one ' Light that lighteth every man that cometh into the world ;' and all mankind, as brought into union and fellowship by that common participation, formed one religious society and communion—one Church." (*Augustinian Doctrine of Predestination,* p. 117.)

Such a Divine element being recognized in Paganism, the next step was that a certain authority was attached by the early Fathers in various instances to ancient Pagan legend and traditions of miraculous appearances and interpositions.

Cases of special Divine interposition in the Gentile world are
recognized in Scripture.

"Scripture gives us reason to believe," says Dr. Newman,
" that the traditions, thus originally delivered to mankind at
large, have been secretly re-animated and enforced by new
communications from the unseen world; though these were
not of such a nature as to be produced as evidence, or used
as criteria and tests, and roused the attention rather than
informed the understandings of the heathen. The book of
Genesis contains a record of the dispensation of natural religion, or paganism, as well as of the patriarchal. The dreams
of Pharaoh and Abimelech, as of Nebuchadnezzar afterwards,
are instances of the dealings of God with those to whom He
did not vouchsafe a written revelation. Or should it be said
that the particular cases merely come within the range of the
Divine supernatural governance which was in their neigh-
bourhood,—an assertion which requires proof,—let the book
of Job be taken as a less suspicious instance of the dealings of
God with the heathen. Job was a Pagan in the same sense
in which the Eastern nations are Pagans in the present day.
He lived among idolaters, yet he and his friends had cleared
themselves from the superstitions with which the true creed
was beset; and, while one of them was divinely instructed by
dreams, he himself at length heard the voice of God out of
the whirlwind, in recompense for his long trial and his faithfulness under it. . . . . If it be objected that Job lived in a less
corrupted age than the times of ignorance which followed,
Scripture, as if for our full satisfaction, draws back the cur-
tain further still in the history of Balaam. There a bad man
and a heathen is made the oracle of true Divine messages
about doing justly, and loving mercy, and walking humbly;
nay, even among the altars of superstition the Spirit of God
vouchsafes to utter prophecy. And so in the cave of Endor,
even a saint was sent from the dead to join the company of
an apostate king, and the sorceress whose aid he was seeking.
Accordingly, there is nothing unreasonable in the notion, that
there may have been heathen poets and sages, or sibyls again,
in a certain extent divinely illuminated, and organs through
whom religious and moral truth was conveyed to their coun-
trymen; though their knowledge of the Power from whom
the gift came, nay, their perception of the gift as existing in
themselves, may have been very faint or defective." (*Arians*,
p. 89.)

But the Fathers went further, and recognized Pagan super-

natural events, as occurring in the common stream of Pagan
history, apart from any connexion with or relation to the
sacred people. Certain Pagan miracles, especially some which
occur in Roman history, had gained a respectable place in the
works of heathen historians, the same list recurs in different
Fathers, and Minutius Felix (*Octavius*, c. 27), Lactantius
(*Divin. Inst.* lib. ii. c. 8), Tertullian (*Apol.* c. 22), and Augustine
(*De Civit. Dei*, lib. x. c. 16), extend a kind of acceptance to
them[a]. The latter Father exhibits perhaps more of a critical
spirit than his predecessors, and in touching on the subject of
natural marvels, especially the existence of certain extraordinary nations which was asserted in geographical books of
that age, says, " Sed omnia genera hominum quæ *dicuntur*
esse credere non est necesse." (*De Civit. Dei*, xvi. 8.) He
supposes himself pressed by an objector who reminds him
that if he discredits the marvels of secular writers he will
have to account for his belief in those of Scripture, but he
disowns the dilemma. " Quod propterea poterunt dicere, ut
respondendi nobis angustias ingerant: quia si dixerimus non
esse credendum, scripta illa miraculorum infirmabimus; si
autem credendum esse concesserimus, confirmabimus numina

---

a Such a partial recognition however of Pagan legends and reports of supernatural occurrences must be distinguished from the appeals which the Fathers
sometimes make to heathen mythology, in defence of Christianity against
heathen objections—appeals which have the force of an *argumentum ad hominem*. Thus when heathen opponents taunted the Christians with the ignominious death of Him whom they asserted to be the Son of God, Justin
Martyr encountered them with facts from their own mythology—the miserable
earthly fates which some of Jove's sons had met—Ἀσκληπιὸν καὶ θεραπευτὴν
γενόμενον, κεραυνωθέντα ἀναλελευθέναι εἰς οὐρανόν· Διόνυσον δὲ διασπαραχθέντα·
Ἡρακλέα δὲ φυγῇ πόνων ἑαυτὸν πυρὶ δόντα. (*Apol.* i. 21.) Though he also
considers these coarse and fabulous pictures of the sufferings of heroism in
pagan mythology as an intentional travesty of the sufferings and persecutions
of the Messiah, inspired by diabolical cunning, in order to confuse men, and
blind them to the notes of the Messiah when He came,—τὰ μυθοποιηθέντα ὑπὸ
τῶν ποιητῶν ἀπάτῃ καὶ ἀπαγωγῇ τοῦ ἀνθρωπείου γένους εἰρῆσθαι ἀποδείκνυμεν κατ'
ἐνέργειαν τῶν φαύλων δαιμόνων. (*Apol.* i. s. 54.) So Tertullian, in speaking of
the Incarnation, says, " Recipite hanc fabulam ; similis est vestris, dum ostendimus quomodo Christus probetur. Sciebant et qui penes vos *ejusmodi fabulas
æmulas ad destructionem veritatis* istiusmodi præministraverunt, venturum
esse Christum." (*Apol.* c. xxi.)

paganorum. Sed nos non habemus necesse omnia credere
quæ continet historia gentium, cum et ipsi inter se historici,
sicut ait Varro, per multa dissentiant." (*De Civ. Dei*, xxi. 6.)
Later writers however of reputation have acknowledged Pagan
miracles; Dante (*De Monarchia*, lib. ii. c. 3) ranks certain recorded in Roman history as evidences, among other proof, of
the Divine authority of the Roman empire.   And even our
theologian Jackson entertains the idea of supernatural visita-
tions under Paganism.

" As the end and purpose which Homer assigns for the
apparitions of his gods, so are both these, and many other
particular circumstances of his gods assisting the ancient
heroics, such as might justly breed offence to any serious
reader, if a man should avouch them in earnest, or seek to
persuade him to expect more than mere delight in them.
Yet I cannot think that he would have feigned such an
assistance, unless the valour of some men in former times had
been extraordinary, and more than natural.   Which supernatural excellency in some before others, could not proceed
but from a supernatural cause.   And thus far his conceit
agrees with Scripture; that there were more heroical spirits
in old times than in later, and more immediate directions
from God for managing of most wars.   And from the experience hereof, the ancient poets are more copious in their
hyperbolical praises of their worthies, than the discreeter sort
of later poets durst be, whilst they wrote of their own times.
Not that the ancient were more licentious, or less observant
of decorum in this kind of fiction than the other; but because
the manifestation of a Divine power in many of their victories
was more seen in ancient than in later times; so that such
fictions, as to the ancient people might seem (by reason of
these extraordinary events then frequent) very probable, would
have been censured as ridiculous and apish in succeeding
ages, wherein no like events were manifested. . . . . . But
why their forefathers should either have invented such
strange reports, or be so inclinable to believe them; if we
search into the depth or first spring of this persuasion, we
cannot imagine any other cause, but the real and sensible
experience of such strange events as they reported to
posterity. . . . . . The often manifestation of an extraordinary power in battles, or presence in oracles, and sensible
documents of revenge from heaven, made the one prone to
entertain any report of the gods, though never so strange;

and the want of like sensible signs of the same power in our
days (while men's minds are still set upon politic means and
practices for their own good) doth make the other so apt to
assent to any *politic* discourse, and so *averse* from belief of the
prophets or sacred writers." (*Comments upon the Creed*, bk. i.
ch. xi, xii.

I quote this passage from Jackson as, though a milder and
more modified specimen, a specimen in a modern divine of the
spirit favourable to Pagan supernatural events in the Fathers.

2. But the difference between the patristic treatment of
the argument of miracles, and its treatment in the hands of
our own popular writers on evidence, is due mainly to another
source, viz. the belief of the Fathers in magic. The Fathers
held the popular ideas of their age on this subject, and wrote
under a strong and genuine conviction that there was such
an art as magic, and that it had real powers and could
produce real supernatural effects; from which effects they
were bound to distinguish true miracles, which came from a
Divine source and were wrought for the proof of a Divine
revelation. The class of enchanters or wizards—*magi, præsti-
giatores*—did not figure in their eyes as the mere creation of
legend and fancy, but as a class possessed of real powers.
The source of these powers was held to be the relation in
which these persons stood to dæmons and evil spirits. The
order of dæmons, their origin, their nature, and the place
which they are permitted to occupy in the world, are discussed with much more boldness and more attempt at accuracy and detail in patristic theology than in modern; and
the early writers introduce, in addition to the Scripture
notices of devils, the material of tradition and the theories
of Alexandrian Platonism. Augustine (*De Civ. Dei*, viii. 14
et seq.) comments upon Porphyry's division of the rational
universe, which was the Platonic one: "Omnium inquiunt
animalium, in quibus est anima rationalis, tripartita divisio
est, in Deos, homines, dæmones. Dii excelsissimum locum
tenent, homines infimum, dæmones medium. Nam deorum
sedes in cœlo est, hominum in terra, in aere dæmonum." (c. 14.)
Augustine does not object to the existence of an order of

dæmons so situated, but only to the Platonic inference from it: "Jam vero de loci altitudine, quod dæmones in aere, nos autem habitamus in terra, ita permoveri ut hinc eos nobis esse præponendos existimemus, omnino ridiculum est. Hoc enim pacto nobis et omnia volatilia præponimus." (*Ibid.* c. 15.) He identifies these dæmons with the evil spirits of Scripture. Tertullian's language is: "Itaque corporibus quidem et valetudines infligunt [dæmones] et aliquos casus acerbos, animæ vero repentinos et extraordinarios per vim excessus. Suppetit illis ad utramque substantiam homines adeundam mira subtilitas et tenuitas sua." (*Apol.* c. 22.) Minutius Felix acquiesces in the Platonic assertion of an intermediate class of beings: "Substantiam inter mortalem immortalemque, i. e. inter corpus et spiritum, mediam, terreni ponderis et cœlestis levitatis admixtione concretam;" which he identifies with the devils of Scripture (*Octavius*, c. 26). Lactantius adopts a tradition: "Cum ergo numerus hominum cœpisset increscere .... misit Deus angelos ad tutelam cultumque generis humani, quibus quia liberum arbitrum erat datum, præcepit ante omnia ne terræ contagione maculati, substantiæ cœlestis amitterent dignitatem. .... Itaque illos cum hominibus commorantes dominator ille terræ fallacissimus [the devil, who according to Lactantius had fallen from envy of the Son of God previously to the creation of these angels, c. 9,] consuetudine ipsa paulatim ad vitia pellexit, et mulierum congressibus inquinavit. Tum in cœlum ob peccata non recepti ceciderunt ad terram. Sic eos Diabolus ex angelis Dei suos fecit satellites." (*Divin. Inst.* lib. ii. c. 15.)

To this order of dæmons, which the Platonists revered, but which the Fathers identified with the lost spirits of Scripture, both Christian and heathen writers in common assigned the authorship of the supernatural effects produced by magic. "Apuleius," says Augustine, "ascribes to these the divinations of the augurs and soothsayers, the foresight of prophets and dreams, and also the miracles of wizards" (*miracula magorum*). (*De Civ. Dei*, viii. 16.) Tertullian attributes the responses of the heathen oracles and other Pagan channels of prophecy, as well as the miracles of magic, to

the same source. "Omnis spiritus ales est: hoc angeli et
dæmones : igitur momento ubique sunt : totus orbis illis
locus unus est: quod ubique generatur tam facile sciunt
quam enuntiant, velocitas divinitas creditur, quia substantia
ignoratur. . . . . Porro et magi phantasmata edunt . . . .
multa miracula circulatoriis præstigiis ludunt, habentes dæmonum assistentem sibi potestatem." (*Apol.* cc. 22, 23.) Justin
Martyr (*Apol.* lib. i. s. 5), Irenæus (*Contra Hær.* ii. c. 32),
Lactantius (*Divin. Inst.* lib. ii. c. 15) use the same language.
So too Minutius Felix : "Magi quoque non tantum sciunt
dæmonas, sed etiam quicquid miraculi ludunt, per dæmonas
faciunt; illis adspirantibus et infundentibus." (*Octavius*, c. 26.)
So too Augustine : "Addimus etiam et humanarum et magi-
carum, id est per homines dæmonicarum artium, et ipsorum
per seipsos dæmonum multa miracula." (*De Civ. Dei*, xxi. 6.)
And he argues for the reality of true or divinely-wrought
miracles from the fact of these miracles of inferior and
diabolical origin : "Quamobrem si tot et tanta mirifica
Dei creatura utentibus humanis artibus fiunt, ut ea qui
nesciunt opinentur esse divina : si magorum opera, quos nostra
Scriptura veneficos et incantatores vocat, in tantum dæmones
extollere potuerunt . . . . . quanto magis Deus potens est
facere quæ infidelibus sunt incredibilia." (*Ibid.*)   Origen
accounts for the power of magicians, by the help partly of
his mysterious theory of *words*, which he applies to this
subject, intimating that a power is exerted over dæmons
by the knowledge and utterance of their true names, in the
language of their own appropriate regions : Διὸ καὶ δύναται
ταῦτα τὰ ὀνόματα λεγόμενα μετά τινος τοῦ συμφυοῦς αὐτοῖς
εἱρμοῦ· ἄλλα δὲ κατὰ Αἰγυπτίαν φερόμενα φωνὴν, ἐπὶ τινῶν
δαιμόνων τῶν τάδε μόνα δυναμένων, καὶ ἄλλα κατὰ τὴν Περσῶν
διάλεκτον ἐπὶ ἄλλων δυναμέων. . . . . . ὍΟτι οἱ περὶ τὴν χρῆσιν
τῶν ἐπῳδῶν δεινοὶ ἱστοροῦσιν, ὅτι τὴν αὐτὴν ἐπῳδὴν εἰπόντα μὲν
τῇ οἰκείᾳ διαλέκτῳ, ἔστιν ἐνεργῆσαι ὅπερ ἐπαγγέλλεται ἡ ἐπῳδή.
(*Contra Cels.* lib. i. s. 24, 25[b].)

---

[b] Professor Blunt, in his "Lectures on the Early Fathers," has a note upon
this theory of names put forth by Origen; in which, however, he erroneously
supposes the theory to be connected in Origen's meaning with Christian

Such being the belief of the Fathers in the reality of
magic, a belief which they expressed either with simplicity
or with ingenious and philosophical additions, according to
the character of the writers, how did they distinguish true
miracles wrought in evidence of a Divine communication
from the supernatural results of magic? They had different
modes of meeting this objection, and establishing the Divine
source of the Gospel miracles. They appealed to the greatness, majesty, and sublimity of the latter, which were of such
a kind that no magic had ever professed to produce anything like them. Our Lord's Resurrection especially was regarded as intrinsically a Divine act, being, as it was, a miracle
sui generis, not wrought by any intermediate agent, any person
intervening between the Invisible Supernatural Power and the
subject of that power, but wrought by our Lord Himself upon
Himself: Himself in death restoring Himself to life. (See below,
p. 245.) "Magicians," says Chrysostom, speaking even of
the miracles of our Lord's ministry, "have wrought miracles,
but not *such* miracles"—γόητες σημεῖα ποιοῦσι, ἀλλ᾽ οὐ τοιαῦτα

exorcism, and the exertion of miraculous powers within the Church, whereas
Origen is not speaking of Christian miracles but of heathen and Jewish *magic*,
and only proposes the theory in that connexion. Professor Blunt thus finds a
difficulty in Origen's implicit disclaimer of the proceedings and powers with
which this theory of names is connected ; whereas such powers being those
of magic, Origen's separation of himself from them and those who practise
them is no difficulty. "Some particulars," Professor Blunt says in the text,
referring to the existence of miraculous powers in the Early Church, "may
embarrass us ;" and among them Origen's theory of names, applied, as he
supposes, to these Christian powers ; an application with which he cannot
reconcile Origen's introduction of Jewish and heathen thaumaturgy in connexion with it ; and he pursues the difficulty in a note. "It is remarkable
that when giving further instances of the like effect produced by the names
Israel, Sabaoth, Adonai, whilst expressed in Hebrew, and of the inefficacy
of the same when translated, he uses the expression ὥς φασιν οἱ περὶ ταῦτα
δεινοί : and again, ἐὰν δὲ τηρήσωμεν αὐτὸ, προσάπτοντες οἷς οἱ περὶ ταῦτα δεινοὶ
συμπλέκειν αὐτὸ ᾠήθησαν—' but if we retain the original word, coupling it with
such other words as *those who are skilful in such matters* are used to couple it '—
(*Contra Cels.* v. s. 45), as though Origen disclaimed all such powers of in-
cantation for himself," &c. (*Blunt,* p. 399.) His speaking of this class as
one with which he has no connexion does not require to be accounted for,
because the class of which he is speaking was not a Christian one, but that
of wizards and practisers of the art of magic.

ποιοῦσι σημεῖα. (tom. xii. p. 32.) " Potestis aliquem nobis designare," says Arnobius, " monstrare ex omnibus illis magis qui unquam fuere per secula, consimile aliquid Christo millesima ex parte qui fecerit?" (*Adv. Gentes*, lib. i. c. 43.) The manner and mode in which Christ wrought His miracles, without any of the low forms and fantastic utterances and repetitions of magic, by a simple word or touch, is also observed. " We may also with St. Irenæus[c] observe," says Barrow, " that Jesus, in performing His cures and other miraculous works, did never use any profane, silly, fantastic ceremonies ; any muttering of barbarous names or insignificant phrases ; any invocation of spirits, or inferior powers ; any preparatory purgations, any mysterious circumstances of proceeding, apt to amuse people ; any such unaccountable methods or instruments, as magicians, enchanters, diviners, circulatorious jugglers, and such emissaries of the devil, or self-seeking impostors, are wont to use ; but did proceed altogether in a most innocent, simple, and grave manner, with a majestic authority and clear sincerity, becoming such an agent of God as He professed Himself to be." (vol. v. p. 205.)

But the great token by which the Fathers distinguished the miracles of the Gospel, those supernatural works which bore witness to our Lord's Divine mission, from the miracles produced by thaumaturgy and the power of inferior spirits, was the evidence of prophecy. The body of miracles which testified to our Lord as the Messiah, coincided and fitted in with a whole series of prophetical indications which had commenced with the beginning of things, i. e. with the fall of the first man, and had been sustained continuously almost to the very advent of our Lord. From the first page of the Old Testament to the last a constant promise was held out of the coming of One who should redeem mankind—a Great Deliverer who should save His people from their sins, and plant a new dispensation, a Divine kingdom in the world. It was evident that when this great Personage, so long pointed out by prophecy, came, there must be tokens by which

---

[c] Contra Hær. ii. 58.

He could be recognized as the Person who was *meant* by such prophecy, who was the true Messiah, to whom all these intimations belonged. When therefore a Personage appeared who claimed *to be* the Messiah, who announced Himself as the Head of this new kingdom in the world,—One whose whole life and teaching corresponded to that pretension, and who moreover authenticated His character and mission by the most remarkable and astonishing miracles; such an exhibition of miraculous power must plainly in reason be looked upon not simply in itself, but also in connexion with that constant voice of prophecy which had heralded the approach of a Messiah. Here was a coincidence—a Great Personage with an extraordinary mission had been *predicted*, One who professed to be this Great Personage had *come*, bringing the testimony of miracles to the truth of His announcement. Such a miraculous demonstration, therefore, could not be regarded in the same light as that in which a sudden unlooked-for outbreak of supernatural power would be, some wonderful outburst which came isolated and disconnected with all circumstances preceding it ; but must be contemplated in conjunction with the antecedent posture of things and the antecedent course of revelation. The miracles fulfilled prophecy ; prophecy therefore was a guarantee to the miracles. It was a security for their Divine source—that they really were tokens from God. The two, as in every case of coincidence, confirmed each other. This was the great distinction then which in the eyes of the Fathers separated the Gospel miracles in character from those miracles which magic and diabolical power could produce. Magic might achieve extraordinary effects for the moment and *at* the moment, but it could not create the long antecedent flow of prophecy, the long expectancy of revelation, the intimations of the Divine Oracle from the beginning of things, the foreshadowings and anticipations which had from the first signified the approach of a Messiah, and had been the standing oracle in the heart of the holy nation, and, in a sense, of mankind. The idea was that miracles, to have their proper effect as evidence, must not be a mere present

exhibition, but that they must have a root in the past, that
they must be the fulfilment of and carry out some great
antecedent plan and promise, that they must fit in with the
course of the Divine dispensation, and that they must testify
to some truth which had already an incipient place in the
authorized religion.

Such is the current answer of the Fathers by which they ·
meet the objection of magic—prophecy. " Should any one
object to us," says Justin Martyr, " that Christ wrought His
miracles by magic, we refer him to the Prophets." (*Apol.* i. 30.)
" If," says Irenæus, " they say that the Lord wrought these
wonders by illusion—φαντασιωδῶς—we refer them to the Prophetical writings, from which we shall shew that all these
things were predicted of Him." (*Contra Hær.* lib. ii. c. 32.)
" Celsus," says Origen, " asserts that if we are asked why
we believe Jesus to be the Son of God, we reply that He
healed the lame and the blind, whereas he himself attributes
these works to magic. I answer that we hold Jesus to be the
Son of God on account of these miracles, but on account
of them as having been foretold by the Prophets." (*Contra·
Cels.* lib. ii. s. 48.) " Know," says Lactantius, " that Christ is
believed by us to be God, not only on account of His miracles,
but because we see in Him all those things accomplished
which were announced by the Prophets. He wrought miracles : we might have thought Him a magician as ye think
Him, and as the Jews did, if all the Prophets had not with
one mouth foretold that He would do those very things.
Therefore we believe Him to be God, not more from His
wonderful deeds than from the Cross itself, because *that* was
foretold. Nor therefore do we repose faith in His divinity,
on account of His own testimony, but on account of the testimony of the Prophets, who long before predicted what He
would do and suffer ;—a kind of proof which cannot belong
to Apollonius, or Apuleius, or any of the magicians." (*Divin.
Inst.* lib. v. c. 3.) Augustine takes his stand upon miracles and
prophecy together : " Exceptis enim tot et tantis miraculis,
quæ persuaserunt Deum esse Christum, prophetiæ quoque
Divinæ fide dignissimæ præcesserunt, quæ in illo, non sicut a

patribus adhuc creduntur implendæ, sed jam demonstrantur impletæ." (*De Civ. Dei*, xxii. 6.)

Jackson represents with tolerable fidelity the patristic view :—

" By Christ's miracles alone considered, *they were not bound absolutely to believe He was the Messias, but by comparing them with other circumstances, or presupposed truths, especially the Scripture's received and approved prophecies of the Messias :* though no one for the greatness of power manifested in it could of itself, yet the frequency of them at that time, and the condition of the parties on whom they were wrought, might absolutely confirm John and his disciples ; because such they were in these and every respect, as the evangelical prophet had foretold Messias should work : for this reason our Saviour delivers His answer in the prophet's own words, as elsewhere He Himself did read them, then best interpreted *by the signs of the time,* that John might see by the event He was the man of whom Isaiah speaks, *He whom the Lord had appointed to preach the gospel to the poor, whom He had sent to heal the brokenhearted, to preach deliverance to the captives, and recovering of sight to the blind, to set at liberty such as were bruised, and that He should preach the acceptable year of the Lord.* . . . . From these instances, to omit others, the reader may resolve himself in what sense Christ's works are said to bear witness of His divinity, or condemn the Jews of infidelity. Both which they manifestly did, yet not in themselves, not as severally considered or sequestered from all signs of times and seasons ; *but as they involved such concurrence of God's providence, or presupposed such prophetical predictions, as have been intimated.* Every miracle was apt of itself to breed admiration, and beget some degree of faith, as more than probably arguing the assistance of a power truly divine. But seeing Moses had forewarned God would suffer seducers to work wonders for the trial of His people's faith, who, besides Him that gave them this liberty, could set them bounds beyond which they should not pass ? who could precisely define the compass of that circle, within which only Satan could exercise the power he had by that permission ? Be it granted (which is all men otherwise minded concerning this point demand) that Beelzebub himself with the help of all his subjects can effect nothing exceeding the natural passive capacity of things created ; he must be as well seeing in the secrets of nature as these subtle spirits are, that can precisely define in all particulars what may be done by force of nature, what not.

Hardly can we (without some admonitions to observe their carriage) discern the sleight of ordinary jugglers : much more easily might the prince of darkness so blind our natural understanding, as to make us believe (were the light of God's word taken away) that were effected by his power which had been wrought by the finger of God, that secret conveyance of materials elsewhere preexistent, into our presence, was a new creation of them. . . . . . Such signs and wonders might be wrought by seducers, that such as would gaze on them, and trust their own skill in discerning their tricks, should hardly escape their snares : *If any man say to you, Lo, here is Christ, or, lo, He is there ; believe it not : for false Christs shall arise, and false prophets, and shall shew signs and wonders, to deceive, if it were possible, the very elect.* And possible it was to have deceived even these, if it had been possible for these not to have *tried their wonders by the written word.*" (*Comments on the Creed*, bk. iii. ch. 20.)

It was this sense and deep estimate of the value of prophecy, as evidence of the Messiah, and as a voucher for the Divine design in, and the authentic nature of the miraculous evidence accompanying Him, that sent the Fathers into the region of heathen prophecy, to discover and collect the scattered traces of that wider and earlier revelation which had from the first shadowed forth this mighty Person, and had spread dimly and irregularly from the fountain-head of prophecy. Their idea was to carry the evidence of a Messiah *back* as far as possible—*back* into the infancy of time, and into the first dawn of inspiration ; not only that inspiration which had been reposited in the sacred books, but that also which had travelled out of the sacred line of testimony into the world at large, and scattered itself with the ramifications and migrations of the human race : it was to connect the Messiah with the first forecast of the future which had been imparted to mankind, and with a great prophetic wish which had thus from the first seated itself in the heart of mankind. Thus the Sibylline prophecies, which contained as interpreted by Virgil the original element of a great anticipation, but which had become corrupted by interpolations, were appealed to by the Fathers with the interest and fondness of writers who delighted to see the expectation of a Messiah rooted in the mind

of the human race. (See Augustine, *De Civ. Dei*, xviii. 23;
Lactantius, *Divin. Inst.* i. 6; iv. 6, 15.)

" It was a sound and healthy feeling," says Neander, "that
induced the apologists of Christianity to assume the existence
of a prophetic element, not in Judaism alone, but also in
Paganism, and to make appeal to this, as the apostle Paul at
Athens, in proclaiming the God of revelation, appealed to the
presentiment of the unknown God in the immediate consciousness of mankind, and to those forms in which this
consciousness had been expressed by the words of inspired
poets. Christianity, in truth, is the end to which all development of the religious consciousness must tend, and of which,
therefore, it cannot do otherwise than offer a prophetic testimony. Thus there dwells an element of prophecy not barely
in revealed religion, unfolding itself beneath the fostering care
of the divine vintager (John xv) as it struggles onward from
Judaism to its complete disclosure in Christianity, but also in
religion as it grows wild on the soil of paganism, which by
nature must strive unconsciously towards the same end. But
though the apologists had a well-grounded right to search
through those stages of culture from which they themselves
had passed over to Christianity, in quest of such points of
agreement,—for which purpose they made copious collections
from the ancient philosophers and poets,—yet it might easily
happen that they would be led involuntarily to transfer their
Christian mode of apprehension to their earlier positions, and
allow themselves to be deceived by mere appearances of resemblance. Add to this, that Alexandrian Jews and pagan
Platonists may have already introduced many forgeries under
the famous names of antiquity, which could serve as testimonies in behalf of the religious truths taken for granted by
Christianity in opposition to pagan Polytheism. And at a
time when all critical skill, as well as all interest in critical
inquiries, were alike wanting, it would be easy for men who
were seeking, under the influence of a purely religious interest, after the testimonies of the ancients, for such a use, to
allow themselves to be imposed upon by spurious and interpolated matter. This happened not seldom with the Christian
apologists.

" Thus, for instance, there were interpolated writings of this
description passing under the name of that mythic personage
of antiquity, the Grecian Hermes (Trismegistus) or the
Egyptian Thoth ; also under the names of the Persian
Hystaspes (Gushtasp), and of the Sibyls, so celebrated in the

Greek and Roman legends, which were used in good faith by
the apologists. Whatever truth at bottom might be lying in
those time-old legends of the Sibylline prophecies, of which
the profound Heraclitus, five hundred years before Christ, had
said, 'Their unadorned, earnest words, spoken with inspired
mouth, reached through a thousand years,' the consciousness
of such a prophetic element in Paganism, that which in these
predictions was supposed to refer to the fates of cities and
nations, and more particularly to a last and golden age of the
world, gave occasion to divers interpretations taken from
Jewish and Christian points of view." (*Church History*, vol. i.
p. 240.)

Lactantius claims the tribute of contemporary oracles to
our Lord, and reports the response of the " Milesian Apollo"
to the question whether Christ " was God or man"—$\theta\nu\eta\tau\grave{o}s$
$\check{\epsilon}\eta\nu$ $\kappa\alpha\tau\grave{\alpha}$ $\sigma\acute{\alpha}\rho\kappa\alpha$, $\kappa.\tau.\lambda.$ (*Divin. Inst.* iv. 13:) The patristic feeling
is again represented by Jackson :—

" Plutarch's relation of his demoniacal spirits mourning
for great Pan's death, about this time, is so strange, that
it might perhaps seem a tale, unless the truth of the common
bruit had been so constantly avouched by ear-witnesses unto
Tiberius, that it made him call a convocation of wise men, as
Herod did at our Saviour's birth, to resolve him who this
great Pan, late deceased, should be. Thamous, the Egyptian
master (unknown by that name to his passengers, until he
answered to it at the third call of an uncouth voice, uttered
sine authore from the land, requesting him to proclaim the
news of great Pan's death, as he passed by Palodes), was
resolved to have let all pass as a fancy or idle message, if
the wind and tide should grant him passage by the place
appointed; but the wind failing him on a sudden, at his
coming thither, he thought it but a little loss of breath to
cry out aloud unto the shore as he had been requested,
' Great Pan is dead.' The words, as Plutarch relates, were
scarce out of his mouth before they were answered with a
huge noise, as it had been of a multitude, sighing and groan-
ing at this wonderment. If these spirits had been by nature
mortal, as this philosopher thinks, the death of their chief
captain could not have seemed so strange ; but that a far
greater than the greatest of them, by whose power the first
of them had his being, should die to redeem his enemies
from their thraldom, might well seem a matter of wonderment and sorrow unto them. The circumstance of the time
will not permit me to doubt, but that under the known name

of Pan was intimated the great Shepherd of our souls, that
had then laid down His life for His flock; not the feigned
son of Mercury and Penelope, as the wise men foolishly
resolved Tiberius." (*Comments on the Creed*, bk. i. ch. 10.)

But because prophecy was in the judgment of the Fathers
wanted to guarantee the Divine source of miracles, and give
them their proper effect as evidence, it is not to be considered that the Fathers superseded the intrinsic force of
miracles, and *merged* it in prophecy. Each of these kinds
of evidence, in their view, stood in need of the other; miracles
to shew who was the object of prophecy, prophecy to mark
the Divine character of the miracles; but neither of these
was regarded as sufficient without the other. It was not
supposed that prophecy of itself would be enough to point
out the Messiah to the world upon His arrival, and give
mankind a justification for fixing upon a particular individual
as being that great Personage. For how does the case stand?
A mighty Deliverer and Redeemer of mankind from sin and
death is announced beforehand, but how is He known when
He does come? His office is principally mysterious and
supernatural, and does not bear witness to itself. The circumstance therefore that One who will fulfil this office is
predicted does not supersede the necessity of some adequate
marks and signs at the time to indicate who the predicted
Person is, and distinguish Him when He arrives from
others. And the natural mark of such a Personage is
miraculous power. This in the idea of the Fathers is wanted
then to point out at the time "the Lamb of God that taketh
away the sin of the world," as prophecy is wanted to mark
that miraculous power as divinely bestowed and indicative of
the Divine will. Prophecy announced beforehand that such
a Personage would come; the signs by which He would be
recognized, when He did come, must depend upon other
considerations, viz. *what are* the natural and adequate evidences of such a Personage, His character and mission. This
is a question of judgment and reason, with which prophecy
has nothing to do. Prophecy in proclaiming Him beforehand implies that He will be known and distinguishable upon
His arrival; which implies that He will be accompanied at

the time by sufficient evidences : but prophecy does not settle
what those evidences are, much less does it supersede the
need of them.

The patristic structure of evidence was indeed, like the
modern, a mixed one, consisting of different materials—
prophecy, miracles; the remarkable peculiarity of the spread
of Christianity in the world, that it ascended from the lower
classes of society to the upper, and not by the reverse process; and that the new religion was first promulgated by
rude men unacquainted with learning and rhetoric, and gained
ground by the force of persuasion, amid persecution and dis-
couragement, in spite of torture and death; the moral result
of Christianity, that it converted men from the lowest sen-
suality to the practice of virtue and piety, and wherever
it had been received had wrought a wonderful change in
the habits of mankind. The patristic argument consisted
of all these considerations, only not collected into the com-
pact body of statement which modern writers have produced,
but given out as each point happened to suggest itself to the
writer's mind, and occurring often in the midst of other and
extraneous matter. Even the professed Apologetic treatises
of the ancients are deficient in plan and method. But the
materials of the modern treatises on evidence are there, and
with the direct proofs of Christianity the collateral also
appear. " Ineruditos liberalibus disciplinis, et omnino,
quantum ad istorum doctrinas attinet, impolitos, non peritos
grammatica, non armatos dialectica, non rhetorica inflatos,
piscatores Christus cum retibus fidei ad mare hujus seculi
paucissimos misit." (*Augustine, De Civit. Dei*, xxii. 5.) Lactantius appeals to the rudeness and simplicity of the first
promulgators of the Gospel as evidence of the genuineness
and sincerity of their own belief in the facts which they
reported (*Div. Inst.* v. 3), to the progress of the faith under
persecution (*Ibid.* v. 13), to the virtues of Christians,
especially their humility and " equity," i.e. their all looking
upon themselves as equal in the sight of God, and the rich
and great among them lowering themselves to the level of the
poor :—" Dicet aliquis, Nonne sunt apud vos, alii pauperes,
alii divites; alii servi, alii domini? Nonne aliquid inter

singulos interest? Nihil: nec alia causa est cur nobis in-
vicem fratrum nomen impertiamus, nisi quia pares esse nos
credimus." (v. 16.) Origen retorts upon Celsus the taunt
of the lowly birth and parentage of Jesus, and draws an
argument *for* the Gospel from the circumstance of our Lord's
surmounting such obstacles : he draws attention to the rapid
spread of His doctrine, the comprehensive power by which it
has drawn over to itself wise and unwise, Greek and bar-
barian, the violent persecutions it enabled them to endure,
the difficult moral virtues which it enabled them to practise.
(*Contra Cels.* i. 27 et seq.)   The *success* of Christianity, that
it *had* gained ground, that it *was* believed by such a large
part of the world,—this matter-of-fact argument has a place in
the patristic evidences : " Nemo Apollonium pro Deo colit,"
says Lactantius (*Div. Inst.* v. 3). This argument has even
more of a place than might have been expected at that early
stage of the progress of Christianity; and even before Augustine talked of the conversion of the " world," which when
the Roman Emperor was gained he might colourably do,
Origen boasted of the " world's " subjugation to the Gospel—
ὡς νικῆσαι ὅλον κόσμον αὐτῷ ἐπιβουλεύοντα (*Contra Cels.* i. 3).

Indeed, Augustine rhetorically pushes the argument of the
success of the Gospel to such an extent that he appears at
first to assert that that success of itself is evidence enough of
the truth of Christianity, and that besides the miracle of this
success no other miracle is wanted.   " Si vero per Apostolos
Christi, ut eis crederetur, Resurrexionem atque Ascensionem
prædicantibus Christi, etiam ista miracula[d] facta esse non credunt : *hoc nobis unum grande miraculum sufficit, quod eam terra-
rum orbis sine* ullis miraculis credidit." (*De Civ. Dei*, lib. xxii.
c. 5.)   But when we examine Augustine's argument we find
that what he asserts is not that Christianity is independent of
the evidence of miracles, but that the evidence of the miracles
is so strong and overwhelming that the fact of their falsehood,

---

[d] " Ista miracula" alludes in Augustine's argument to the miracles of
the *Apostles*, by which they confirmed their testimony to our Lord's Resurrection and Ascension. " If you do not believe in these miracles," he says,
"you have to believe in as great a miracle, the belief in the Resurrection,
without them." The special allusion, however, to the Apostolic miracles is
not necessary to the argument.

in spite of this evidence, would be more extraordinary than the fact of their truth. He is arguing for the doctrine of the resurrection of the body against the heathen philosophers who thought it incredible: "*Sed videlicet homines docti atque sapientes acute sibi argumentari videntur contra corporum resurrexionem.*" (*De Civ. Dei*, xxii. 4.) And against this notion of the incredibility of the resurrection of the body, he urges the *fact* of our Lord's bodily resurrection. This fact, he says, is now accepted by the whole world. "*Sed incredibile fuerit aliquando: ecce jam credidit mundus sublatum terrenum Christi corpus in cœlum, resurrectionem carnis et ascensionem.*" (c. 5.) But that the whole world, he says, should believe that a thing intrinsically incredible has taken place is itself incredible. He thus reduces the philosophers to the dilemma that they must believe something incredible, either the incredible fact itself or the incredible belief in it; and therefore that the apparent incredibility of the miracle of Christ's Resurrection is no reason against it. The argument is rhetorical and not a rigid specimen of evidential reasoning; but what the argument aims at is the proof of the truth of the miracle of our Lord's Resurrection, not the conclusion of the truth of Christianity being independent of that miracle. "Si rem incredibilem crediderunt, videant quam sint stolidi [the heathen sceptics against whom he is arguing] qui non credunt: si autem res incredibilis credita est, etiam hoc utique incredibile est sic creditum esse quod incredibile est." (*Ibid.*) Why should the resurrection of the body and the particular resurrection of our Lord's body be disbelieved as incredible, when if we disbelieve *that*, we must believe something else which is quite as incredible? We meet the same argument in Chrysostom: Πόθεν τὸ ἀξιόπιστον ἔσχον; ὅπερ γὰρ ἔφθην εἰπὼν, εἰ σημείων χωρὶς ἔπεισαν, πόλλῳ μεῖζον τὸ θαῦμα φαίνεται. (*Hom. vi. in Cor.* tom. x. p. 45.)

So again Augustine says (*Contra Ep. Manichæi*, c. 5)— "Ego vero Evangelio non crederem, nisi me catholicæ ecclesiæ commoveret auctoritas,"—which some might interpret to mean that he accepted the Gospel upon the testimony of the Church solely, and did not require the proof of miracles. But Thorndike in commenting on this passage

distinguishes between two functions and capacities of the
Church, one false, the other true; one, according to which
the Church was an infallible asserter, and her assertion
enough; the other, according to which the Church was a
body of men witnessing to the transmission of certain doctrines and scriptures, upon certain evidence; witnessing, i.e.
to the *evidence* of those credenda, as well as to the credenda
themselves—such evidence being principally miracles. This
is Thorndike's fundamental distinction in treating of the
authority of the Church and the inspiration of Scripture—
his answer to the dilemma, to which the Roman divines
profess to reduce us upon the latter question, urging that
we receive the inspiration of Scripture upon the authority
of the Church; and that therefore we stand committed to
the principle of the authority of the Church in the fact of
our belief in the Bible. We do, is Thorndike's reply, but
not to the authority of the Church as an infallible asserter,
but as a body *witnessing* to the transmission of certain evidence *for* the inspiration of Scripture, contained in Apostolic
history,—viz. the assertion of their own inspiration by the
Apostles, attested by miracles. He explains then Augustine's
statement in accordance with this discriminating view. " The
question is, whether the authority of the Church as a corpora-
tion would have moved St. Augustine to believe the Gospel,
because they held it to be true; or the credit of the Church
as of *so many men of common sense attesting the truth of those
reasons which the Gospel tenders,* why we ought to believe.
. . . . . The miracles done by those from whom we have the
Scriptures is the only motive to shew that they came from
God, and that therefore we are obliged to receive what they
preached, and by consequence the Scriptures that contain it.
. . . . . For as true as it is that if God has provided such
signs to attest His commission, then we are bound to believe;
so true is it that if all Christians *agree* that God did procure
them to be done, then did He *indeed* procure them to be
done. For so great a part of mankind cannot be out of their
wits all at once." (*Principles of Christian Truth,* bk. i. ch. iii.)

The Fathers indeed assign other inferior uses to miracles
besides the most important purpose of evidence; such as

those of exciting and stimulating, awakening men from the
torpor of custom; and in the light of this advantage they
speak of miracles as an accommodation to human weakness.
Thus Augustine: " Quamvis itaque miracula visibilium na-
turarum videndi assiduitate viluerunt, tamen cum ea sa-
pienter intueamur inusitatissimis rarissimisque majora sunt.
Nam et omni miraculo quod fit per hominem majus miraculum est homo. Quapropter Deus qui fecit visibilia, cœlum
et terram, non dedignatur facere visibilia miracula in cœlo
et terra *quibus ad se invisibilem colendum excitet animum adhuc visibilibus deditum.*" (*De Civ. Dei*, x. 13.) Chrysostom
looks upon miracles in the same light, when he accounts for
the cessation of the gift of tongues by remarking that Christians of that later day did not *need* such wonders to move
their faith. " Tongues, as Paul saith, are for a sign not
to them that believe, but to them that believe not. Ye see
that God has removed this sign, not to disgrace but to
honour you; designing to shew that your faith does not
depend upon tokens and signs." (tom. ii. p. 464.)

In this light too the Fathers would seem to view miracles,
when they join the current miracles of their own age to
those of Scripture in the evidential office. The Fathers
assert *uno ore* that miracles had then ceased; yet they speak
of miracles taking place in the Church then, and even of
these miracles witnessing in a sense to the truth of the
Gospel. We must reconcile these two conflicting statements
by supposing that they recognized certain powers working
in and events taking place in the Church, which, though
not rising up to the level of the miracles of Scripture, still
shewed extraordinary Divine action, and in the degree in
which they did possessed an evidential function, and kept
alive the faith of the Church. " Christian doctrine," says
Origen, " has its proper proof in the demonstration, as the
Apostle says, of the Spirit and of power; of the Spirit in
prophecy, of power in the miracles which Christians could
then work, and of which *the vestiges still remain among those*
who live according to the Christian precepts—ἴχνη ἔτι σώ-
ζεσθαι." (*Contra Cels.* lib. i. s. 2.) " It is a magnificent act of
Jesus, that even to this day those whom He wills are healed

in His name." (*Ibid.* ii. 33.) Irenæus, after asserting that our Lord's miracles were verified by prophecy, which shewed Him to be the Son of God, adds, " Wherefore in His name His true disciples now perform deeds of mercy :" he mentions exorcisms, cures, &c. (*Contra Hær.* ii. 32.) " That Jesus," says Justin Martyr, " was made man for the sake of the believers, and for the subversion of dæmons, is manifest from what is done before your eyes all over the world ; when those who are vexed by dæmons, whom your own enchanters could not cure, are healed by our Christians abjuring and casting out the dæmons in the name of Jesus." (*Apol.* ii. s. 6.) " O si audire eos velles," says Cyprian, " quando a nobis adjurantur et torquentur. . . . . Videbis nos rogari ab eis quos tu rogas, timeri ab eis quos tu times." (*Ad Demetr.* xv.) Augustine, speaking of the miracles attributed to the interference of the martyrs, says, " Cui nisi huic fidei attestantur ista miracula in qua prædicatur Christus resurrexisse in carne, et in cœlum ascendisse in carne ? Quia et ipsi martyres, . . . pro ista fide mortui sunt, qui hæc a Domino impetrare possunt, propter cujus nomen occisi sunt." (*De Civ. Dei,* xxii. 9.)

I have endeavoured to state the patristic use of the evidence of miracles, and the characteristics by which it was distinguished from the modern popular argument. With respect, however, to the Fathers' appeal to this evidence, it must be remembered that their recognition of the evidential value of miracles, and of the need of them to attest the truth of the Divine nature and office of our Lord, is seen more as a great *assumption* underlying the whole fabric of patristic reasoning on this subject, than as anything formally expressed and developed in statement. The Fathers undoubtedly made deductions from the force of miracles as evidence, but that the person of the Messiah and Son of God who came to be the mediator between God and man, and to atone by His death for the sins of the whole world, would, when He came, be known and distinguished wholly without any miraculous element in His birth, life, or death, simply living in and passing through the world in that respect like an ordinary man—was an idea which never even occurred to the mind of any Father, and which, had it been

presented to him, he would have at once discarded. The
ancients, in their whole representation of the evidence of
Christ's nature and supernatural office—the evidence that
He was what He professed to be, the only-begotten Son
of God, the Lamb of God that took away the sin of the
world—*assumed* the great miracles of His Birth, Resurrection,
and Ascension; the Creed was used not only as a statement
of our Lord's Divine character, but as the proof of it as
well.   Christ as a superhuman Personage, the Head of a
supernatural dispensation, must be known from other men
by some adequate marks of distinction : the Fathers always
took for granted that that distinction must be by means
of something miraculous : that where there was an invisible
supernatural, which it was necessary to believe, the sign
and token of it would be the visible supernatural.   The Creed
stated this miraculous proof, so far as it attached to the
person of our Lord—His Birth, Resurrection, and Ascension.
The Creed was thus in essence a *defence* as well as an
assertion of our Lord's supernatural character, a defence of
it upon miraculous grounds.   In the very act of *worshipping*
Jesus Christ, the Fathers indeed assumed the miraculous
evidence of who Jesus Christ *was;* for to worship a person
who had lived and died like an ordinary man, with however
excellent gifts endowed, was an idea which they could not
have conceived; the miraculous testimony to His own assertion of His nature was taken for granted in the simple
prayer, " O Son of David, have mercy on us !"

" The facts of Christianity," says Archdeacon Lee, " are
represented by some as forming no part of its ' essential doctrines;' they rank, it is argued, no higher than its ' external
accessories.'   It is impossible to maintain this distinction.   In
the Christian revelation the *fact* of the Resurrection is the cardinal doctrine, the doctrine of the Incarnation is the fundamental fact.   Christianity exhibits its most momentous truths
as actual realities, by founding them upon an historical basis,
and by interweaving them with transactions and events which
rest upon the evidence of sense." (*On Miracles*, p. 5.)

Let us beware, in conclusion, of depreciating the ground-

work of Christian evidence laid down by the Fathers, because
these ancient writers entertained some points of belief relating to the class of inferior spirits and the art of Magic
which are not accepted at the present day. Such partial.
thaumaturgic pretensions as the art of Magic displayed,
even could we suppose them real, would not interfere with
the proper force of the miraculous evidences of the Gospel;
nor therefore was the belief in them inconsistent with a
true insight into Christian evidence. Nor must we forget
that the most indiscriminating belief in magic and witchcraft
continued up to very recent times in the Christian world.
The divines of the sixteenth and seventeenth centuries, whether
English or Continental, must have been singularly removed
from the prejudices and ideas of their times if they were not
more or less under the influence of the belief in these
powers[e]. Yet we should justly complain if upon this ground
any one refused to allow those divines the credit of being
able to weigh Christian evidence. Jackson, Hammond,
Thorndike, and others lived when the popular impression of the power of witchcraft to produce sensible supernatural effects upon human bodies and minds was strong,
and not confined to the lower and untaught classes, but shared
by the educated. Yet Christian evidence was in their day
a definite department of theology. Grotius had produced a
treatise which reigned in our schools, and Pascal meditated
another, of which the fragmentary beginnings are preserved
in his "Thoughts." Our divines all that time discussed the
miraculous proofs of Christianity, and shewed themselves quite
adequate to that task. Sir Matthew Hale, in the year 1665,
declared his own belief in witchcraft upon the occasion of condemning two women to death for that crime; yet it would
be a very mistaken inference to draw from the existence of
such a belief in that eminent Christian lawyer, that he could

[e] "All the nations of Christendom," says Dr. Hey (Norrisian Professor
1780-1795), "have so far taken these powers for granted, as to provide legal
remedies against them. At this time there subsist in this University one if
not several foundations for annual sermons to be preached against them."
(*Bishop Kay's Tertullian*, p. 171.)

not have a correct perception of the evidences of Christianity,
or was unequal to draw up a sound and rational statement of
those evidences. The Fathers partook of the popular ideas
of their age, which did not however incapacitate them for
judging of Christian evidences, or neutralize their statements
on this subject.

NOTE 3, p. 24.

" I THEREFORE proceed," says Spinoza, " to the consideration
of the four principles which I here propose to myself to demonstrate, and in the following order :—1st, I shall begin by
shewing that nothing happens contrary to the order of
nature, and that this order subsists without pause or interruption, eternal and unchangeable. I shall at the same time
take occasion to explain what is to be understood by a
miracle. 2nd, I shall prove that miracles cannot make known
to us the essence and existence of God, nor consequently His
providence, these great truths being so much better illustrated and proclaimed by the regular and invariable order
of nature. . . . . .

" (1) . . . . . As nothing is absolutely true save by
Divine decree alone, it is evident that the universal laws
of nature are the very decrees of God, which result necessarily from the perfection of the Divine nature. If,
therefore, anything happened in nature at large repugnant
to its universal laws, this would be equally repugnant to
the decrees and intelligence of God; so that any one who
maintained that God acted in opposition to the laws of
nature, would at the same time be forced to maintain that
God acted in opposition to His proper nature, an idea than
which nothing can be imagined more absurd. I might shew
the same thing, or strengthen what I have just said, by
referring to the truth that the power of nature is in fact
the Divine Power; Divine Power is the very essence of God
Himself. But this I pass by for the present. *Nothing, then,
happens in nature which is in contradiction with its universal
laws[f].* Nor this only; nothing happens which is not in

---

[f] Spinoza says in a note,—" By nature here I do not understand the material universe only, and its affections, but besides matter an infinity of other
things."

accordance with these laws, or does not follow from them:
for whatever is, and whatever happens, is and happens
by the will and eternal decree of God; that is, as has
been already shewn, whatever happens does so according
to rules and laws which involve eternal truth and necessity.
Nature consequently always observes laws, although all
of these are not known to us, which involve eternal truth
and necessity, and thus preserves a fixed and immutable
course. . . . .

"From these premises, therefore, viz. that *nothing happens
in nature which does not follow from its laws;* that these laws
extend to all which enters into the Divine mind; and, lastly,
that nature proceeds in a fixed and changeless course; it
follows most obviously that the word miracle can only be
understood in relation to the opinions of mankind, and signifies nothing more than an event, a phenomenon, the cause
of which cannot be explained by another familiar instance,
or, in any case, which the narrator is unable to explain.
I might say, indeed, that a miracle was that the cause of
which cannot be explained by our natural understanding
from the known principles of natural things. . . . .

"(2) But it is time I passed on to my second proposition,
which was to shew that from miracles we can neither obtain
a knowledge of the existence nor of the providence of God;
on the contrary, that these are much better elicited from
the eternal and changeless order of nature. . . . . . But
suppose that it is said that a miracle is that which cannot be explained by natural causes; this may be understood in two ways: either that it has natural causes which
cannot be investigated by the human understanding, or that
it acknowledges no cause save God, or the will of God. But
as all that happens, also happens by the sole will and power
of God, it were then necessary to say that a miracle either
owned natural causes, or if it did not, that it was inexplicable
by any cause; in other words, that it was something which
it surpassed the human capacity to understand. But of
anything in general, and of the particular thing in question,
viz. the miracle, which surpasses our powers of comprehension, nothing whatever can be known. For that which
we clearly and distinctly understand must become known
to us either of itself, or by something else which of itself is
clearly and distinctly understood. *Wherefore, from a miracle,
as an incident surpassing our powers of comprehension, we cannot
understand anything,* either of the essence or existence, or any
other quality of God or nature. . . . . .

Wherefore, as regards our understanding, those events which we clearly and distinctly comprehend, are with much better right entitled works of God, and referred to His will, *than those which are wholly unintelligible to us*, although they strongly seize upon our imagination and wrap us in amazement; inasmuch as those works of nature only which we clearly and distinctly apprehend render our knowledge of God truly sublime, and point to His will and decrees with the greatest clearness. . . . . . For if miracles be understood as interruptions or abrogations of the order of nature, or as subversive of its laws, *not only could they not give us any knowledge of God, but, on the contrary, they would destroy that which we naturally have*, and would induce doubt both of the existence of God and of everything else." (*Tractatus Theologico-Politicus*, c. vi.)

The argument of Spinoza under the first head is based upon an ambiguity in the meaning of " Nature," one sense of which it uses in the premiss, and another in the conclusion. In the premiss, Spinoza uses " Nature" in the sense of the universe both spiritual and material; in which sense it is true that " nothing happens in nature which is in contradiction with its universal laws." For even a miracle, though contrary to the order of the material world, or an interruption of it, is in agreement with the order of the universe as a whole, as proceeding from the power of the Head of that universe, for a purpose and end included in the design of the universe. In the conclusion he slides from the universal sense of nature to the sense of nature as this material order of things. The miracle, or violation of the order of nature which is pronounced impossible, is the literal historical miracle, which is only a contradiction to this visible order of nature. The conclusion, then, is not got legitimately out of the premiss. God cannot act in opposition to the law and order of the whole universe, in which case He would be acting against His own intelligence and will. But it does not follow that God may not act in contradiction to the order of a *part*, because the part is subordinate to the whole; and therefore an exception to the order of a part may be subservient to the order and design of the whole. Spinoza, it may be added, from the term " law " extracts

" a fixed and immutable course of things," or necessity : but
" law" in this sense is a pure hypothesis, without proof.

The argument of Spinoza under the second head is based
upon overlooking a miracle as an *instrument,* its acting as
a note and sign of the Divine will, and only regarding it
as an anomaly beginning and ending with itself. Emerson
adopts Spinoza's aspect of a miracle, when he says,—" The
word Miracle, as pronounced by Christian Churches, gives
a false impression; it is a Monster. It is not one with the
blowing clouds and the falling rain." (*Lee on Miracles,*
p. 92.)

NOTE 4, p. 30.

WHETHER or not Mahometanism stands in need of miracles
to attest its truth, must depend upon what Mahometanism *is;*
whether or not it pretends to be a revelation in the strict
sense; i. e. a revelation which communicates truths undiscoverable by human reason. Were Mahometanism simply
Deism, or rather Monotheism; did it only inculcate upon
mankind the great principle of the Unity of God; impressing together with that doctrine the obligation of worship and other moral and religious duties which were obvious
to reason; in that case Mahometanism could not require the
evidence of miracles to witness to its truth. Because the principle of the Unity of God is one which naturally approves
itself to the enlightened understanding of man, and is accepted upon its own intrinsic reasonableness. Had Mahomet
therefore only come before the world as a preacher of this
great truth, had he taken his stand upon those great arguments of reason which support it, and upon the strength of
those arguments called upon the idolatrous Arabian tribes to
throw away their idols and turn to the One living and true
God, the religion which he taught and established would
have had its proof complete without miracles : its proof would
be contained in itself. Nor, again, had Mahomet, not resting
this great truth upon grounds of reason and intrinsic evidence,
preached it as a truth of *revelation,* but of *an old and already*

T

existing revelation which was attested, when it was communicated, by its own miraculous credentials, would he in that case either have stood in need of miraculous proof for the religion which he taught, because such proof had been already given, and no new proof of the kind was wanted.

1. But Mahomet did not adopt this position; he did not confine himself to the ground of human reason, or to the ground of an old and existing revelation, but professed to have a new and express revelation of his own to communicate to mankind, a revelation which came to him straight from heaven. "We reveal unto thee this Koran[g]," God is representing as saying to Mahomet in that book; "Thou hast certainly received the Koran from the presence of a wise and knowing God." (chap. xxvii.) He professed to have had this revelation imparted to him by the medium of an angel, the angel Gabriel: "Gabriel (God is represented as speaking) hath caused the Koran to descend upon thine heart, by the permission of God." (chap. ii.) It is true that this revelation to Mahomet is exhibited as a supplementary one, not, i. e. as a revelation which contradicts and supersedes the former revelations of the Law and the Gospel, but which carries them out and advances a further step upon them; but this light in which the Koran is put, does not shew that it does *not*, but that it *does* profess to be an express and separate revelation to Mahomet. It is plain that the Gospel, though a development of the Law, was a separate revelation from the Law, on which account it was attested by its own special and appro-

---

[g] "Which we have sent down in the Arabic tongue." (*Koran*, chap. xii.) Sale says: "The Mahommedans absolutely deny the Koran was composed by their prophet himself, or any other for him; it being their general and orthodox belief that it is of divine original, nay that it is eternal and uncreated, remaining, as some express it, in the very essence of God; that the first transcript has been from everlasting by God's throne, written on a table of vast bigness, called the preserved table, in which are also recorded the divine decrees past and future; that a copy from this table, in one volume on paper, was, by the ministry of the angel Gabriel, sent down to the lowest heaven, in the month of Ramadan, on the night of power: from whence Gabriel revealed it to Mahommed by parcels, some at Mecca and some at Medina, at different times, during the space of twenty-three years, as the exigency of affairs required." (*Preliminary Discourse*, sect. iii.)

priate credentials: the revelation to Mahomet therefore, if it stood in a like supplementary relation to both of these former revelations together, was a revelation additional to both, a new revelation to mankind which required its own credentials, as the Gospel did when it succeeded to the Law.

"The Koran," says Mr. Forster, "was delivered by Mahomet, professedly as the complement of the former Scriptures of the Law and the Gospel, as a *further revelation*, that is to say, perfective of both; and advancing in its turn on the revelation of the Gospel, as this had previously advanced on that of the Mosaic Law. . . . . . Passages in the Koran directly class the Mahometan Bible so-called with the Old and New Testaments :—

"'We have surely sent down the Law, containing direction and light: thereby did the prophets, who professed the true religion, judge those who judaized.

"'We also caused Jesus, the Son of Mary, to follow the footsteps of the Prophets; confirming the Law, which was sent down before him : and we gave him the Gospel, containing direction and light; confirming, also, the Law, which was given before it.

"'We have also sent down unto thee (Mahomet) the Book of the Koran, with truth; confirming that Scripture which was revealed before it, and preserving the same from corruption.'

"In these passages the Koran formally challenges its place beside the sacred volumes of the Law and the Gospel, as sent to perfect both; and as forming, together with them, the sum of God's written revelation." (*Mahometanism Unveiled*, vol. ii. p. 14.)

The supernatural communication then of God to Mahomet, the Divine mission of Mahomet, needed attestation, to oblige a rational assent to and belief in it; attestation of that kind which is appropriate to truths undiscoverable by human reason. "Revelation," says Bp. Butler, "is miraculous, and miracles are the proof of it." That Mahomet stood in these supernatural relations to the Divine Being was a mysterious truth which no man could ascertain by the natural exercise of his reason. The Divine intercourse with him was a fact which belonged in its own nature to the invisible and supernatural world. Mahomet's assertion then was not proof of it, neither was his success. The prophetic mission of Mahomet then to establish a supplementary dispensation, which is rehearsed in the Mahometan's fundamental formula of faith, needed miraculous evidence, and being without that evidence is without proper proof.

2. But besides the Divine mission of Mahomet to establish a new dispensation, the substance of the Mahometan revelation itself is in many parts wholly undiscoverable by human reason. The great principle of Monotheism is so prominent in Mahometanism, as a system of religious belief, that we are apt to regard it as the only one, and so to look upon the religion in a light in which it can dispense with miraculous evidence. But besides the great doctrine of the Divine Unity, many most important articles of belief are divulged in the Koran—articles relating to the intermediate state, the mode of the general resurrection, the proceedings of the last judgment, the state of purgatory, its pains and duration; the happiness of heaven and the torments of hell. Minute revelations are made on these subjects, which are of overpowering interest to the Mahometan believer; but which are entirely supernatural communications, and undiscoverable by human reason. Such information then relating to the mysterious and invisible world, stands in need of some mark or guarantee to attest its correctness; nor can it rationally oblige the belief of those to whom it is given, unless it can produce such a voucher. But no such is produced in Mahometanism.

But besides the doctrines and revelations relating to the invisible world, Mahometanism also contains a large mass of rules and usages relating to practice, all of which rest upon a ground of express revelation, and are regarded upon that account as obligatory; and which therefore imply some direct guarantee attaching to them, in proof that they are Divine commands. General precepts indeed for the observance of the duty of prayer, almsgiving, &c., do not require any special voucher for their authority, because moral duties carry their

own evidence with them, and conscience accepts them upon
their own intrinsic ground. But positive institutions and
regulations, which are not binding upon any moral or natural
ground, can only be rendered obligatory by some direct sign
and warrant that the command to observe them comes from
God. What tokens then do the positive institutions of
Mahometanism present as credentials of their Divine origin, and in proof of their obligatoriness? There is no
adequate evidence of this Divine legislation, for the natural evidence of such rules and institutions having been
founded and imposed by Divine command, is a visible token
from God to that effect, or miraculous evidence; which
Mahometanism does not possess. The positive rules and institutions of the Mosaic law exhibited such a warrant, but
those of Mahometanism can only present the assertion of
Mahomet to that effect, joined to his success. The minute
regulations prescribed for the performance of prayer, the
observance of sacred seasons and days, the institution of pilgrimage, and much other ceremonial matter, all stand in the
Mahometan religion upon the express ground of a Divine
command; so do the prohibitions or negative ordinances of
external observance in that religion; a large body even of
civil law stands upon the same footing. But of this special
Divine authority no rational proof is given.

Mahometanism then comprehending, as it does, besides the
tenet of Monotheism, the express belief in the inspiration of
Mahomet and the Divine messages to him, a large body
of important revelations relating to the invisible world and a
future state, and finally, an immense mass of positive regulations, all imposed as matter of Divine command; belief in
it without the evidence of miracles is in its very form irrational, because it is belief in a revelation undiscoverable by
human reason, without the rational guarantee for the truth of
such revelation. Should the Mahometans ever alter the basis
of their religion, and place their creed and their institutions
upon another footing; should they reduce the inspiration of
their Prophet to the insight of a deep religious mind into the
great truth of the Unity of God; accept that belief as resting

upon grounds of reason, and discard all the revelations of the
Koran relating to the invisible world and a future state;
should they transfer the positive institutions of Mahometanism from the ground of a Divine command to that
of expediency, and so from being sacred and unchangeable
lower them into alterable human arrangements;—in that
case their religion would not need miracles, but then their
religion would cease to be Mahometanism. Such a religion
would be Deism, or natural religion. But Mahometanism,
as it is, is more than Deism; it is a professed revelation, and
the revelation of what is undiscoverable by human reason;
the belief in which, not only without that degree but without
that *kind* of proof which a revelation requires, is in its very
form irrational belief, though thousands not only of rational
but intelligent persons may *hold* it.

LECTURE II.

NOTE 1, p. 34.

Bishop Butler in the Introduction to the "Analogy" called
attention to the deficiency in the philosophical treatment of
the argument from experience, that the nature and *ground*
of it had not been gone into;—a part of the subject however
which he declines pursuing himself, as not being necessary to
the particular object with which he was concerned. "It is
not my design," he says, "to inquire further into the nature,
the foundation, and measure of probability; or whence it proceeds that *likeness* should beget that presumptive opinion and
full conviction which the human mind is formed to receive
from it, and which it does produce in every one. This belongs to the subject of Logic, and is a part of that subject
which has not yet been thoroughly considered." The "Analogy" came out in 1736, and Hume's "Treatise of Human
Nature," which entered upon this new field of inquiry, and
took up for the first time in philosophy the question of the

ground of the argument of experience, by a curious coincidence, followed the notice of the want in the " Analogy" by an interval of only two years, coming out in 1738.

NOTE 2, p. 54.

The general definition of Induction, that it is " a process of inference from the known to the unknown;" the operation of the mind by which we infer that what we know to be true in particular cases will be true in all similar cases, that what is true at certain times will be true in similar circumstances at all times, (*Mill's Logic*, vol. i. p. 297,) is universally assented to. The peculiarity of the process is confessed to be that it gets out of facts something more than what they actually contain; extends them further than they actually go. To pronounce upon what is wholly unknown, and say that it, the unknown thing, is or will be so and so, because the known is so and so, *is* thus to extend known facts beyond themselves; but unless this is done, there is no induction. " Any operation involving no inference, any process in which what seems the conclusion is no wider than the premisses from which it is drawn, does not fall within the meaning of the term." (*Mill*, i. 297.) " Did he [a philosopher] infer anything that had *not* been observed, from something else which *had?* Certainly not." There was no induction then. (p. 301.) " There was not that transition from known cases to unknown which constitutes induction." (p. 313.) " The process of induction," says Dr. Whewell, " includes *a mysterious step* by which we pass from particulars to generals, of which step the reason always seems to be inadequately rendered by any words which we can use." (*Philosophy of Discovery*, p. 284.)

But after the first general definition of induction Dr. Whewell and Mr. Mill disagree. In Mr. Mill's view induction is in its essence a simple direct process of arguing from some things to other things, from particulars to particulars, without the medium of the conscious contemplation of those known particulars in a general form, that is to say, the medium of language or general propositions. The mind simply passes on from several individual cases known to another individual case not known. " Not only may we reason from particulars to particulars without passing through generals, but we perpetually do so reason. All our earliest inferences are of this nature. From the first dawn of our intelligence we draw inferences, but years elapse before we learn the use of general language. The child who, having burnt his fingers, avoids to thrust them again into the fire, *has reasoned or inferred*, though he has never thought of the general maxim, ' Fire burns.' He knows from memory that he has been burnt, and on this evidence believes, when he sees a candle, that if he puts his finger into the flame of it he will be burnt again. He believes this in every case which happens to arise, but without looking in each instance beyond the present case. He is not generalizing, *he is inferring a particular from particulars. In the same way also brutes reason.* There is no ground for attributing to any of the lower animals the use of signs, of such a nature as to render general propositions possible. But those animals profit by experience, and avoid what they have found to cause them pain, in the same manner, though not always with the same skill, as a human creature. Not only the burnt child, but the burnt dog dreads the fire." (*Mill*, i. 210.) " *All inference is from particulars to particulars.* General propositions are merely *registers* of such inferences already made, and short formulæ for making more . . . . . the real logical antecedent or premisses being the particular facts from which the general proposition was collected by induction." (p. 216.) " If we have a collection of particulars sufficient for grounding an induction, we need not frame a general proposition : *we may reason at once from those particulars to other particulars.*" (p. 220.) The idea of the essence of the inductive process contained in these passages agrees with that of Hume, who regards it as an instinctive process, performed in no argumentative way, or by any argumentative medium. The idea also agrees with Hume's idea of the process as being no part of the distinctive human reason, or resting upon grounds of human reason, but being common to rational and irrational natures. "Experimental reasoning," says Hume, "we possess in common with beasts;" Mr. Mill says, "In this way (i. e. in inferring unknown particulars from known ones) brutes reason."

Dr. Whewell, however, differs from this account of induction as being an inference direct from particulars; as well as from the idea of induction as a process in essence common to rational and irrational natures; he regards it as essential to the idea of induction that it should be a conscious philosophical process, carried on by means of "general propositions, or observations consciously looked at in a general form." "Not only a general *thought* but a general *word* or phrase is a requisite element in induction[h]." (*Philosophy of Discovery*, pp. 241, 245.) Whether then a "general proposition" or "word" or "conscious general form of knowledge" is *essential* to induction as a process carried on in intelligent minds, is a question which must be decided by the examination of the fact—the consideration of what by the inspection of our own minds we perceive ourselves to do in induction. On examining then what goes on in our own minds, when as *intelligent and rational beings* from known particulars we infer what is unknown and beyond them—which is induction, it does not appear to be at all necessary or essential to that proceeding, that those particular observations should pass through the medium of a general proposition. The inductive inference naturally and with full propriety attaches itself to an observation a certain number of times made; upon the mere repetition of the fact observed the mind goes on to an inference respecting what is not observed, viz. that the latter will be like the former; the observations may be rational and intelligent ones, made with sagacity and discernment, but that they should have been made time after time, and should simply exist in the memory as a series or succession of particular facts, is enough in order that the inductive inference

[h] "The elements and materials of science," the writer adds, "are *necessary truths* contemplated by the intellect: it is by consisting of such elements and such materials that science is science." (p. 244.) But has *inductive* science to do with necessary truths?

may attach constitutionally to them. It has happened so, this and that and the other time, *therefore* it will so happen again, under the same circumstances. A physician has observed in so many patients the connexion of a disease with certain symptoms; he expects the same connexion in the next patient. This is an inference from particulars simply, but it is rational induction.

Indeed, as Mr. Mill observes, particulars are not only enough to infer from, and the inductive inference legitimate from them, without any medium of a general proposition, but in the nature of the case particulars are the only ground which we really have for induction to proceed upon, and the essential argument is in every case of induction *from* particulars. Particulars are all we know of, and therefore all we can possibly argue from. It is true we may introduce if we please a general proposition into the affair, and instead of proceeding straight from the particular facts and getting the inference from them as an *in*duction, turn the particular facts into a general proposition from which we obtain the inference as a *de*duction. Instead of saying, 'Alexander, Cæsar, Queen Elizabeth, Peter, Robert, William, (the list might be supposed extended to all who ever lived, and still be only a list of particular persons,) have died; therefore I shall die;' I may say, 'All men die,' which is a general proposition, and infer my own death as included in it. But this is a mere difference of form or arrangement which does not affect the substance of an inductive argument, or divorce it from its real basis in particulars. " The mortality of John, Thomas, and company," says Mr. Mill, " is, after all, the only evidence we have for the mortality of the Duke of Wellington. Not one iota is added to the proof by interpolating a general proposition. Since the individual cases are all the evidence we can possess, evidence which no logical form into which we choose to throw it can make greater than it is . . . . I am unable to see why we should be forbidden to take the shortest cut from these premises to the conclusion, and constrained to travel the 'high priori road' by the arbitrary fiat of logicians." (vol. i. p. 209.)

A general proposition introduced into an inductive argument cannot be inserted as any real or true ground of it; for if it is inserted as a truth, it is a *petitio principii*, and should therefore be immediately ejected. But if it is only introduced as a formal medium or mode of statement, it is not of the essence of the rational and scientific argument of induction.

The general proposition, so far as it comes in correctly at all, is indeed the *conclusion* of the inductive argument, and therefore cannot be the premiss of it. A general proposition however, i. e. a universal proposition, is not properly even the conclusion of the inductive argument, i. e. it is only used as such from the necessities of language, and because we have no other available formula for expressing the true conclusion in our mind. The inductive conclusion which really exists in the mind is indeed neither a general propositition nor a particular proposition. It is a vague indefinite *expectation* of a practical kind that when a thing has happened so repeatedly, it will continue to happen so under the same circumstances. But this indefinite expectation in our minds, this anticipatory look-out into the future or unknown, is not correctly expressed by a general proposition; because this is *more* than the true internal conclusion. A general proposition is the universal statement that the sun will always rise, but this is a statement which we do not really make in our minds, and is in excess of and beyond our actual mental condition and attitude on the subject. A general proposition is thus to the real inductive conclusion within the mind a case which is too large for its contents, which sticks out on all sides with unsubstantial amplitude. The inductive conclusion is not knowledge, and therefore if we give it the form of knowledge by means of a universal assertion, we still do not make it knowledge any the more by so doing, but only use a formula, with an understanding with ourselves about it. But neither, on the other hand, is the inductive conclusion a 'particular' in the strict sense; we reason *from* particulars, but not properly *to* particulars. If because the sun has always risen hitherto, I say it will rise to-morrow morning, or the morning after; that is a *limitation* of the real inductive conclusion in the mind, just as the general proposition is an *excess* of it. I do not adequately express the anticipation of which I am possessed, by this particular,—to-morrow morning, or another morning. When I make this particular prophecy, I plainly make it on the ground of a more general one. It is indeed exactly the same really, whether I say the sun will rise to-morrow, or the sun will rise always; I have the same meaning in my mind in both expressions. The same general anticipation speaks under both forms. All men hitherto have died; *I* shall die. This latter is a particular. But it is evidently exactly the same really, whether I say, '*I* shall die,' or '*All* men will die;' it is actually in the mind the same anticipation in either case.

For the argument of the Second Lecture it is enough, if without entering into the comparison of the inductive process as it goes on in rational creatures with the same process as it goes on in irrational, that process looked at in itself is admitted to be unaccountable and not founded on reason : for if —that which is identical with this process—the belief in the order of nature does not rest upon reason, the ground is gone upon which it can be maintained that a contradiction to that order is as such contrary to reason. The language however of philosophers, even when most cautious upon this subject, shews that if we look only to the inductive *inference itself* purely and simply, as distinguished from the facts from which it *is* an inference, and as unaffected by the difference in the character and rank of these facts; that if we regard it only as the attaching of continuance to whatever it is which has been repeated; it is impossible to make out any positive difference between that inference in rational natures and irrational. It is so difficult wholly to abstract the inference from the facts *from which* it is an inference, that we do not get the idea of the pure inference itself into our minds. According to the received language however of philosophers this inference is wholly unaccountable and altogether non-logical in *rational* natures : "to pass from particulars to generals is a mysterious step," says Dr. Whewell, however scientific the material to

which it is applied :—" there must necessarily be a logical
defect in it"—" the rules of the syllogism do not authorize
the answers of the inductive generalizing impulse." (*Philosophy of Discovery*, pp. 284, 451, 457.)   But if the inductive
impulse is thus in rational natures instinctive, mechanical, and
non-logical, in what does it differ from the same impulse in
irrational natures?   Man is a rational being, but if he does
not draw the inductive inference *with* his reason, that inference is not affected by his peculiar and distinctive gift of
the rational faculty.   Man knows indeed, when he contemplates himself and compares his actions and calculations with
the grounds and motives upon which they rest, that he *is* the
subject of a mechanical impression, which brutes, who have
not the self-contemplative faculty, do not know; and he
shews that this operation has taken place in his mind by
propositions, whereas irrational beings only shew that it has
by action; but do consciousness and language touch the
nature of the operation itself?   Mr. Mill, though he has
admitted that brutes " reason" (vol. i. p. 210) and draw instinctively the inductive inference, yet " objects" with Dr.
Whewell " to the application of the term induction to any
operation performed by mere instinct; that is from an animal
impulse, without the exertion of any intelligence." (*Note*,
vol. i. p. 295.)   Nor is such a restriction in the application of
the term otherwise than proper, because we associate with the
term induction not only the mysterious and unreasoning
step beyond the facts which have been described, but also the
scientific search for and discovery of the facts themselves;
but this restriction of the term does not touch the question
which we have been considering :—a question however which,
as I have observed, is more a curious than important one, if
only the main fact of the unreasoning nature of the inductive
inference is admitted.

What it is which constitutes the ground of induction or
the inference from the known to the unknown has been since
Hume's time a matter of dispute among philosophers, all of
whom however agree in the negative point, that the inference
does not rest upon any ground of reason.   " The ingenious

author of the Treatise of Human Nature," says Dr. Reid, "first
observed that our belief of the continuance of the laws of
nature cannot be founded either upon knowledge or probability; but far from conceiving it to be an original principle of the mind, he endeavours to account for it from his
favourite hypothesis. . . . . . However, we agree with the
author of the Treatise of Human Nature in this, that our
belief in the continuance of nature's laws is not derived from
reason.   It is an instinctive prescience of the operations of
nature. . . . . . Antecedently to all reasoning we have by our
constitution an anticipation that there is a fixed and steady
course of nature. . . . . . And this prescience I call the
inductive principle." (*Reid on Human Mind*, sect. xxiv.)
Brown disagrees with Hume's rationale of *custom* as the
ground of the inference from the known to the unknown.
" Custom may account for the mere suggestion of one object
by another, as a part of a train of images, but not for that
belief of future reality which is a very different state of mind.
The phenomenon *A*, a stone has a thousand times fallen to
the earth; the phenomenon *B*, a stone will always, in the
same circumstances, fall to the earth—are propositions that
differ as much as the propositions, *A*, a stone has *once* fallen
to the earth; *B*, a stone will *always* fall to the earth.   At
whatever link of the chain we begin, we must still meet with
the same difficulty—the conversion of the past into the
future.   If it be absurd to make this conversion at one stage
of inquiry, it is just as absurd to make it at any other stage."
His own rationale is " succession of thought"—" the natural
tendency of the mind to exist in certain states after existing
in certain other states."   The general expectation which succeeds to the facts of experience, he conceives, is only an
instance of this principle.   " This belief is a state or feeling
of the mind as easily conceivable as any other state of it—
a new feeling arising in certain circumstances," in the same
way in which *other* states of feeling arise.   " To have our
nerves of taste or hearing affected in a certain manner, is not
indeed to taste or to hear, but it is immediately afterwards to
have those particular sensations; and this merely because the

mind was originally so constituted, as to exist directly in the
one state after existing in the other. To observe, in like
manner, a series of antecedents and consequents, is not, in the
very feeling of the moment, to believe in the future similarity,
but, in consequence of a similar original tendency, it is immediately afterwards to believe, that the same antecedents will
invariably be followed by the same consequents. That this
belief of the future is a state of mind very different from the
mere perception or memory of the past, from which it flows,
is indeed true; but what resemblance has sweetness, as a sensation of the mind, to the solution of a few particles of sugar
on the tongue; or the harmonies of music to the vibration of
particles of air. All which we know, in both cases, is, that
these successions regularly take place; and in the regular
successions of nature, which could not, in one instance more
than in another, have been predicted without experience,
nothing is mysterious, or everything is mysterious. It is
wonderful, indeed,—for what is not wonderful?—that any
belief should arise as to a future which as yet has no existence; and which therefore cannot, in the strict sense of the
word, be an object of our knowledge. But when we consider
who it was who formed us, it would in truth have been more
wonderful if the mind had been so differently constituted that
the belief had not arisen; because, in that case, the phenomena of nature, however regularly arranged, would have been
arranged in vain." (*Brown's Philosophy of the Human Mind,—
Chapter on Objects of Physical Enquiry*, vol. i. p. 190.) The
criticism to which both these explanations of the inference
from experience is open, is that they are only ingenious statements of the fact. Reid's "instinctive prescience" is as a
phrase inaccurate, because we have not prescience or *knowledge*
of the future; such prescience can only really mean expectation; and then the explanation becomes only a statement of
the fact that we *do* expect the future to be like the past.
Brown's explanation approaches more to the nature of an
explanation, and yet at bottom it is only the statement that
after experience of the past we *have* expectation of the future,
that the former state of mind succeeds the latter. Hume's

rationale of custom, though undoubtedly deficient, has the advantage of connecting the argument of experience with a great principle in nature, which is not identical with it, with which however it appears to be connected; and thus approaches more to the nature of an explanation than these two. The question, however, what *is* the nature of the inductive inference, and to what principle we are to refer it, is an ulterior question which does not affect the argument of this Lecture, for which it is enough to say what it is *not*, viz. that it is not grounded on reason.

The nature of this remarkable assumption, again, upon which all induction rests, is discussed in the article on the " Immutability of Nature," in the Quarterly Review (No. 220, 1861) :—

" But then Science will turn to that axiom upon which, after all, the cogency of induction must rest. From the human mind, not from outward experience, as Dr. Whewell so wisely reiterates, we must derive the idea that ' similar causes will produce similar effects.' Our belief in the universality and immutability of the operations of nature must rest ultimately upon this internal instinct. Trace that belief, with Hume, to custom; or with others to association; or with others to a separate principle in the human mind; call it the generalizing principle, or the inductive principle : whatever account we give of it, this only, and not experience, can be our authority for assuming the continuity and stability of nature. And if it be a law of mind, a law like our moral principles, so stamped upon our being as to bear the marks of a revelation from God, then upon our faith in the veracity of God, upon our conviction that He would never engrave ineffaceably and unalterably upon the tables of our hearts and souls anything but truths (in one word, after all, upon faith, and not on proof), we may found our science of induction. But is it so stamped by God? Is it more than an instinct, a tendency, an impulse, requiring, like so many other tendencies of our nature, to be narrowly watched, balanced, and corrected by opposite tendencies ? All our sins and vices may be traced up to tendencies and principles, all implanted in our being by nature, but not therefore to be blindly followed without control or qualification. Are we yet sufficiently acquainted with the nature of this principle to decide this question ? Are there not obvious marks which class it rather with our instincts than with our reason—with imperfect impulses of our compound nature, rather than with absolute revelations from God? We can break its links. We cannot believe gratitude to be a sin, or falsehood meritorious; but we can imagine and believe in the existence of a world, where all the combinations of nature may be totally different from our present experience. The connexion between death and the swallowing of arsenic is of a totally different kind from that between injustice and the punishable character of injustice. No one would affirm of moral truths, as Science affirms of material causes and effects, that our knowledge of them rests wholly upon experience.

"That the principle has been so little studied, is so little understood, would suffice to warn us against asserting at once its Divine authority and sanction for the universal immutability of Nature. It would seem partly to be a result of the mechanical association of ideas, by which the mind spontaneously and unconsciously recalls and suggests combinations once observed, forming thus our memory, our habits, our character, our pleasures, our imagination, and a very large proportion of our practical reasoning. But every step we take in life compels us to keep this associating tendency under the strictest control, to regard it as a hundred other tendencies in our nature necessary to existence—valuable as a prompter—but . . . requiring at every step to be kept in check by experience, by faith in testimony."

It may be objected to the ordinary account of induction as based upon repetition and recurrence, that in the case of *experiments* repetition is *not* wanted to produce the feeling of assurance in the mind; i. e. that this is not the basis of the practical certainty we have in the result of experiments: that our assurance of this is not *gradually* acquired, slight at first and increasing afterwards every time the experiment is tried; but that after *one* chemical experiment, shewing the properties of a substance, or the effects of the union of two substances, we feel as sure that the same properties and effects will appear again as we do after the experiment has been fifty times repeated; or that if we do not, the want of such certainty arises from the doubt whether the experiment has been properly tried, it being possible, e. g. that some chance ingredient may have got in; not from the need of repetition supposing the accuracy of the experiment.

This is a question, then, which does not at all concern the nature of the ground of induction or the inference from experience, that it is instinctive and not founded on reason. Because were it true that the certainty of an experiment after one performance is as great as it is ever after, and that this certainty is strictly of an inductive kind, the instance would only shew, not that inductive certainty was not of the instinctive kind asserted, but only that inductive certainty, being of this nature, sometimes arose upon one case, instead of always requiring repetition. The difference would shew that there were difficulties in the interior of the subject of induction which were not yet solved, but it would not shew that the inductive inference from experience, whether arising upon a single case or upon repetition, rested upon a ground of reason.

It admits, however, of a considerable question, whether in the intelligent attitude of the mind toward an experiment, the certainty reposed in an experiment *is* an inductive certainty. There is indeed a posture of mind in which experiments are regarded simply as phenomena of experience, phenomena presented to the eye apart from their object and rationale; and the confidence in experiments, regarded in this light, does not seem other than an *inductive* confidence; but then in this light experiments do not seem free from but to come under the law of repetition; for we should anticipate the issue of an old familiar experiment that had been performed in all laboratories and lecture-rooms for years, with more confidence and more as a matter of course than we should the issue of a new one which had only been tried once or twice. But in the intelligent attitude of the mind toward an experiment it draws a distinction between the natural properties of a substance which are *supposed and taken for granted as being* such and such, and their mere exhibition to the eye by means of an experimental process. We take it for granted upon the ordinary instinctive ground, that the substance before us is exactly the same substance with exactly the same properties as the substance upon which the late experiment was tried; but *upon* this assumption, the fact that such and such *is* the property of the substance before us, is, after the late experiment, no step of induction, but an article of *knowledge*. We know that the property is there, which the second experiment only makes visible to the eye and does not prove to the mind. It must be observed that in the case of an experiment we have, to begin with, the advantage of the common instinctive induction of the identity of the substance before us with the last substance, already existing as our groundwork; and, upon this groundwork assumed, the result of the second experiment is *contained* in the result of the first; and therefore this result is not, upon this ground assumed, an inductive one. If it be said that the inductive nature of this *groundwork* still continues, that is true, and so far the result of the *experiment* is inductive. So far as it is not an absolute certainty that this is the same substance, with the same properties, as the last one, so far it is not a certainty that the result of the experiment will be the same: but in attending to the experiment the mind puts aside the uncertainty, whatever there may be, of the groundwork of it, and does not consider it.

I say, (p. 54,) " The first part of the inductive process is not reasoning, but observation; the second is not reasoning, but instinct." The first part of the inductive process may with general truth be described as " observation," in distinction to reasoning, because the sagacious observation of facts is all that is *necessary* to found an induction, and the great mass of inductions are founded simply upon facts of observation. Such facts, i. e. facts of scientific observation, Dr. Whewell calls " selected facts," the selection of them being by means of certain *conceptions* of the mind, by which facts are perceived in their proper relation, which he calls " colligation." (*Philosophy of Ind. Sciences*, vol. ii. chaps. ii–iv.) " In the progress of science," says Dr. Whewell, " facts are *bound together* by the aid of suitable conceptions. This part of the formation of our knowledge I call the *colligation* of facts ; and we may apply the term to every case in which by an act of the intellect we establish a precise connexion among the phenomena which are presented to our senses." (p. 36.) Even to the old, and as it happens untrue, Aristotelian fact of the longevity of "acholous" animals the writer applies the term "conception." "It is a *selected* fact, a fact selected and compared in several cases, which is what we mean by a conception. . . . . He applied the conception *acholous* to his observation of animals. This conception divided them into two classes, and these classes were, he fancied, long-lived and short-lived respectively." (*Philosophy of Discovery*, p. 455.)

It may, however, happen that particular facts upon which inductions are founded, are not the results of observation solely, but that the ascertainment of them involves reasoning, e. g. astronomical facts, the distance of the moon, the globular form of the earth, &c. In particular cases it is disputed whether an observation involves more than simple observation or not; as e. g. Kepler's discovery of the curve of the orbit of Mars. Mr. Mill says, this was only "the sum of the observations," not an induction from them;—the sum of the observations with the addition of the "curve the different observed points would make supposing them all to be joined together,"—which was *description*. Dr. Whewell says "that the intermediate positions between the several observations are an induction, [quoting Mr. Mill himself to that effect,] and that therefore the whole curve must be an induction." "Are particular positions to be conceived as points of a curve without thinking of the intermediate positions as belonging to the same curve?" (*Philosophy of Discovery*, p. 248.) What proves the curve would perhaps be as much the argument of coincidence as that of induction; it appearing to be a moral impossibility that the fitting in of so many points in the orbit with the figure of an ellipse should be a mere chance, the other *unobserved* points *not* fitting in with it. I have mentioned these cases to illustrate the point that observation, popularly so called, sometimes involves regular reasoning. But though the observation of facts which constitute the first part of induction involves in particular cases reasoning, observation alone is all that is required for induction, and this is the main faculty at work in this stage.

NOTE 3, p. 54.

" The very essence of the whole argument is the invariable preservation of the principle of *order:* not necessarily such as we can directly recognise, but the universal conviction of the unfailing subordination of everything to *some* grand principles of *law,* however imperfectly apprehended or realised in our partial conceptions, and the successive subordination of such laws to others of still higher generality, to an extent transcending our conceptions, and constituting the true chain of universal causation, which culminates in the sublime conception of the Cosmos.

" It is in immediate connexion with this enlarged view of *universal immutable natural order,* that I have regarded the narrow notions of those who obscure the sublime prospect, by imagining so unworthy an idea as that of occasional interruptions in the physical economy of the world.

" The only instance considered was that of the alleged sudden supernatural origination of new species of organised beings in remote geological epochs. It is in relation to the broad principle of law, if once rightly apprehended, that such inferences are seen to be wholly unwarranted by science, and such fancies utterly derogatory and inadmissible in philosophy; while, even in those instances properly understood, the real scientific conclusions of the *invariable and indissoluble chain of causation* stand vindicated in the sublime contemplations with which they are thus associated.

" To a correct apprehension of the whole argument, the one essential requisite is to have obtained a complete and satisfactory grasp of this *one grand principle of law pervading nature, or rather constituting the very idea of nature;*—which forms the vital essence of the whole of inductive science, and the sole assurance of those higher inferences, from the inductive study of natural causes, which are the indications of a supreme intelligence and a moral cause.

" *The whole of the ensuing discussion must stand or fall with the admission of this grand principle.* Those who are not prepared to embrace it in its full extent, may probably not accept the conclusions: *but they must be sent back to the school of inductive science, where alone it must be independently imbibed and thoroughly assimilated* with the mind of the student in the first instance.

" On the slightest consideration of the nature, the foundations, and general results of inductive science, we see abundant exemplification at once of the *legitimate objects* which fall within the *province* of physical philosophy, and the *limits* which, from the nature of the case, must be imposed on its investigations. We recognise the powers of intellect fitly employed in the study of nature, but indicating no conclusions *beyond* nature; yet pre-eminently leading us to perceive *in nature*, and in the invariable and universal constancy of its laws, the indications of *universal, unchangeable, and recondite arrangement, dependence, and connexion* in reason." (*Powell on the Order of Nature*, p. 228.)

" The case of the alleged external attestations of Revelation is one essentially involving considerations of *physical* evidence. It is not one in which such reflections and habits of thought as arise out of a familiarity with human history and moral argument will suffice. These no doubt, and other kindred topics, with which the scholar and the moralist are familiar, are of great and fundamental importance to our general views of the whole subject of Christian evidence; but the particular case of *miracles*, as such, is one specially bearing on purely *physical* contemplations, and on which no general moral principles, no common rules of evidence or logical technicalities, can enable us to form a correct judgment. It is not a question which can be decided by a few trite and common-place generalities as to the moral government of the world and the belief in the Divine Omnipotence, or as to the validity of human testimony, or the limits of human experience. It involves, and is essentially built upon, those grander conceptions of the order of nature, those comprehensive primary elements of all physical knowledge, those ultimate ideas of universal causation, *which can only be familiar to those thoroughly versed in cosmical philosophy in its widest sense.*

" In an age of physical research like the present, all highly cultivated minds and duly advanced intellects have imbibed, more or less, the lessons of the inductive philosophy, and have at least in some measure learned to appreciate the grand foundation conception of universal law—to recognise the impossibility even of *any two material atoms* subsisting together without a determinate relation—of any action of the one on the other, whether of equilibrium or of motion, without reference to a physical cause—of any modification whatsoever in the existing conditions of material agents, unless through the invariable operation of a series of eternally impressed consequences following in some necessary chain of orderly connexion." (*Powell's Study of the Evidences of Christianity,* p. 133.)

"The entire range of the inductive philosophy is at once based upon, and in every instance tends to confirm, by immense accumulation of evidence, the grand truth of the universal order and constancy of natural causes, as a primary law of belief; so strongly entertained and fixed in the mind of every truly inductive inquirer, that he can hardly even conceive the possibility of its failure." (p. 108.)

"The enlarged critical and inductive study of the natural world cannot but tend powerfully to evince the inconceivableness of imagined interruptions of natural order, or supposed suspensions of the laws of matter, and of that vast series of dependent causation which constitutes the legitimate field for the investigation of science, whose constancy is the sole warrant for its generalizations." (p. 110.)

"No amount of attestation of innumerable and honest witnesses would ever convince any one versed in mathematical and mechanical science, that a person had squared the circle or discovered perpetual motion. Antecedent credibility depends on antecedent knowledge, and enlarged views of the connexion and dependence of truths; and the value of any testimony will be modified or destroyed in different degrees to minds differently enlightened." (p. 141.)

A writer in the Quarterly Review has forcibly pointed out that such language as this violates "the very caution prescribed and commanded by the logic of induction, which rigidly confines statements of facts to actual experience, refraining from any admixture with these of assumption or hypothesis." The "Immutability of the Laws of Nature" is, he observes, such an assumption or hypothesis, and is therefore an offence against "inductive logic—that logic whose nobleness and potency is centred in a rigid discrimination of experience from imagination." (*Article on the Immutability of Nature,* 1861.)

NOTE 4, p. 59.

MR. MILL aims at providing induction with a complete logical basis, and discards the idea that the uniformity of nature rests upon any antecedent ground or assumption in

the mind. " I must protest," he says, "against adducing
as evidence of the truth of a fact in external nature the
disposition, however general, of the human mind to believe
it. *Belief is not proof, and does not dispense with the necessity
of proof*. . . . . To demand evidence when the belief is
ensured by the mind's own laws is supposed to be appealing
to the intellect against the intellect. But this I apprehend is
a misunderstanding of the nature of evidence. By evidence
is not meant anything and everything which produces belief.
There are many things which generate belief besides evidence : a mere strong association of ideas often causes a belief
so intense as to be unshaken by experience or argument.
Evidence is not that which the mind does or must yield to,
but that which it ought to yield to." (vol. ii. p. 95.) We
could not have a more decided announcement that the writer
intended to establish law in nature, or the belief in the uniformity of nature, upon a logical and argumentative as distinguished from an instinctive ground. He disproves the
latter by another argument : " Were we to suppose (what is
perfectly possible to imagine) that the present order of the
universe were brought to an end, and a chaos succeeded in
which there was no fixed succession of events, and the past
gave no assurance of the future; and if a human being were
miraculously kept alive to witness this change, *he surely would
soon cease to believe in any uniformity, the uniformity itself no
longer existing.* If this is admitted, *either the belief in uniformity is not an instinct,* or it is an instinct conquerable, like
all other instincts, by acquired knowledge." (vol. i. p. 97.)

The reply to this argument is, that when the belief in the
future uniformity of nature is pronounced to be instinctive,
it is only pronounced to be instinctive upon the condition
of her *past* uniformity. The belief which is pronounced to be
instinctive absolutely, is the belief that the unknown will
be like the known. It depends therefore upon what the
known or past is, what we believe the unknown or future
will be. If the past has been order, we believe the future
will be order; if the past has been chaos, we believe the
future will be chaos. The instinctive belief which is spoken

of is the belief according to which the future in our minds instinctively reflects the past, whatever that past may be.

Discarding, then, altogether the instinctive or antecedent ground, as the ground of the legitimate belief in the uniformity of nature, Mr. Mill proceeds to provide this belief with real evidence, or to place it upon a full logical basis. And the first ground which he puts forward is that this belief is "verified by experience." "Some believe it," he says, "to be a principle which, *antecedently to any verification by experience,* we are compelled by the constitution of our thinking faculty to assume as true;" but he, on the other hand, pronounces that this principle both requires and has the verification of experience. "The assumption with regard to the course of nature and the order of the universe," i. e. the belief in its uniformity, he says, "is an assumption involved in every case of induction. And if we consult the actual course of nature *we find that the assumption is warranted.* The universe we find *is* so constituted, that whatever is true in any one case is true in all cases of a similar description. This *universal fact* is a warrant for all inferences from experience. . . . . The justification of our belief that the future will resemble the past, is that the future *does* resemble the past: and the logician is bound to demand this outward evidence, and not to accept as a substitute for it a supposed internal necessity." (vol. i. 316; v. 2, 97.)

I am at a loss to understand what Mr. Mill can mean by saying that the assumption of the uniformity of nature is "verified by experience," "is warranted by a universal fact;" and by saying that "the justification of our belief that the future *will* resemble the past, is that the future *does* resemble the past." If, indeed, I make use of "experience" in such a way as to *combine it* with an instinctive or antecedent ground, that is the ground upon which the belief in the uniformity of nature is ordinarily put; the ground, viz. that although such a belief of course implies a past experience, and would be impossible without it, the belief is instinctive *upon* this past experience. The sun *having* risen up to this morning, which is past experience, I believe that it *will* rise to-morrow, which is an instinctive belief or assumption *upon* that past experience. But if I use the "verification of experience" in *distinction* to an antecedent or instinctive ground, in that case the "verification" of my belief in the sun's rising to-morrow "by experience" can only mean the verification of it by the *fact itself of the sun's rising to-morrow.* Such an "experimental proof" of induction would indeed convert any inductive conclusion into a universal proposition; for a conclusion which is "*proved*" and "verified" by "experience," as distinguished from any "general disposition of the human mind to believe it," is undoubtedly an actual and true fact. But such an "experimental proof" of induction cannot be stated without an absurdity; for we cannot without a contradiction in terms speak of the subject of inductive belief being verified by experience when that belief is by the very supposition an advance upon our experience: my belief that the sun *will* rise to-morrow cannot be verified by the fact of the sun's rising to-morrow, when as yet by the very form of the expression that fact has not yet taken place. Such a kind of verification could only be expressed by saying, 'I believe that the sun *has* risen, *to-morrow.*' Whatever amount of experience we may have backward, that experience can only verify the belief that preceded it—the belief in those particular facts of which that experience was the verification; that past experience cannot possibly verify my belief in a fact which is now future: yet this is what Mr. Mill verbally states,—"The justification of our belief that the future will resemble the past, is that the future *does* resemble the past." That which *was once* a future fact may have become in ten thousand instances a present fact, and, when it became present, have resembled the past; but we cannot possibly pronounce that what is *now* future resembles the past, because that future does not now exist. Whatever past verifications there may have been of the once future, *that which is at this time future* cannot be included in them; and for our belief in *it* we must depend upon an antecedent ground or assumption in our minds that the future will resemble the past. The order or uni-

formity of nature could indeed be verified by experience, were
it a *past* order or uniformity only ; but it is a future order as
well ; and the belief respecting that future must rest upon an
assumption by which we connect that past *with* this future.

As Mr. Mill, however, advances further in the construction
of a logical basis for induction, his argumentative phraseology changes, and the principle of the uniformity of nature
is asserted, instead of being "verified by experience" to be
"founded on prior generalizations or inductions." Of "the
fundamental principle or axiom of induction that the course
of nature is uniform," he says, "it would be a great error to
offer this large generalization as any explanation of the inductive process. On the contrary, I hold it to be itself an
instance of induction, an induction by no means of the most
obvious kind. Far from being the first induction we make, it
is one of the last. . . . . . This great generalization is itself
founded on prior generalizations." (vol. i. p. 317.) "The
belief we entertain in the universality throughout nature of
the law of cause and effect [which is the same with the order
or uniformity of nature] is itself an instance of induction ;
we arrive at this universal law by generalization from many
laws of inferior generality." (vol. ii. p. 97.) The general
axiom then of the uniformity of nature is founded upon a
number of particular inductions. Upon what are the particular inductions founded? The particular inductions are,
according to Mr. Mill, founded upon the general axiom.
"This assumption with regard to the course of nature and
the order of the universe *is involved in every case of induction.*"
(vol. i. p. 316.) But the construction of such a ground of
induction as this appears to shew that induction does *not*,
rather than that it *does*, rest upon a logical basis. For what
is the state of the case? The general assumption of the
uniformity of nature rests upon particular cases of induction ;
those particular cases of induction rest upon that general
assumption of the uniformity of nature. The large generalization rests upon prior generalizations ; the prior generalizations upon the large one. But if the two grounds or bases
of induction rest upon each other, what is this but to say

that induction as a whole is foundation*less;* that it stands
upon no ground of reason. If in every case of induction
there is an assumption, and that assumption rests upon those
cases of induction; both together are argumentatively suspended in space.

Mr. Mill of course perceives the objection to which his
ground is open, and replies; but instead of shewing that
his ground furnishes that " proof" or " evidence " with
which, he has said, induction cannot dispense, he appears
to disclaim the very intention of giving such proof or evidence at all. " In what sense can a principle which is so
far from being our earliest induction be regarded as a warrant
for all others? In the only sense in which, as we have
already seen, the general propositions which we place at the
head of our reasonings when we throw them into syllogisms
ever contribute to their validity . . . . . *not contributing at
all to prove* the conclusion, but being a necessary condition of
its being pro*v*ed; since no conclusion is proved for which
there cannot be found a true major premiss." (vol. i. p. 318.)
The general assumption then of the uniformity of nature has
only the place in the inductive process of a major premiss in
the syllogism, which, Mr. Mill says, " is a *petitio principii,*"—
" no real part of the argument, but an intermediate halting-
place for the mind, interposed by an artifice of language
between the real premiss and the conclusion." (vol. i. p. 225.)

In another passage, however, Mr. Mill seems to promise
such an explanation of the apparent circular reasoning upon
which he has based induction as will shew that the circularity
in it is only apparent, and that it is at the bottom real proof.
" If we assume the universality of the very law which these
cases [particular inductions] do not at first sight appear to
exemplify [i.e. the very law which is founded upon *them*],
is not this a *petitio principii?* Can we prove a proposition
by an argument which takes it for granted? And if not, on
what evidence does it rest?" (vol. ii. p. 94.) Mr. Mill's explanation then is, that the large generalization rises upon *some*
particular cases, and being gained proves the others. " The
more obvious of the particular uniformities suggest and give

evidence of the general uniformity, and the general uniformity once established enables us to prove the remainder of the particular uniformities." (vol. ii. p. 97.) But this is no answer to the argumentative objection which has been urged. For how were the more obvious particular inductions, upon which the whole structure rests, themselves made? By assuming the *general* principle of uniformity—"This is an assumption involved *in every case of induction.*" (vol. i. p. 316.) The general principle then still remains an assumption ; for those cases which assumed it evidently did not prove it.

Again, he reminds us that one part of induction may be *founded* on another and yet may *correct* that other. The principle of universal law or uniformity in nature, though a great philosophical principle, he says, is *founded* upon unscientific and empirical inductions; for the precariousness of this early and loose kind of induction diminishes "as the subject-matter of observation widens ;" and the law now mentioned is "an empirical law coextensive with all human experience." But the principle of universal law or uniformity once proved corrects and improves upon the looser and earlier inductions ; and "we substitute for the more fallible forms of the process, an operation grounded on the same process in a less fallible form." (vol. ii. p. 98.) But though it is true that, looking upon induction in its *results,* one part corrects another ; the correction of the results of induction has nothing to do with the philosophical *ground* of induction, which Mr. Mill still leaves in the state which has been described ; the general law of uniformity resting on the particular cases, and the particular cases on the general law.

The representation, then, of the uniformity of nature as being, in distinction to an antecedent assumption, " a universal fact," " certain," " absolute," " proved ;" the assertion that " the justification of our belief that the future will resemble the past is that the future does resemble the past ;" this identification of a law of nature with a universal proposition falls to the ground, and with it the following statements :—" We cannot admit a proposition as a law of nature and yet believe a fact in real contradiction to it. We must disbelieve the alleged fact, or believe that we were mistaken in admitting the supposed law." "If an alleged fact be in contradiction, not to any number of approximate generalizations, but to a completed generalization grounded on a rigorous induction, it is said to be impossible." "An impossibility is that the truth of which would conflict with a complete induction." (vol. ii. pp. 157, 159, 164)

It is proper, however, to add, that when Mr. Mill arrives at the point that he has to make a statement on the subject of belief in miracles, that statement appears not to agree with and carry out this account of induction, but to be in opposition to it. He says :—

" But in order that any alleged fact should be contrary to a law of causation, the allegation must be, not simply that the cause existed without being followed by the effect, for that would be no uncommon occurrence; but that this happened in the absence of any adequate counteracting cause. Now in the case of an alleged miracle, the assertion is the exact opposite of this. It is, that the effect was defeated, not in the absence, but in consequence of a counteracting cause, namely, a direct interposition of an act of the will of some being who has power over nature; and in particular of a being whose will, being assumed to have endowed all the causes with the powers by which they produce their effects, may well be supposed able to counteract them. A miracle (as was justly remarked by Brown) is no contradiction to the law of cause and effect, it is a new effect supposed to be produced by the introduction of a new cause. Of the adequacy of that cause, if present, there can be no doubt; and the only antecedent improbability which can be ascribed to the miracle, is the improbability that any such cause existed." (vol. ii. p. 159.)

This statement then certainly implies that a miracle is not impossible, and admits of being rationally believed. For a miracle is pronounced to be possible *if* there is an adequate cause in counteraction to natural causes to account for it: " the interposition of an act of the will of some being who has power over nature" is admitted to be such an adequate counteracting cause; and it is implied that there is nothing contrary to reason in the belief in such a being. But such

a statement as to the possibility of a miracle does not agree
with the previous position which Mr. Mill has laid down;
because he has said that a fact in contradiction to a completed induction is impossible, and we know that a miracle is
such a fact. That men, e. g. do not after death return to life
again is "a completed induction;" and therefore the resurrection of a man after death is a contradiction to a "completed
induction." It is true that a miracle is not in contradiction to
a law of causation, in the sense of causation by an act of the
Divine will; but the law of causation of which Mr. Mill has
all along spoken, and the contradiction to which he has pronounced to be an impossibility, is a law which consists simply
in a succession of uniform facts; it is physical law simply,
the chain of natural causes, which natural causes are only
another word for recurrent facts. A miracle, though it is
not contrary to a law of causation which includes the Divine
will as a cause, is contrary to this law of natural causation or
the order of nature. Mr. Mill's test of impossibility has
been all along a strictly matter-of-fact test—"a completed
generalization," a "completed induction." In this last statement, however, he adopts another test, that, viz. of causation
absolutely, and refuses to pronounce upon the impossibility
of a fact so long as, though contrary to the order of natural
causes, it can be referred to an adequate counteracting cause.
I gladly accept Mr. Mill's statement on the subject of belief
in miracles, but if this statement is true Mr. Mill's previous
language requires correction[h].

---

[h] Mr. Mill's statement of Hume's argument, as only asserting that "no
evidence can prove a miracle to any one who did not previously believe the
existence of a Being with supernatural power," is an incorrect one. Hume
asserts that the existence of a God makes no difference to his argument; and
rightly; because his argument rests simply upon a comparison of the respective
contradictions to experience in the two facts themselves—the truth of the
miracle, and the falsehood of the witness; the former of which two contradictions, he says, is greater than the latter. But if this argument is correct,
it is equally correct whether a Deity is supposed or not. For if experience is
our only guide, it is the only test also of the will of the Deity; which will,
therefore, is no additional consideration to experience, but is identical with and
is merged in it.

The sense of abstract possibility indeed in Mr. Mill's mind,
revealed by him in various statements in his works, cannot
be said to be too jealous, or timid, or narrow. This idea,
which is cherished by him as a philosophical liberty and
right, includes in it many results so stupendous and overwhelming that no miracle can be compared with them. " I
am convinced," he says, " that any one accustomed to abstraction and analysis, who will fairly exert his faculties for this
purpose, will, when his imagination has once learned to entertain the notion, find no difficulty in conceiving that in some
one, for instance, of the many firmaments into which sidereal
astronomy now divides the universe, events may succeed one
another at random without any fixed law." (ii. 96.) " In
distant parts of the stellar regions, where the phenomena
may be wholly unlike those with which we are acquainted, it
would be folly to affirm confidently that this general law [of
uniformity] prevails. The uniformity in the succession of
events, otherwise called the law of causation, must not be
received as a law of the universe, but of that portion of
it only which is within the range of our own observation."
(p. 104.) It must be remarked that this reign of enormity,
contradictory at its very root to our order of nature, and
involving all the miracles, did they take place on this earth,
which the wildest fancy can even picture to itself, has not,
according to Mr. Mill's conception, its possible locality in
another and invisible world, but in this very material universe in which we are living; the distance of this portentous
scene from this planet, however long, is a certain definite distance. Such conceptions as these have subjected Mr. Mill to
much criticism, but to whatever charge they are open it is not
to the charge of a limited sense of possibility. The objection
made to miracles is that they are divergences from the laws
of the material world introduced *into* the material world ; the
same persons who would admit any amount of strangeness in
another invisible world objecting to the introduction of divergence or strangeness into this world. Mr. Mill's conception
violates this distinction conspicuously, and so involves the
great point objected to in miracles.

LECTURE III.

NOTE 1, p. 81.

" No extent of physical investigation can warrant the *denial* of a *distinct order* of impressions and convictions wholly different in kind, and affecting that portion of our compound constitution which we term the moral and spiritual.

" That impressions of a spiritual kind, distinct from any which positive reason can arrive at, may be made on the internal faculties of the soul, is an admission which can contravene no truth of our constitution, mental or bodily. Nor can it be reasonably disputed on any physical ground that, under peculiar conditions, such spiritual impressions or intimations, in a peculiarly exalted sense, may be afforded to some highly-gifted individuals, and worthily ascribed to a Divine source, thus according with the idea we attach to the term ' revelation.'

" On other grounds it may perhaps be argued, that such a mode of communicating high spiritual truth is suitable to the truths communicated; that spiritual things are exhibited by spiritual means; moral doctrines conveyed through the fitting channel of the moral faculties of man. But all we are at present concerned to maintain is, that both the *substance* and the *mode* of the disclosure are thus wholly remote from anything to which *physical* difficulties can attach, or which comes under the province of *sense* or *intellect*.

" But then, in accordance with its *nature*, the *objects* to which such a revelation refers must be *properly* and *exclusively* those belonging to *moral and spiritual conceptions :* whether as related to what we experience within ourselves, or pointing to and supposing a more extended and undefined world of *spiritual, unseen, eternal existence, above and beyond* all that is matter of sense or reason, of *which science gives no intimation—* apart from the world of material existence, of ordinary human action, or even of metaphysical speculation, wholly the domain and creation of faith and inspiration. Such a world, it is acknowledged, is disclosed by Christianity as the subject of

a peculiar revelation, presenting objects which are wholly and
exclusively those of faith, not of sense or knowledge.

"Thus it follows, in regard to revelation in general, that so
far as its objects are properly those which are in their nature
restricted to *purely religious* and *spiritual* truths, we must
acknowledge that in these, its more characteristic and essential elements, *it can involve nothing which can come into contact
or collision with the truth of physical science or inductive uniformity; though* wholly *extraneous* to the world of positive
knowledge, *it can imply nothing at variance with any part of it*,
and thus can involve us in *no difficulties on physical grounds*.

"And those who reason most extensively on the Divine
perfections are usually foremost to allow that our most worthy
conception of Divine interposition is that of spiritual manifestation in the disclosure of the Divine will and purposes for
the salvation of man.

"It is the very aim and object of philosophy to point to
broad principles of unity, continuity, and analogy in all
physical events; though there are many who (as one of the
ablest writers of the age has expressed it), being 'unable to
compare, suppose that everything is isolated, simply because
to them the continuity is invisible.'

"But in matters altogether alien from physical things, or
even the·moral order of this world,—in spiritual, unseen, and
heavenly things, from their very nature, no such analogies
can be formed or expected; they are essentially distinct in
kind and order.

"Thus, a purely *spiritual* revelation, as such, stands on
quite distinct grounds from the idea of *physical* interruption.
Yet this distinction has been continually lost sight of, while
it is of the most primary importance for vindicating the
acceptance of such revelation as the source of spiritual truth."
(*Powell's Order of Nature*, p. 276.)

"The progress of opinion on such questions has been in
some measure indicated in the historical survey before taken.
The *metaphysical* spirit of an older philosophy indisposed or
disqualified even the most philosophical inquirers from perceiving the relative importance and bearing of physical truth.
Their Theistic arguments were based on technical abstrac-
tions, and overruled all physical inferences. Hence both
the belief and the scepticism of different ages has taken its
character. Men formerly, and even at present under metaphysical influences, have cavilled at *mysteries*, but acquiesced in
miracles. Under a more *positive* system, the most enlightened are the first to admit spiritual *mysteries* as matters of

faith, utterly beyond reason, though they find deviations from *physical* truth irreconcilable to science." (*Ibid.* p. 292.)

" In the foregoing survey of the relations of Christianity to the physical order of things, and especially to miracles, in the form which any view of that question necessarily takes in the present day, it has been observed that the point to which opinion seems from various quarters to be converging, both among enlightened believers and thinking and inquiring minds, even of very different schools, is to recede from the precise and formal arguments once so much insisted on, but now seen to involve so many physical difficulties, and to recur to more purely *spiritual* considerations and the ground of *faith* in the reception of revelation ;—a view which so eminently harmonises with its nature as a disclosure of spiritual mysteries of the unseen world.

" If in what has preceded no reference has been made to such high mysteries as the Trinity, the union of the Divine and human natures in Christ, the Atonement by His death, the influence of the Holy Spirit, or Sacramental grace, it is because these and the like tenets of the Church do not properly fall under the present discussion; since though in some few points touching upon material things,—on the human existence and death of Christ, and on the nature of man,—yet they involve no consideration of a *physical* kind infringing on the visible order of the natural world, and thus cannot be open to any difficulties of the kind here contemplated : in fact, all the objections which have been raised against them are of a metaphysical, moral, or philological nature.

" But if, in other cases, the highest doctrines are essentially connected with the narrative of miracles, we have seen that the most earnest believers contemplate the *miracle* by the light of the *doctrine,* and both solely with the eye of *faith ;* and thus when, as in some of the chief articles of the Christian formularies, the invisible world seems to be brought into immediate connexion with the visible,—the region of faith with that of sense,—when heavenly mysteries are represented as involved in earthly marvels,—the spirit of faith obviates the difficulties of reason by claiming them to its own province and prerogative. . . . . .

" Thus the resurrection of Christ is emphatically dwelt upon, not in its physical letter, but in its doctrinal spirit ; not as a physiological phenomenon, but as the corner-stone of Christian faith and hope, the type of spiritual life here, and the assurance of eternal life hereafter.

" So, in like manner, the transcendent mysteries of the

Incarnation and the Ascension are never alluded to at all by
the Apostles in a historical or material sense, but only so far
as they are involved in points of *spiritual* doctrine, and as
objects of *faith;* as connected with the Divine manifestation
of the 'Word made flesh,' 'yet without sin,'—with the *in-
scrutable* work of redemption on earth and the *unseen* intercession in heaven,—with the *invisible* dispensations of the
gift of grace from above, and with the *hidden* things of the
future, which 'eye hath not seen, nor ear heard, nor have
entered the heart of man,'—with the *predicted* return of
Christ to judge the world,—and the eternal triumph of His
heavenly kingdom.

"And in this spiritualised sense has the Christian Church
in all ages acknowledged these Divine mysteries and miracles,
'not of sight, but of faith,'—not expounded by science, but
delivered in traditional formularies,—celebrated in festivals
and solemnities,—by sacred rites and symbols,—embodied in
the creations of art, and proclaimed by choral harmonies;—
through all which the spirit of faith adores the 'great mystery of godliness,—manifested in the flesh,—justified in the
spirit,—seen of angels,—preached unto the Gentiles,—believed on in the world,—received up to glory.'" (*Ibid.* p. 456.)

NOTE 2, p. 87.

"L'unité jointe à l'infini ne l'augmente de rien, non plus
qu'un pied à une mesure infinie. Le fini s'anéantit en présence
de l'infini, et devient un pur néant. Ainsi notre esprit devant
Dieu; ainsi notre justice devant la justice divine. . . . .

"Nous connaissons qu'il y a un infini et ignorons sa nature,
comme nous savons qu'il est faux que les nombres soient finis :
donc il est vrai qu'il y a un infini en nombre, mais nous ne
savons ce qu'il est. Il est faux qu'il soit pair, il est faux
qu'il soit impair; car, en ajoutant l'unité, il ne change point
de nature : cependant c'est un nombre, et tout nombre est
pair ou impair; il est vrai que cela s'entend de tous nombres
finis. . . . . .

"Nous connaissons l'existence de l'infini et ignorons sa
nature, parce qu'il a étendue comme nous, mais non pas des
bornes comme nous." (*Pascal, ed. Fougeres,* vol. ii. pp. 163,
164.)

"The idea of space or extension," says Locke, "naturally leads us to think that space in itself is actually boundless. For it being considered by us either as the extension of body, or as existing by itself, without any solid matter taking it up (for of such a void space we have not only the idea, but I have proved, as I think, from the motion of body, its necessary existence), it is impossible the mind should be able ever to find or suppose any end of it, or be stopped anywhere in its progress in this space, how far soever it extends its thoughts. Any bounds made with body, even adamantine walls, are so far from putting a stop to the mind in its farther progress in space and extension, that it rather facilitates and enlarges it; for so far as that body reaches, so far no one can doubt of extension; and when we are come to the utmost extremity of body, what is there that can put a stop, and satisfy the mind that it is at the end of 'space, when it perceives it is not; nay, when it is satisfied that body itself can move into it? For if it be necessary for the motion of the body that there should be an empty space, though ever so little, here amongst bodies; and it be possible for body to move in or through that empty space; nay, it is impossible for any particle of matter to move but into an empty space; the same possibility of a body's moving into a void space, beyond the utmost bonds of body, as well as into a void space interspersed amongst bodies, will always remain clear and evident; the idea of empty pure space, whether within, or beyond the confines of all bodies, being exactly the same, differing not in nature, though in bulk; and there being nothing to hinder body from moving into it. So that wherever the mind places itself by any thought, either amongst or remote from all bodies, it can, in this uniform idea of space, nowhere find any bounds, any end; and so must necessarily conclude it, by the very nature and idea of each part of it, to be actually infinite. . . . . .

" *What is positive, what negative, in our idea of infinite?* The idea of infinite has, I confess, something of positive in all those things we apply to it. When we would think of infinite space or duration, we, at first step, usually make some very large idea, as, perhaps, of millions of ages or miles, which possibly we double and multiply several times. All that we thus amass together in our thoughts is positive, and the assemblage of a great number of positive ideas of space or duration. But what still remains beyond this we have no more a positive distinct notion of, than a mariner has of the

depth of the sea where having let down a large portion of his
sounding-line he reaches no bottom; whereby he knows the
depth to be so many fathoms and more, but how much that
more is he hath no distinct notion at all; and could he always
supply new line and find the plummet always sink, without
ever stopping, he would be something in the posture of the
mind reaching after a complete and positive idea of infinity.
In which case, let this line be ten or ten thousand fathoms
long, it equally discovers what is beyond it, and gives only
this confused and comparative idea, that this is not all, but
one may yet go farther. So much as the mind comprehends
of any space, it has a positive idea of; but in endeavouring to
make it infinite, it being always enlarging, always advancing,
the idea is still imperfect and incomplete. So much space as
the mind takes a view of in its contemplation of greatness, is
a clear picture, and positive in the understanding; but infinite
is still greater. 1. Then the idea of so much is positive and
clear. 2. The idea of greater is also clear, but it is but a
comparative idea, viz. the idea of so much greater as cannot
be comprehended; and this is plainly negative, not positive.
For he has no positive clear idea of the largeness of any extension (which is that sought for in the idea of infinite) that
has not a comprehensive idea of the dimensions of it; and
such nobody, I think, pretends to in what is infinite. For to
say a man has a positive clear idea of any quantity, without
knowing how great it is, is as reasonable as to say he has
the positive clear idea of the number of the sands on the sea-
shore, who knows not how many there be, but only that they
are more than twenty. For just such a perfect and positive
idea has he of an infinite space or duration who says it is
larger than the extent or duration of ten, one hundred, one
thousand, or any other number of miles or years, whereof he
has, or can have, a positive idea; which is all the idea, I
think, we have of infinite. So that what lies beyond our
positive idea towards infinity, lies in obscurity; and as the
indeterminate confusion of a negative idea, wherein I know I
neither do nor can comprehend all I would, it being too large
for a finite and narrow capacity; and that cannot but be very
far from a positive complete idea, wherein the greatest part of
what I would comprehend is left out, under the indeterminate
intimation of being still greater. For to say that having in
any quantity measured so much, or gone so far, you are not
yet at the end, is only to say that that quantity is greater.
So that the negation of an end, in any quantity, is, in other

words, only to say that it is bigger : and a total negation
of an end is but carrying this bigger still with you in all
the progressions your thoughts shall make in quantity ; and
adding this idea of still greater, to all the ideas you have,
or can be supposed to have, of quantity.   Now, whether such
an idea as that be positive, I leave any one to consider."
(*Locke on Human Understanding*, bk. ii. ch. 17.)

"Omne quod est, igitur, nulla regione viarum
Finitum est ; namque extremum debebat habere :
Extremum porro nullius posse videtur
Esse, nisi ultra sit quod finiat, ut videatur,
Quo non longius hæc sensus natura sequatur.
Nunc extra summam quoniam nihil esse fatendum est,
Non habet extremum ; caret ergo fine modoque :
Nec refert, quibus assistas regionibus ejus:
Usque adeo, quem quisque locum possedit, in omneis
Tantundem parteis infinitum omne relinquit.
    Præterea, si jam finitum constituatur
Omne, quod est, spatium, si quis procurrat ad oras
Ultimus extremas, jaciatque volatile telum,
Id validis utrum contortum viribus ire,
Quo fuerit missum, mavis, longeque volare,
An prohibere aliquid censes, obstareque posse ?
Alterutrum fatearis enim sumasque, necesse est,
Quorum utrumque tibi effugium præcludit, et omne
Cogit ut exempta concedas fine patere.
Nam sive est aliquid, quod prohibeat efficiatque,
Quo minu' quo missum est veniat, finique locet se ;
Sive foras fertur, non est ea fini' profecto.
Hoc pacto sequar, atque, oras ubicumque locaris
Extremas, quæram, quid telo denique fiat.
Fiet, uti nusquam possit consistere finis ;
Effugiumque fugæ prolatet copia semper."

Lucretius, i. 957.

NOTE 3, p. 88.

One particular argument of Bishop Butler in opposition to the presumption against miracles is drawn from the fact of creation, as being itself a miracle, or of the nature of one, and so a precedent for miracles; there being no presumption, when a power different from the course of nature was exerted in the first placing of man here, against that power going on to exert itself further in a revelation.

"There is no presumption, from analogy, against some operations which we should now call miraculous; particularly none against a revelation at the beginning of the world: nothing of such presumption against it, as is supposed to be implied or expressed in the word *miraculous*. For a miracle, in its very notion, is relative to a course of nature; and implies somewhat different from it, considered as being so. Now, either there was no course of nature at the time which we are speaking of, or, if there were, we are not acquainted what the course of nature is upon the first peopling of worlds. And therefore the question, whether mankind had a revelation made to them at that time, is to be considered, not as a question concerning a miracle, but as a common question of fact. And we have the like reason, be it more or less, to admit the report of tradition concerning this question, and concerning common matters of fact of the same antiquity; for instance, what part of the earth was first peopled.

"Or thus: when mankind was first placed in this state, there was a power exerted totally different from the present course of nature. Now, whether this power, thus wholly different from the present course of nature, for we cannot properly apply to it the word *miraculous;* whether this power stopped immediately after it had made man, or went on, and exerted itself farther in giving him a revelation, is a question of the same kind as whether an ordinary power exerted itself in such a particular degree and manner or not.

"Or suppose the power exerted in the formation of the world be considered as miraculous, or rather, be called by that name; the case will not be different: since it must be acknowledged that such a power was exerted. For supposing it acknowledged, that our Saviour spent some years in a course of working miracles: there is no more presumption, worth mentioning, against His having exerted this miraculous power, in a certain degree greater, than in a certain degree less; in one or two more instances, than in one or two fewer; in this, than in another manner." (*Analogy*, part ii. ch. ii.)

This argument does not appear to be interfered with by anything which science has brought to light since Butler's time. It assumes indeed a " beginning of the world," and scientific authorities state that there are no evidences *in nature* of a beginning[1]. But supposing this to be the case, science still does not assert that there is no beginning, but only deny that the examination of nature exhibits proof that there is one.

Science would indeed appear to be in the reason of the case incompetent to pronounce that there was no beginning in nature; because however far back she may trace the history of the formation of the material world, she can only assert what she has discovered, viz. the farthest point backward reached; she cannot assert what succession lies beyond the last ascertained point, still less that this succession is infinite.

[1] " It has been already observed that strict science offers no evidence of the *commencement* of the existing order of the universe. It exhibits indeed a wonderful succession of *changes*, but however far back continued, and of however vast extent, and almost inconceivable modes of operation, still *only changes :* occurring in recondite *order*, however little as yet disclosed, and in obedience to physical laws and causes, however as yet obscure and hidden from us. Yet in all this there is no *beginning* properly so called ; no commencement of existence when nothing existed before : no *creation* in the sense of origination out of non-existence, or formation out of nothing. The nebular theory may be adopted in cosmology, or the development hypothesis in palæontology—or any other still more ambitious systems reaching back in imagination into the abysses of past time ; yet these are only the expositions of ideas theoretical and imaginary, but still properly within the domain of *physical order*, and even by them we reach no proper commencement of existence. More than half a century ago, Dr. Hutton announced the first ideas of a natural geology, and boldly declared, ' In the economy of the world I can find no traces of a beginning, no prospect of an end,' and all the later progress of science has pointed, as from its nature it must do, to the same conclusion, nor can any other branch of science help us farther back than geology. In a word, geology (as Sir C. Lyell has so happily expressed it) is ' the autobiography of the earth,' but, like other autobiographies, it cannot go back to the birth." (*Powell's Order of Nature*, p. 250.)

It may be said that when the process of research has gone on for a long time, and when it always has been found hitherto that however back we have gone, there has been something discovered farther back still; the presumption is raised that this retrogression could be seen to go on for ever, if we could only continue to trace it. But this is no more than a presumption, which ought to give way to other considerations, if there are such of a weighty and urgent kind, for believing the contrary.

The value indeed of the fact of there being no scientific *evidence* of a beginning in nature as a proof there *is* no beginning, must depend on the consideration whether there would or could be scientific evidence of a beginning, supposing there to *be* one. For if, supposing a beginning, no search or analysis of nature might or could afford evidence of it, in that case no proof of the want of a beginning is given in the absence of scientific evidence for one. Evidence of a beginning, we must remember, is only another word for *our being able* to trace and find one; that is to say, evidence is only another expression for our faculties. Have we then the faculties for discovering by analysis a beginning in nature? In reply to this question it may be worth remarking, that we cannot be sure of the extent to which our faculties go in investigating nature; that we do not know the degree of their strength and subtlety, nor therefore, on this account, what conclusion is to be drawn from their failure. But, indeed, there appears to be another and a stronger reason to allege why we cannot draw the conclusion of there being no beginning from our not finding one, or from there being no evidences of one; for can there in the nature of the case be evidences and proofs from analysis of a beginning in nature, when all that analysis can ever possibly discover is the existence of some earlier fact than all hitherto ascertained ones, which is not a beginning, and no evidence of one[k].

---

[k] Mr. Baden Powell supposes that he enhances his statement of fact that science contains no evidence of a beginning by the addition that to " imagine a beginning is altogether out of the domain of science :"—which is the same as supposing that the testimony of a witness that a fact did not take place, is

Science then is opposed to a certain conception of creation, but not to creation itself.　It is opposed to creation conceived as an instantaneous operation, as an act of the Almighty will calling at once and in a moment by its fiat the whole world, material, animal, and rational, into existence, without graduation, progression, succession of steps.　But all that is essential to creation is that it should have a *beginning ;* and what succeeds this beginning—whether the end, the whole and finished work, immediately succeeds it, or whether a long and extended series of stages commencing with the lowest forms of organic nature, and terminating in the existing result, are all included within the creative work—is altogether irrelevant to the idea of creation.　Science then is in no disagreement with the idea of creation in that which is essential to it, although the facts which science has brought to light in connexion with the formation of this world are inconsistent with one conception and notion of creation.　Physical science at least is only opposed to that which is essential to creation, or to a beginning, in the way which has been mentioned, viz. as raising, by her past researches farther and farther backward, a kind of impression in the mind of the absolute interminableness of this process.　But such an impression cannot be urged as any proof that this series *is* interminable, because we possess no knowledge whatever of what exists beyond the last discovered fact; so that in the nature of the case the conclusion that this series *is* interminable, i.e. that this world has existed from all eternity, and is uncreated, cannot be pronounced by science.

strengthened by the circumstance that, not being on the spot, he could not have seen it if it *had* taken place.

That we cannot however in *material* nature by *physical analysis* discover a beginning, is not inconsistent with that beginning admitting of legitimate proof when we include in nature the order of *intelligent* beings, and apply to nature so understood certain principles of *reasoning* inherent in the very constitution of our minds.　Because we conclude from the existence of the universe some self-existent being, we conclude from the order of intelligent beings in the universe, and the appearances of design in it, the *intelligence* of that Self-existent Being ; and we conclude from the Original Being being intelligent, and matter not, that the material world cannot be that Original Being, i. e. must have a beginning. (*Clarke's Demonstration,* Prop. viii.)

Upon whatever ground, then, the existence of a *Creator* and Governor of the world was assumed in the " Analogy," upon the same it may be assumed now, and with the assumption of a creation goes the argument respecting miracles *from* the creation.

Again, the part of Butler's argument relating to the particular miracle of a revelation to man, supposes, in the mode in which it is put, that mankind was placed in this world at the beginning of this world; and these two phrases, " mankind being first placed in this state," and " the beginning " or " formation of the world," are used in the same meaning : a supposition which is opposed to recent science. But this supposition makes no difference to the argument so long as the former of these two events, whether contemporaneous with the other or not, is in itself correctly described in the argument ; for if " when mankind was first placed in this state there was a power exerted totally different from the present course of nature," the argument correctly proceeds, " whether this power stopped, or went on," &c. But that the power exerted upon that occasion *was* extraordinary is not disproved or contradicted by modern science; for all that modern science has ascertained is, that man came in subsequently to a long succession of irrational species ; but that there was a preceding succession of irrational species does not make the introduction of the human species any the less, when it took place, a new fact in the world, indicating the exertion of " a power totally different from the course of nature ;" both from that course of nature which was going on at the time, when man as yet did not exist, and from the present course of nature, when we only see his continuance, not his beginning.

Taking the facts of science, indeed, as they stand, and abstracted from any hypothesis respecting them, the several introductions of new species, antecedently to man, were severally " exertions of a power different from the course of nature." These species may be said indeed to constitute a succession or a series, and nature in the successive introduction of them may be said to exhibit marks of a plan or programme. But

a mere succession of events does not of itself constitute an
order or course of nature; that depends on the mode or continuity of the succession. If there are long breaks in the
chain, and if these several introductions or beginnings of new
forms of life take place at vast and irregular intervals, embracing lengths of intervening time almost transcending our
conception, these several new introductions would no more
form an order of nature, than particular instances of resurrection after death, at intervals of hundreds or thousands of
years, since the creation of mankind, would form a law of
resurrection. These several introductions of new life would
still be each of them a change in the order of nature existing
at the time of their respectively taking place ; and, inasmuch
as everything that is produced must have a cause, they would
be each the exertion of power different from the course of
nature, then and now. Such a progress of creation, indeed,
as that of which Mr. Darwin has set forth the hypothesis,
would be inconsistent with any event belonging to that progress being different from the order of nature; because the
order of nature and creation would then be identical; the
formation of new species would be a process always going on
in all its stages, earlier or later, according to the particular
instances; and the production of each new species, as each
was produced, would be only so slight an advance upon the
previous step, that it would not be a difference from, but only
an instance of, a constantly changing and advancing order of
nature. The miraculous stage indeed, if any, would be not
that of creation, which was a continuous order of nature, but
the present era of the world, when this order of nature has
stopped. Mr. Darwin's hypothesis supplies the links and
fills up the chasms in the progress of creation. But without
anything to fill up the immense chasms and breaks in the
order of creation as it stands, the new species as they make
their appearance in the record before us are entirely new and
original phenomena, starting up whole, at incalculable intervals
from each other.

Nor—though it may be hardly worth while making the
observation—can any " creational law " which does not fill

up these voids, but leaves them standing as they are, make any difference in the character of these phenomena. A "creational law" which coexists with such gaps and breaks can only be a theory of Divine action, a conception of the mind, not a law of nature; having the same relation to the productions of new species that Mr. Babbage's law of miracles has to miracles: a law which, as I observed in Lecture VI., does not touch the miraculous character of miracles. Secondary causes in order to constitute an order of nature must be visible; in the absence of which visibility their results are still anomalous and strange facts. The philosopher however, when he speaks of a creational law, or "a continuously operative secondary creational power[1]," only *means* the hypothesis that there is, though unascertained, a law of nature in this department, or that new facts constituting an adequate continuity of succession *will* be discovered.

The "first placing of man in this world," however, was a change in the order of nature so different in kind from all previous changes, that even supposing an order of nature up to his introduction, that introduction of him was still "the exertion of a power different from that order of nature." Of this new phenomenon, then, Sir Charles Lyell says,—"In our attempt to account for the origin of species we find ourselves brought face to face with the working of a law of development of so high an order as to stand nearly in the same relation as the Deity Himself to man's finite understanding; a law capable of adding new and powerful causes, such as the moral and intellectual faculties of the human race, to a system of nature which had gone for millions of years without the intervention of an analogous cause." (*Antiquity of Man*, ch. xxiii.)

To the hypothesis of a creational law made in this statement, I apply the remarks made above. But Sir Charles Lyell advances a further step, and while acknowledging the mystery of the origin of man, makes a cautious attempt to bring that mystery within the limits of a class and order of known mysterious phenomena, which have come into

[1] Owen's Palæontology, p. 444.

observation in the actual present course of nature, and within the region of human history and tradition.

"The inventors of useful arts, the poets and prophets of the early stages of a nation's growth, the promulgators of new systems of religion, ethics, and philosophy, or of new codes of laws, have often been looked upon as messengers from heaven, and after their death have had divine honours paid to them, while fabulous tales have been told of the prodigies which accompanied their birth. Nor can we wonder that such notions have prevailed when we consider what important revolutions in the moral and intellectual world such leading spirits have brought about; and when we reflect that mental as well as physical attributes are transmissible by inheritance, so that we may possibly discern in such leaps the origin of the superiority of certain races of mankind. In our own time, the occasional appearance of such extraordinary mental powers may be attributed to atavism; but there must have been a beginning to the series of such rare and anomalous events. . . . .

"To say that such leaps constitute no interruption to the ordinary course of nature, is more than we are warranted in affirming. In the case of the occasional birth of an individual of superior genius, there is certainly no break in the regular genealogical succession; and when all the mists of mythological fiction are dispelled by historical criticism, when it is acknowledged that the earth did not tremble at the nativity of the gifted infant, and that the face of heaven was not full of fiery shapes, still a mighty mystery remains unexplained, and it is the *order* of the phenomena, and not their *cause*, which we are able to refer to the usual course of nature." (*Antiquity of Man*, ch. xxiv.)

Such genealogical leaps then having, as the writer supposes, actually taken place in the intellectual nature of mankind, within the region of historical tradition,—which though it has imparted to its descriptions the shape of popular poetry and imagination, has still preserved in them the substance of true facts,—human nature he conceives to have been a leap of the same kind; only that instead of being a transition from lower man to higher man, it was a transition from the brute to the man. "If in conformity with the theory of progression, we believe mankind to have risen slowly from a rude and humble starting-point, such leaps may have successively introduced not only higher and higher forms and grades of intellect, but at a much remoter period may have cleared at one bound the space which separated the highest stage of the unprogressive intelligence of the inferior animals from the first and lowest form of improveable reason manifested by man."

But, without entering into the question whether differences in the scale of humanity, even if derived from the cause here assigned, would be a parallel to the difference between a state probationary for immortality and one not, i.e. between the human and the brutal; is there any evidence of differences in the scale of humanity having taken place from this cause, i.e. by physical transmission? any evidence that great and leading men who made their appearance in the early ages of society transmitted their own superior faculties by physical descent, and that a permanent rise in the subsequent intellectual level of mankind was produced by the operation of a genealogical law? Historical tradition, indeed, speaks of heroes and legislators who rose from time to time in the first ages of the world, and developed and improved the social and intellectual condition of the nations to which they belonged by education, by new codes and institutions, by new arts and inventions; but not of men who raised the intellect of mankind and founded " the superiority of certain races" by the natural transmission of their own higher qualities of mind, which thus became the hereditary property and new nature of posterity. Sir C. Lyell admits indeed that such facts as these " have a mighty mystery unexplained in them," and that though the facts themselves " are to be referred to the usual course of nature," " their *cause* lies wholly beyond us;" that is to say, he does not deprive the course of nature of mystery, but he conceives, nevertheless, that the leap from animal to human nature is paralleled by facts which have appeared in the existing course of nature. Neither history, however, nor tradition discloses such facts as Sir C. Lyell needs for the purpose of his parallel. We see indeed genealogical ascents of intellect, but those ascents are not permanent, and found no new intellectual nature: for the son having risen above the intellectual level

of his father, *his* son returns back to the lower stage.
Again, we see permanent ascents in the intellect of man,
but those ascents are not genealogical; they are not produced
by physical transmission, but by education, by civilization,
and instruction in the arts of life.   Human nature, before
and after the rise of the great and the wise teachers who have
appeared at different epochs, was the same; only in its former
state uninstructed, in the latter enlightened by new truths
and discoveries.   Permanent ascents gained by physical inheritance are the facts which Sir C. Lyell needs for the purpose of his parallel; but these do not present themselves.

NOTE 4, p. 89.

It is not perhaps sufficiently considered that, whatever
criterion we adopt of the rightness or wrongness of actions,
i.e. what makes actions right or wrong, the particular standard
we apply to the actions does not affect the question of the
principle of "right," or moral obligation being necessary to
bind those actions upon the individual.   Thus the standard of
expediency applied to actions is perhaps popularly supposed
to conflict and to dispense with the principle of moral obligation in the individual; the notion being that, because expediency is the criterion of the actions, therefore the actions
cannot be performed in obedience to the moral sense or sense
of right, but because they are expedient.   But in truth the
standard of expediency no more dispenses with the sense of
moral obligation in the individual than any other standard,
nor is it correct to conceive that if actions are performed
because they are expedient, therefore they are not performed
under a sense of moral obligation; because after the criterion
has done its part and fixed upon the actions on account
of their expediency, the question still remains, Under what
obligation am I to do what is expedient, what conduces
to general happiness?   Unless this additional step can be
made out, the actions may be proved to be ever so useful
and advantageous to the community, but the link which
connects them with the duty of the individual is wanting.

The system of Bentham is defective in this important link—
the medium between the community and the individual, by
which what is useful to the community becomes binding upon
the individual. He gives with great copiousness of statement his *definition* of right and wrong in actions, viz. their
being advantageous or disadvantageous to the whole social
body, including the individual himself. "Only so far as it
produces happiness or misery can an act be properly called
virtuous or *vicious.*" (*Deontology*, vol. i. p. 141.) "Will
clamouring for 'ought' or 'ought not,' that perpetual *petitio
principii*, stand in the stead of utility? Men may wear out
the air with sonorous and unmeaning words; those words will
not act upon the mind; nothing will act upon it but the
apprehensions of pleasure and pain. . . . . . Avow then that
what is called duty to oneself is but prudence, and what is
called duty to others is effective benevolence." (*Introduction
to Deontology*, vol. ii.) But supposing this criterion of rightness in actions themselves to be adopted, viz. their producing
happiness, the question still remains, "Why must I perform
these actions? what have I to do with the happiness of
others?" If the principle of "ought" then is admitted,
and the sense of "ought" allowed to exist in our minds,
there is a tie which binds the individual to society. He
cannot neglect the happiness of others without self-reproach,
and without the right of others to reproach him. But without this sense of "ought" how does the matter stand? A
certain class of actions are attended by most valuable results,
and it is undoubtedly highly for the interest of the community that they should be performed. But all that is by
the very profession proved is the interest of the community.
What difference does it make *in the individual*, not doing
them? Is he himself at all in a *different state* whether he
does them or not? Why should he reproach himself, what
right have others to reproach him, if he does not do them?
Without the sense of "ought" in the individual, there is
a large amount of human happiness laid before us as the
result of certain actions, but there is nothing to bind the
individual to those actions, or make him responsible for that

happiness. Society is lucky, and is to be congratulated upon its good fortune, if it obtains such a class of actions from him; but society cannot say, 'You *ought* to do them,' for there is no such thing as the principle or sense of "ought." If he has not done them, all that can be said is that he *has not* done them—a fact which is no more a reflection upon him than the omission of anything else which was not incumbent upon him. Without the principle of "ought" to supplement the criterion of expediency, the virtuousness of an action is identical with certain advantageous effects, and *means* these effects, and has no other meaning. But these effects are wholly outside the individual agent, and do not affect him in the slightest degree as attaching any quality to him, or making any difference in his inward condition. Praise or blame can only attach to him in the *sense* in which these terms must be used and to which they must be confined in this philosophy, viz. as the assertion of one or another set of effects; in which sense they assert external, or, as we may say, historical facts only, and do not touch the man.

Bentham's position, then, is not true—"The elements of pain and pleasure give to the deontologist instruments sufficient for his work. 'Give me matter and motion,' said Descartes, 'and I will make a physical world.' 'Give me,' may the utilitarian teacher exclaim, 'give me the human sensibilities —joy and grief, pain and pleasure—and I will create a moral world. I will produce not only justice, but generosity, patriotism, philanthropy, and the long and illustrious train of sublime and amiable virtues.'" (*Introduction to Deontology*, vol. ii.) "Deontology" does not supply the link between the good of society and the individual. It may be said that the principle of benevolence exists in the human mind as a passion or affection, independently of the sense of "ought" or duty; and that this is the link which connects the individual with society. But the mere affection of benevolence is only such a link so long as the affection is carried on by its own impulse, as the appetite of hunger or curiosity or any other is; when benevolence becomes an *effort*, unless there is the sense of "ought" to supply the place of the

force of the appetite, society's hold upon the individual goes.
For though benevolence, while it was in force, was advantageous to the community, the want of it cannot be charged
as a *fault*, there being no "ought" or "ought not" in the
system. A "fault" in it can only mean a disadvantageous
consequence of an action regarded as a productive thing,
which is not a fault in the moral sense. Yet, unaccountable
as it may seem, it is only when benevolence *does* become an
effort, and therefore depends entirely upon the sense of
"ought" for its exertion, that it is admitted to be a virtue
by Bentham. "But though the test of virtue be usefulness,
or, in other words, the production of happiness—virtue being
that which is beneficial and vice that which is pernicious
to the community—there is no identity between virtue and
usefulness, for there are many beneficial actions which do not
partake of the nature of virtue. *Virtue demands effort.*"
(*Deontology*, vol. i. p. 146.) But why should a man make
the effort? Bentham cannot say he "ought" to make it,
and no other reason, applying to the individual, can be
alleged. His very definition of virtue then makes it dependent just on that principle which in his philosophy is *omitted*.
He is possessed indeed of certain "sanctions or inducements
to action," such as the fear of punishment and the desire
for approbation. But the former of these two motives can
only apply to a very small proportion of human actions, if
by punishment we mean civil or physical punishment; and
the approbation of others is founded upon the sense of
"ought" in those who give it, and its force as a motive
depends upon the sense of "ought" in him who is the
subject of it. Abstracted from this the approbation of others
is merely their assertion of certain facts which to the individual make no difference. To prudential actions the
obligation is stronger than to benevolent, because interest
in himself is more of a necessary feeling in a man than interest in others; but even here the obligation is not moral; nor
if a man chooses not to regard or consult for his own interest
can blame attach to him; blame at least can only mean in this
philosophy the assertion of certain consequences of his conduct.

THE secularist position is stated thus by its chief promulgator :—

"You cannot live for both worlds, because you do not
know *both*. You know but *one*. Live for the one you do
know." (*Secular Miscellany*, p. 26.)

"Secular principles relate to the present existence of man,
and to methods of procedure the issues of which can be tested
by the experience of this life. A person holding secular principles as general rules of life, concerns himself with present
time and materiality, neither ignoring nor denying the future
and spiritual, which are independent questions. Secularity
draws the line of distinction between the things of time and
the things of eternity. That is secular which pertains to this
world. The distinction may be seen in the fact that the cardinal propositions of theology are proveable only in the next
life, and not in this. If I believe in a given creed, it may
turn out to be the true one, but one must die to find out
that. . . . . Pure secular principles have for their object to fit
men for time. Secularism purposes to regulate human affairs
by considerations purely human. Its principles are founded
upon nature, and its object is to render men as perfect as
possible in this life." (*Principles of Secularism*, p. 6.)

"We desire to *know* and not to *hope*. We have no wants,
and wish to have none which truth will not satisfy. We
would realize this life—we would also *deserve* another, but
without the selfishness which craves it, or the presumption
which expects it, or the discontent which demands it." (*Secularism Distinguished from Unitarianism*, p. 16.)

The philosophy of universal necessary law, alluded to at
p. 90, which puts man and material nature under the same
head, and which argues that if man is not under that law,
neither can nature be asserted to be, i. e. that if free-will is
allowed in man, miracles may be allowed in nature, is thus
stated :—

"Step by step the notion of evolution by law is trans-
forming the whole field of our knowledge and opinion. . . . .
Not the physical world alone is now the domain of inductive
science, but the moral, the intellectual, and the spiritual are
being added to its empire. . . . . It is the crown of philo-

sophy to see the immutable even in the complex action of human life. In the latter, indeed, it is but the first germs which are clear. No rational thinker hopes to discover more than a few primary axioms of law, and some approximating theory of growth. Much is dark and contradictory. . . . .

" Why this rigorous repudiation of all disorder in the material world, whilst insisting on stupendous perturbations of the moral? Why are all facts contrary to science rejected, and theories contrary to history retained? Why are physical miracles absurd, if spiritual miracles abound? Why are there no suspensions of the laws of matter, yet cardinal suspensions of the laws of mind? . . . . They see 'the grand foundation—conception of universal law,' 'the invariable operation of a series of eternally impressed consequences following in some necessary chain of orderly causation.' Such a law, we conceive, is read in all human history, life and spirit." (*Article on Neo-Christianity, Westminster Review, Oct.* 1860.)

LECTURE IV.

NOTE 1, p. 96.

" At the utmost a physico-theology can only teach a supreme mind evinced in the laws of the world of matter, and the relations of a Deity to physical things essentially as derived from physical law.

" A moral or metaphysical theology (so far as it may be substantiated) can only lead us to a Deity related to mind, or to the moral order of the world.

" Physical science may bring us to a God of nature, moral or metaphysical science to a God of mind or spirit. But all philosophy is generalisation, and therefore essentially implies universal order; and thus in these sublime conclusions, or in any inferences we may make from them, that principle must hold an equally prominent place. If we indulge in any speculations on the Divine perfections we must admit an element of immutable order as one of the chief.

" The firm conception of the immutability of order is the first rudiment in all scientific foundation for cosmo-theology. Our conclusion cannot go beyond the assumption in our evidence. Our argument can lead us only to such limited notions of the Divine attributes as are consistent with the principle of 'Cosmos.' If we speak of 'wisdom,' it is as evinced in laws of profoundly-adjusted reason; if of 'power,' it is only in the conception of universal and eternal maintenance of those arrangements; if of 'infinite intelligence,' it is as manifested throughout the infinity of nature; and to whose dominion we can imagine no limit, as we can imagine none to natural order.

"If we attempt to extend the idea of 'power,' to infinity, or what we call the attribute of 'Omnipotence,' in conformity with a strictly *natural* theology, it can only be from the boundless extent to which we find these natural arrangements kept up in incessant activity, but unchangeable order; the unlimited, and we believe illimitable expansion, both in time and space, of the same undeviating regularity with which the operations of the universally connected machinery are sustained. The difficulty which presents itself to many minds, how to reconcile the idea of *unalterable law* with *volition* (which seems to imply something changeable), can only be answered by appealing to those immutable laws as the sole evidence and exponent we have of supreme volition; a volition of immutable mind, an empire of fixed intelligence.

"The simple argument from the invariable order of nature is wholly incompetent to give us any conception whatever of the Divine Omnipotence, except *as maintaining, or acting through, that invariable universal system of physical order and law.* Any belief which may be entertained of a different kind must essentially belong to an order of things wholly beyond any conclusions derived from physical philosophy or cosmo-theology. A Theism of *Omnipotence in any sense deviating from the order of nature* must be derived entirely from *other teaching:* in fact it is commonly traceable to early religious impressions derived, not from any real deductions of reason, but from the language of the Bible.

"Natural theology does not lead us to the *supernatural,* being itself the essential and crowning principle of the *natural:* and pointing to the supreme moral cause or mind in *nature, manifested* to us as far as the invariable and universal series and connexion of physical causes are disclosed; *obscured* only when they may be obscured; hidden only when they may be imagined to be interrupted.

"The supernatural is the offspring of ignorance, and the parent of superstition and idolatry; the natural is the assurance of science, and the preliminary to all rational views of Theism.

" The highest inferences to which any physical philosophy
can lead us, though of *demonstrative force* as far as they can
reach, are confessedly of very *limited extent.* It is a mistake
to confound with the deductions of science these more sublime conceptions and elevated spiritual views of a Deity,—a
personal God,—an Omnipotent Creator,—a moral governor,
—a Being of infinite spiritual perfections,—holding relations
with the spirit of man ;—the object of worship, trust, fear,
and love ;—all which conceptions *can originate only from some
other source than physical philosophy.* These are conclusions
which science must confess entirely to transcend its powers,
as they are beside its province to substantiate." (*Powell's
Order of Nature,* p. 245.)

" The belief in Divine interposition must be essentially
dependent on what we *previously* admit or believe with respect
to the *Divine attributes.*

" It was formerly argued that every Theist must admit the
credibility of miracles ; but this, it is now seen, depends on
the *nature* and *degree* of his Theism, which may vary through
many shades of opinion. It depends, in fact, on the precise
view taken of the Divine attributes ; such, of course, as is
attainable *prior* to our admission of revelation, or we fall
into an argument in a vicious circle. The older writers on
natural theology, indeed, have professed to deduce very exact
conclusions as to the Divine perfections, especially *Omnipotence ;* conclusions which, according to the physical argument already referred to, appear carried beyond those limits
to which reason or science are competent to lead us ; while,
in fact, all our higher and more precise ideas of the Divine
perfections are really derived from that very revelation whose
evidence is the point in question. The Divine Omnipotence
is entirely an inference *from the language of the Bible,* adopted
on the assumption of a belief in revelation. That ' with God
nothing is impossible,' is the very declaration of Scripture ;
yet on this the whole belief in miracles is built, and thus,
with the many, that belief is wholly the *result,* not the *antecedent* of faith." (*Powell's Study of Evidences of Christianity,*
p. 113.)

NOTE 2, p. 100.

PHILOSOPHERS have applied the term "demonstrative" to
certain proofs of the existence of a God ; and were these
reasonings demonstrative in the strict mathematical sense it

would not be correct to say that this great truth rested on
a ground of faith.   But the term "demonstrative" does not
appear to be used in this instance, by those who apply it, in a
strict and mathematical sense.   These kind of reasonings do
indeed proceed upon axioms which instinctively approve themselves as rational; and the axioms being admitted, a chain of
irresistible consequences finally educes from them this cardinal
truth : but the axioms, though upon the broad ground of
reason and common sense obligatory, do not possess the rigid
force of mathematical axioms ; and the structure of reasoning
which is built upon them shares in the same defect.   If we
take the very first axiom, e.g. which lies at the foundation
of the fabric, viz. that everything that begins to exist must
have a cause, however near to the nature of a mathematical
axiom this principle may be, we yet perceive a distinct difference
between this principle and an axiom of mathematics, when
we compare the two together.   We cannot say, e. g. that
exactly the same self-evident certainty belongs to this truth
that belongs to the axiom that things that are equal to the
same are equal to one another.   Nor therefore, when upon
the basis of the axiom that everything that begins to exist
must have a cause, the argument proceeds,—Therefore there
must always be existence antecedent to what begins ; therefore something must have from eternity existed; an eternal
succession of Beings being neither caused from without nor
self-existent, is an inconsistency : therefore what has existed
from eternity is one Being; that one Being as existing from
eternity is the cause of all being that begins ; as existing
necessarily is omnipresent, for the necessity is the same everywhere ; and as the cause of intelligent beings, is Himself
intelligent, — does this superstructure of reasoning possess
the strict force of a mathematical proof.   The demonstrative
argument for the existence of a God is indeed the accurate
working out of some strong instinctive maxims of reason,
but when we endeavour to pursue these maxims and the
reasoning upon them to the point of necessity, we are not
able to do so; the subject eludes our grasp, because in truth
we have not faculties for perceiving demonstration or necessary

connexion upon this subject-matter. Nor therefore do such reasonings, though called demonstrative, when we consider the astonishing nature of the great truth which is educed from them, appear to dispense with faith in the acceptance of and dependence upon them.

Locke strongly asserts the demonstrative nature of the proof of the existence of a God. "It is as certain that there is a God, as that the opposite angles, made by the intersection of two straight lines, are equal." (*Essay on the Human Understanding*, bk. i. ch. iv. s. 16.) "But though this be the most obvious truth that reason discovers, and though its evidence be, if I mistake not, equal to a mathematical certainty; yet it requires thought and attention, and the mind must apply itself to a regular deduction of it from some part of our intuitive knowledge, or else we shall be as uncertain and ignorant of this as of other propositions, which are in themselves capable of clear demonstration. . . . . We have a more certain knowledge of the existence of a God than of anything our senses have not immediately discovered to us. Nay, I presume I may say that we may more certainly know that there is a God, than that there is anything else without us. When I say we know, I mean that such knowledge is within our reach, which we cannot miss if we will but apply our minds to that, as we do to several other inquiries." The proof comes under these heads :—" Man knows that he himself is ;" " He knows also that nothing cannot produce a being, therefore something eternal ;" " Two sorts of beings, cogitative and incogitative ;" " Incogitative beings cannot produce a cogitative ;" "Therefore there has been an eternal wisdom." (Book iv. chap. x.)

Clarke says—

"I proceed now to the main thing I at first proposed ; namely, to endeavour to shew, to such considering persons as I have already described, that the Being and Attributes of God are not only possible or barely probable in themselves, but also strictly *demonstrable* to any unprejudiced mind, from the most uncontestable principles of right reason. . . . . .

"Now many arguments there are by which the Being and Attributes of God have been undertaken to be *demonstrated ;*

and perhaps most of those arguments, if thoroughly understood, rightly stated, fully pursued, and duly separated from the false or uncertain reasonings which have sometimes been intermixed with them, would at length appear to be substantial and conclusive. But because I would endeavour, as far as possible, to avoid all manner of perplexity and confusion, therefore I shall not at this time use any variety of arguments, but endeavour by one clear and plain series of propositions necessarily connected and following one from another, to demonstrate the certainty of the Being of God, and to deduce in order the necessary Attributes of His nature, so far as by our finite reason we are enabled to discover and apprehend them. And because it is not to my present purpose to explain or illustrate things to them that believe, but only to convince unbelievers, and settle them that doubt, by strict and undeniable reasoning; therefore I shall not allege anything, which however really true and useful, may yet be liable to contradiction or dispute; but shall endeavour to urge such propositions only as cannot be denied without departing from that reason which all atheists pretend to be the foundation of their unbelief." (*Demonstration, &c., Introduction.*)

Mr. Goldwin Smith, while arguing that what *does* rest upon probable evidence is not essential to religion, maintains, though without any special reference to these reasonings, that the evidence upon which the existence of a God rests is *not* expressed by the phrase " probable evidence :"—

" I confess that I, for one, enter with the less anxiety into any question concerning the validity of mere historical evidence, because I am convinced that no question concerning the validity of mere historical evidence can be absolutely vital to religion. Historical evidence is not a ground upon which religion can possibly rest; for the human testimony of which such evidence consists is always fallible; the chance of error can never be excluded : and the extraordinary delusions into which great bodies of men have fallen shew that even in the case of a multitude of witnesses that chance may be present in a considerable degree, particularly if the scene of the alleged fact is laid in an uncritical age or nation. Probable evidence, therefore, is the highest we can have of any historical fact. In ordinary cases we practically need no higher. The great results of history are here; we have and enjoy them as certainly as we have and enjoy any object of sense; and it signifies little by what exact agency in any particular case the work of human progress was carried on. But in the case of a religion probable evidence will not suffice. Religion is not a speculation which we may be content to hold subject to a certain chance of error, nor is it a practical interest of the kind which Butler has in his mind when he tells us that we must act on this, as in other cases, on probability. It is a spiritual affection which nothing less than the assured presence of its object can excite. We may be quite content to hold that the life of Cæsar was such as it is commonly taken to have been, subject to certain chances of error arising from his own bias as an autobiographer, and from the partiality, prejudice, or imperfect information of his contemporaries; but we should not be content to hold any vital fact of our religion under the same conditions. We may be ready to stake, and do constantly stake, our worldly interests, as Butler truly observes, upon probabilities, when certainty is beyond our power. But our hearts would refuse their office if we were to bid them adore and hold communion with a probable God." (*Rational Religion, &c.,* p. 108.)

When the evidence, however, of a Deity is described as "demonstrative" or "not probable," such a description does not appear to exclude a ground of *faith* in the acceptance of such evidence; the conclusion being of so immense and astonishing a nature that faith is required for relying upon any reasoning or evidence, however strong, which leads to it; the mind naturally desiring the verification of such proof.

It must be observed that it is not only a *Moral* Deity whose existence is an object of faith; but a Deity at all, i.e. such as is distinguishable from a mere universal force. Language is sometimes used as if the ground of faith only applied to the moral attributes of the Deity, and the mere existence of a Supreme Intelligent Being were the conclusion of reason without faith. But the ground of faith comes in prior to the moral attributes of the Deity, because the existence of a God at all in any sense which comes up to the notion of the existence of a Personal Infinite Being is of itself —before going into any further question—such an amazing and supernatural truth that it cannot be embraced without faith. Although, if we first suppose an Infinite Intelligent Being, we cannot but go on to suppose that that Being possesses a character; and, some character supposed, it cannot but be, notwithstanding the confusion of things here, more natural and easy for us to believe that that character is the Moral or Righteous one, than that it is any other.

NOTE 3, p. 107.

" BUT were these views of the Divine attributes, on the other hand, ever so well established, it must be considered that the Theistic argument requires to be applied with much caution; since most of those who have adopted such theories of the Divine perfections, on abstract grounds, have made them the basis of a precisely opposite belief, rejecting miracles altogether; on the plea that our ideas of the Divine perfections must directly discredit the notion of occasional interposition; that it is derogatory to the idea of Infinite Power and Wisdom to suppose an order of things so imperfectly established that it must be occasionally interrupted and violated when the necessity of the case compelled, as the emergency of a revelation was imagined to do. But all such Theistic reasonings are but one-sided, and if pushed further must lead to a denial of all active operation of the Deity whatever; as inconsistent with unchangeable, infinite perfection. Such are the arguments of Theodore Parker, who denies miracles *because* 'everywhere I find law the constant mode of *operation of an infinite God;*' or that of Wegscheider, that the belief in miracles is irreconcilable with the idea of an *eternal God consistent with Himself,*" &c. (*Powell's Study of the Evidences of Christianity,* p. 113.)

The writer admits that when the miraculous action of the Deity is denied upon *Theistic reasonings,* the denial affects the action of the Deity generally. But has not the same denial the same result when built upon *physical* reasonings?

NOTE 4, p. 107.

" ALL *religion,* as such, ever has been and must be a thing entirely *sui generis,* and implies mystery and faith, however rightly allied to knowledge, and susceptible of a variety of external forms, according to the diversity of human character and the stages of human enlightenment." (*Powell's Order of Nature,* p. 197.)

NOTE 5, p. 108.

" Advancing philosophy unhesitatingly disowns contradiction to physical truth in matters properly amenable to science, however they may have been associated with religious belief; but, beyond the province of scientific knowledge, reason acknowledges a blank and a void, which can only be filled up by conceptions of a totally different order, originating from higher sources, in no way opposed to reason, as they present no ideas cognisable by it, but solely objects of spiritual apprehension derived from Divine revelation." (*Powell's Order of Nature*, p. 217.)

" I have spoken of the necessary *limits* of all scientific deduction. To obviate serious misconception it is material to insist on the distinction, that while the boundary line, by which the deductions of science are so necessarily limited, is thus carefully drawn, this is by no means to be misunderstood as if it were meant as a *negation* of higher truths, but only that they are of *another order*. On the contrary, the point especially insisted on in the former essays was, that the extremely limited extent of strict inferences from the order of nature forms the very ground for looking to *other* and *higher sources* of information and illumination, if we would rise to any of those more exalted contemplations. In any conceptions of the nature or attributes of God, or man's relations to Him, we can only look to other sources of information and conviction of quite a different order from those which science can furnish. Those higher aspirations, which so many pure and elevated minds own, can only be satisfied by disclosures belonging, not to the province of natural philosophy or any deductions from it,—whose utmost limits in this respect we have thus far endeavoured to indicate,—but to something beyond, and properly belonging to the higher jurisdiction of moral or spiritual convictions. But cosmo-theology, though *incapable of anticipating* any such sublime truths of a moral and spiritual revelation, is in *no way opposed* to them; but, on the contrary, as far as it extends may be serviceable, as in some measure opening the way for them." (*Ibid.* p. 249.)

The attempt to disconnect religion with physics in one remarkable instance is thus commented on by Dr. Heurtley :—

" The miracles which are connected with our Lord's Person and office are ' never,' we are told, ' insisted on in their physical details, but solely in their spiritual and doctrinal application.' The resurrection, for instance, is 'emphatically dwelt upon, not in its physical letter, but in its doctrinal spirit.'

"One is at a loss to conceive how any one could make such an assertion as this, unless he thought by his bold confidence to impose upon himself and overbear the reclamations of others. Most persons would rise from the perusal of the 15th chapter of the First Epistle to the Corinthians with the thorough conviction that how much use soever the Apostle may make of our Lord's resurrection doctrinally, he does most emphatically dwell upon it in its *physical letter.* Its *literal truth* as a 'physiological phenomenon' is the very basis and substratum of all that is said on the subject. It is implied throughout the whole of the Apostle's argument. 'I delivered unto you first of all,' says the Apostle, reminding the Corinthians of the doctrine which he had taught at Corinth, 'that which I also received, how that Christ died for our sins according to the Scriptures; and that He was buried, and that He rose again the third day, according to the Scriptures; and that He was *seen* of Cephas, then of the twelve. After that He was *seen* of above five hundred brethren at once. . . . . . After that He was *seen* of James; then of all the Apostles; and last of all, He was *seen* of me also. . . . . Now if Christ be preached that He rose from the dead, how say some among you that there is no resurrection of the dead? But if there be no resurrection of the dead, then is Christ not risen; *and if Christ be not risen, then is our preaching vain, and your faith is also vain. Yea, and we are found false witnesses of God; because we have testified of God that He raised up Christ; whom He raised not up, if so be that the dead rise not.* For if the dead rise not, then is not Christ raised; *and if Christ be not raised, your faith is vain; ye are yet in your sins.* Then they also which are fallen asleep in Christ are perished. . . . . . *But now is Christ risen from the dead, and become the first-fruits of them that slept.*'

"Will any one venture, after such a passage as this, to talk of a merely 'spiritualized sense,' as though the resurrection of the 'fullest development of apostolic Christianity' were of a different kind from that which was recognised on the very day on which the history relates that it occurred, when our Lord shewed the assembled disciples His hands and His feet, and bade them handle Him and see that His body was a real body, and by consequence His resurrection a real resurrection, literally and physically true." (*Replies to Essays and Reviews,* p. 172.)

LECTURE V.

NOTE 1, p. 120.

In the proof of miracles divines assume the existence of
a Deity. Butler "takes for proved that there is an intelligent Author of Nature and natural Governor of the World,"
before he enters upon the external and other evidences of
revelation. (*Analogy, Introduction.*) Paley assumes in like
manner, as the basis of his proof of the Christian miracles,
an intelligent and personal Supreme Being. "Suppose the
world we live in to have had a Creator; suppose it to appear
from the predominant aim and tendency of the provisions
and contrivances observable in the universe, that the Deity
when He formed it consulted for the happiness of His sen-
sitive creation; suppose the disposition which dictated this
counsel to continue; suppose a part of the creation to have
received faculties from their Maker by which they are capable
of rendering a moral obedience to His will. . . . . . Suppose,
nevertheless, almost the whole race, either by the imperfection
of their faculties, the misfortune of their situation, or by the
loss of some prior revelation, to want this knowledge, and not
to be likely without the aid of a new revelation to attain it;
under these circumstances, is it improbable a revelation should
be made? is it incredible that God should interpose for such
a purpose?" (*Evidences of Christianity, Preparatory Considerations.*) "The Christian argument of miracles," says Archdeacon Lee, "takes for granted two elementary truths—the
Omnipotence and the Personality of God." (*On Miracles,*
p. 39.)

NOTE 2, p. 126.

"There is a very strong presumption against common
speculative truths, and against the most ordinary facts,
before the proof of them; which yet is overcome by almost
any proof. There is a presumption of millions to one against

the story of Cæsar, or of any other man. For suppose a
number of common facts so and so circumstanced, of which
one had no kind of proof, should happen to come into one's
thoughts; every one would, without any possible doubt,
conclude them to be false. And the like may be said of a
single common fact. And from hence it appears, that the
question of importance, as to the matter before us, is, concerning the degree of the peculiar presumption supposed
against miracles; not whether there be any peculiar presumption at all against them. For, if there be the presumption of millions to one against the most common facts, what
can a small presumption additional to this amount to, though
it be peculiar? It cannot be estimated, and is as nothing."
(*Analogy*, part ii. ch. 2.)

Butler would appear in this passage to confound two
different kinds of improbability, which Mr. Mill calls improbability before the fact, and improbability after [m]. According to this statement the main and principal presumption against a miracle is that presumption which lies against
all, even the most ordinary facts, when they are imagined
antecedently. The presumption against any occurrence
taking place which it comes into one's head to *imagine*
taking place, is immense; and there is this presumption
beforehand, Butler says, against any miracle taking place;

[m] "The mistake consists in overlooking the distinction between (what
may be called) improbability before the fact, and improbability after it; two
different properties, the latter of which is always a ground of disbelief; the
former is so or not, as it may happen. . . . . . In the cast of a perfectly fair die
the chances are five to one against throwing ace; that is, ace will be thrown
on an average only once in six throws. But this is no reason against believing
that ace was thrown on a given occasion, if any credible witness asserts it;
since, although ace is only thrown once in six times, *some* number which is
only thrown once in six times *must* have been thrown, if the die was thrown
at all. The improbability, then, or in other words, the unusualness of any
fact, is no reason for disbelieving it, if the nature of the case *renders it certain
that either that or something equally improbable*, that is, equally unusual, did
happen. . . . . . We are told that A. B. died yesterday; the moment before
we were so told, the chances against his having died on that day may have
been ten thousand to one; but since he was certain to die at some time or
other, and when he died must necessarily die on some particular day, while
the chances are innumerable against every day in particular, experience affords
no ground for discrediting any testimony which may be produced to the event
having taken place on a given day." (*Logic*, vol. ii. p. 166.)

Z

but according to his statement, this presumption which
a miracle has against it *in common* with all facts whatever, is the great and main presumption against a miracle;
and any additional to this, which may be peculiar to it,
or attach to it because it is a miracle, amounts to nothing.
" What can a small presumption additional to this amount
to, though it be peculiar?" But this statement is not an
adequate representation of the presumption against a miracle,
and does not carry our common sense along with it, because
it does not distinguish between the different natures of an
improbability beforehand—upon a ground of mere random
anticipation—of *any* event, and improbability upon the
ground of the *kind* of event. He regards the *latter* as a mere
infinitesimal addition in *quantity* to the immense body of
already existing *former* presumption; whereas the latter is
a presumption different in *nature* and kind from the former.
The presumption which there was beforehand against *any*
particular event is one which in its own nature immediately
gives way to the least evidence of such an event occurring,
because its sole ground was the want of evidence, which is
ipso facto removed by evidence. A random guess is in other
words the entire absence of evidence; but the mere absence
of proof offers no resistance to proof. Whereas the improbability upon the ground of the *kind* of event goes on along
with the proof of that event, and *resists* that proof;—resists it,
even though it ultimately yield to it. " The chances against
an ordinary event," says Bishop Fitzgerald, " are not *specific*
but *particular:* they are chances against *this* event, not
against *this kind* of event." (*Article on Miracles: Dictionary
of the Bible.*) On the other hand, the presumption against
a miracle is presumption against the *kind* of event. Whereas
then Butler represents the " particular" presumption against
a miracle, which is the same that there is against any common fact beforehand, as the principal improbability of a
miracle, and the " specific" presumption as so minute an
addition to this as to be incapable of being estimated, the
order and value of the presumptions ought to be reversed;
the former being in truth nothing of a presumption, that is

to say, a presumption which does not tell in the least as soon as ever evidence is offered; the latter being a presumption which acts when evidence is offered. In this particular case Butler's criterion is not a natural one; for the objection to the *kind* of event a miracle is, is plainly our natural objection to a miracle.

" Butler," says Bishop Fitzgerald, " seems to have been very sensible of the imperfect state, in his own time, of the logic of probability; and though he appears to have formed a more accurate conception of it than the Scotch school of philosophers who succeeded and undertook to refute Hume; yet there is one passage in which we may perhaps detect a misconception of the subject in the pages even of this great writer.

" It is plain that in this passage Butler lays no stress upon the peculiarities of the story of Cæsar, which he casually mentions. For he expressly adds, ' or of any other man;' and repeatedly explains that what he says applies equally to any ordinary facts, or to a single fact. . . . . .

" The way in which he proposes to estimate the presumption against ordinary facts is, by considering the likelihood of their being anticipated beforehand by a person *guessing at random*. But surely this is not a measure of the likelihood of the facts considered in themselves, but of the likelihood of the *coincidence of the facts* with a rash and arbitrary anticipation. The case of a person guessing beforehand, and the case of a witness reporting what has occurred, are essentially different. In the common instance, for example, of an ordinary die, before the cast, there is nothing to determine my mind, with any probability of a correct judgment, to the selection of any one of the six faces rather than another; and therefore we rightly say that there are five chances to one against any one side, considered as thus arbitrarily selected. But when a person who has had opportunities of observing the cast, reports to me the presentation of a particular face, there is evidently no such presumption against the coincidence of *his* statement and the actual fact; because he has, by the supposition, had ample means of ascertaining the real state of the occurrence. And it seems plain that, in the case of a credible witness, we should as readily believe his report of the cast of a die with a million of sides as of one with only six; though in respect of a random guess beforehand, the chances against the correctness of the guess would be vastly greater in the former case, than in that of an ordinary cube. . . . . .

" The truth is, that *the chances* to which Butler seems to refer as a presumption against ordinary events, are not in ordinary cases overcome by testimony at all. The testimony has nothing to do with them ; because they are chances against the event considered as the subject of a random vaticination, not as the subject of a report made by an actual observer. It is possible, however, that throughout this obscure passage, Butler is arguing upon the principles of some objector unknown to us ; and, indeed, it is certain that some writers upon the doctrine of chances (who were far from friendly to revealed religion) have utterly confounded together the questions of the chances against the coincidence of an ordinary event with a random guess, and of the probability of such an event considered by itself." (*Dictionary of the Bible: Article on Miracles.*)

Archdeacon Lee disagrees with Bishop Fitzgerald. " So far is Bishop Butler from ignoring the distinction between ' probability before and after the fact,' or, as he expresses himself with greater precision, ' before and after proof,' that his whole argument proceeds upon its recognition." (*On Miracles*, p. 75.) Bishop Butler's argument recognizes *two states of the case*, before and after proof of the fact ; nor could it avoid doing so : but this is not the same as recognizing the two kinds of probability " before" and " after." He recognizes improbability before proof, and certainty after proof ; but not that improbability which conflicts *with* proof, that which is meant by " improbability after the fact." The writer adds :—

" The two instances selected by Mr. Mill are indeed, as he states, ' things in strict conformity to the usual course of experience,' ' the chances merely being against them ;' but they are not in the least analogous to the instances on which Bishop Butler founds his proposition. The great difference is, *that we do know all the chances in the one case, and that we do not know all the chances in the other.* There are but six sides to the die ; the chances, therefore, are but five to one against ace, at any throw. The years of human life cannot exceed a definite number, to which we can approximate within moderate limits ; but the probability of the events on which the ' Analogy' depends cannot be thus estimated. The history of Cæsar, or of any other man, or common facts, are matters incapable of being submitted to calculus of probabilities. The events of human life present a variety to which no bounds can be set. What human calculation can make full allowance for the influence of human motives; or foresee all the possible outbursts of human passion; or reduce the contingencies of political change to the dominion of unvarying law?" (*On Miracles*, p. 75.)

But does it make any difference in the nature of the improbability before proof, now spoken of, whether or not we can *calculate* the chances in question? We know that the chances are five to one against the throw of ace in the cast of the die, and that they are millions to one, or incalculable, against the story of any common man, imagined beforehand; but the difference in the number of the opposing chances, which constitutes improbability beforehand, makes not the slightest difference in the *weight* of that improbability, when evidence is given of the fact; which weight is then nothing, equally whether the antecedent chances are units or thousands. One die has six sides, another, let us suppose with Bishop Fitzgerald, has a million; beforehand therefore the chances, in these two cases, were respectively five to one and a million to one against any particular throw; but this difference in the number of chances beforehand would not make a particular throw *when made* at all more difficult to believe or make it require at all more evidence in the case of one die than in the case of the other; because the weight of the improbability before the fact would, upon evidence of the fact, vanish and disappear at once alike, whether that improbability was five to one or a million to one. A die, whether it has the one or the other number of sides, is equally obliged to fall on *some* side; which fall therefore is in either case equally devoid of strangeness, and therefore an equal subject of evidence. In like manner any common man's history has antecedently an incalculably greater number of chances against it than some one given ordinary event has, but one does not require greater evidence than the other.

NOTE 3, p. 128.

"THIS of course turns on the general grounds of our antecedent convictions. The question agitated is not that of mere testimony, of its value, or of its failures. It refers to those *antecedent* considerations which must govern our entire view of the subject, and which being dependent on higher laws of belief, must be paramount to all *attestation*, or rather belong to a province distinct from it. What is alleged is a case of the supernatural; but no testimony can reach to the supernatural; testimony can apply only to apparent sensible facts; testimony can only prove an extraordinary and perhaps inexplicable occurrence or phenomenon: that it is due to supernatural causes is entirely dependent on the previous belief and assumption of the parties. . . . . . If a number of respectable witnesses were to concur in asseverating that on a certain occasion they had seen two and two make five, should we be bound to believe them?

"This, perhaps it will be said, is an extreme case. Let us suppose another. If the most numerous ship's company were all to asseverate that they had seen a mermaid, would any rational persons at the present day believe them? That they saw something which *they believed* to be a mermaid would be easily conceded. No amount of attestation of innumerable and honest witnesses would ever convince anyone versed in mathematical and mechanical science, that a person had squared the circle or discovered perpetual motion. Antecedent credibility depends on antecedent knowledge, and enlarged views of the connexion and dependence of truths; and the value of any testimony will be modified or destroyed in different degrees to minds differently enlightened.

"Testimony, after all, is but a second-hand assurance; it is but a blind guide. Testimony can avail nothing against reason." (*Powell's Study of Evidences,* pp. 107, 141.)

NOTE 4, p. 131.

"THE essential question of miracles stands quite apart from any consideration of *testimony*; the question would remain the same if we had the evidence of our own senses to an alleged miracle, that is to an extraordinary or inexplicable fact. It is not the *mere fact*, but the *cause* or *explanation* of it, which is the point at issue." (*Powell's Study of Evidences*, p. 141.)

"But material as, in reference to the study of the last remark, is the discussion of *testimony*, it must still be observed that in the general and abstract point of view this is really but *adventitious* to the question of *miracles;* and that, supposing all doubt as to *testimony* were entirely removed, as in the case of an actual witness having the evidence of *his own senses* to an *extraordinary* and perhaps *inexplicable* fact, still the material enquiry would remain, *Is it a miracle?* It is here, in fact, that the essence of the question of credibility is centred—not in regard to the mere external apparent *event*, but to the *cause* of it." (*Powell's Order of Nature*, p. 286.)

"We have observed that a *miracle* is a matter of *opinion;* and, according to the ordinary view, the precise point of *opinion* involved in the assertion of a miracle is that the event in question is a *violation* or *suspension* of the laws of nature; a point on which *opinions* will chiefly vary according to the degree of acquaintance with physical philosophy and the acceptance of its wider principles; especially as these principles are now understood, and seem to imply the grand conception of the universal Cosmos, and the sublime conclusions resulting from it or embodied in it." (*Ibid.* p. 291.)

"Of old the sceptic professed he would be convinced by *seeing* a miracle. At the present day, a visible miracle would but be the very subject of his scepticism. It is not the *attestation*, but the *nature* of the alleged marvel, which is now the point in question." (*Ibid.* p. 296.)

NOTE 5, p. 132.

" THERE are still some who contend that it is idle to object
to miracles as violations of natural laws, because we know
not the extent of creation ; . . . . . that we are surrounded
by phenomena whose causes or nature we are not and probably never shall be able to explain. . . . . . None of these
or the like instances are at all of the same kind, or have any
characteristics in common with the idea of what is implied
by the term ' miracle,' which is asserted to mean something
at variance with nature and law.   There is not the slightest
analogy between an unknown or inexplicable phenomenon
and a supposed suspension of a known law !" [*e.g.* the fact of
a suspension of gravitation.—*Order of Nature*, p. 271.]—
(*Study of Evidences*, p. 109.)
   "The philosopher denies the credibility of alleged *events*
professedly in their nature at variance with all physical analogy." (*Ibid.* p. 135.)
   " The literal sense of *physical events* impossible to science
cannot be essential to spiritual truth." (*Order of Nature*,
p. 376.)
   " Questions of this kind are often perplexed by want of
due attention to the laws of thought and belief, and of due
distinction in ideas and terms.   The proposition ' that an
event may be so incredible as intrinsically to set aside any
degree of testimony,' in no way applies to or affects the
honesty or veracity of that testimony, or the reality of the
impressions on the minds of the witnesses, so far as relates to
the matter of sensible fact only.   It merely means : that
from the nature of our antecedent convictions, the probability
of some kind of mistake or deception somewhere, though we
know not where, is greater than the probability of the *event
really happening* in the way and from the causes assigned."
(*Study of Evidences,* p. 107.)
   The transference indeed everywhere insisted upon by this
writer, of miracles from the region of history to that of *faith*
(see following note), indicates of itself that the thing pronounced to be incredible, and to be incapable of being
accepted as real, is not the *cause* of the miraculous facts, but
the miraculous facts themselves as recorded.   For were the
miracles credible as *facts,* and the supernatural causes alone
denied, why should not they be matters of history, to be

accepted upon historical evidence—the facts accepted, however the causes were disputed? But miracles are denied the character of historical events, and relegated to the domain of faith; which shews that, in the mind of the writer, the facts themselves rank as incredible, and not the cause only.

NOTE 6, p. 135.

" The main point on which I would remark as evinced in these and numerous other passages to the same effect, is, that the acceptance of miracles as such seems to be here distinctly recognised as the sole work of a *religious principle of faith*, and not an *assent of the understanding* to *external evidence*, the appeal to which seems altogether disowned and set aside. Conviction appears to be *avowedly* removed from the basis of testimony and sensible facts, and placed on that of spiritual impression and high religious feeling." (*Powell's Order of Nature*, p. 367.)

"The belief in miracles, whether in ancient or modern times, has always been a point *not* of *evidence* addressed to the *intellect*, but of *religious faith* impressed on the *spirit*. The mere fact was nothing: however well attested, it might be set aside; however fabulous, it might be accepted,—according to the predisposing religious persuasion of the parties. If a more philosophical survey tend to ignore suspensions of nature, as inconceivable to reason, the spirit of faith gives a different interpretation, and transfers miracles to the more congenial region of spiritual contemplation and Divine mystery." (*Ibid.* p. 439.)

"To conclude, an alleged miracle can only be regarded in one of two ways; either abstractedly as a physical event, and therefore to be investigated by reason and physical evidence, and referred to physical causes, possibly to *known* causes, but at all events to some higher cause or law, if at present unknown; . . . . . or, as connected with religious doctrine, regarded in a sacred light, asserted on the authority of inspiration. In this case it ceases to be capable of investigation by reason, or to own its dominion; it is accepted on religious grounds, and can appeal only to the principle and influence of faith.

"Thus miraculous narratives become invested with the character of articles of faith." (*Powell's Study of the Evidences of Christianity*, p. 142.)

NOTE 7, p. 136.

"THE case indeed of the *antecedent* argument of miracles is very clear, however little some are inclined to perceive it. In nature and from nature, by science and by reason, we neither have nor can possibly have any evidence of a *Deity working miracles ;*—for that we must go out of nature and beyond reason. If we could have any such evidence *from nature*, it could only prove extraordinary *natural* effects, which would not be *miracles* in the old theological sense, as isolated, unrelated, and uncaused; whereas no *physical* fact can be conceived as unique, or without analogy and relation to others, and to the whole system of natural causes." (*Powell's Study of the Evidences of Christianity*, p. 141.)

NOTE 8, p. 137.

"IF miracles were in the estimation of a former age among the chief *supports* of Christianity, they are at present among the main *difficulties* and hindrances to its acceptance." (*Powell's Study of the Evidences of Christianity*, p. 140.)

"In the popular acceptation, it is clear the Gospel miracles are always *objects*, not *evidences* of faith; and when they are connected specially with doctrines, as in several of the higher mysteries of the Christian faith, the sanctity which invests the point of faith itself is extended to the external narrative in which it is embodied; the reverence due to the mystery renders the external events sacred from examination, and shields them also within the pale of the sanctuary; the *miracles* are merged in the *doctrines* with which they are connected, and associated with the declarations of spiritual things which are, as such, exempt from those criticisms to which physical statements would be necessarily amenable." (*Ibid.* p. 143.)

LECTURE VI.

NOTE 1, p. 147.

" CONSIDER why it is that, with exactly the same amount of evidence, both negative and positive, we did not reject the assertion that there are black swans, while we should refuse credence to any testimony which asserted that there were men wearing their heads underneath their shoulders. The first assertion was more credible than the latter. But why more credible? So long as neither phenomenon had been actually witnessed, what reason was there for finding the one harder to be believed than the other? Apparently, because there is less constancy in the colours of animals than in the general structure of their internal anatomy. But how do we know this? Doubtless, from experience. It appears, then, that we need experience to inform us, in what degree, and in what cases, or sorts of cases, experience is to be relied on. Experience must be consulted in order to learn from it under what circumstances arguments from it will be valid. We have no ulterior test to which we subject experience in general; but we make experience its own test. Experience testifies that among the uniformities which it exhibits, or seems to exhibit, some are more to be relied on than others; and uniformity, therefore, may be presumed, from any given number of instances, with a greater degree of assurance, in proportion as the case belongs to a class in which the uniformities have hitherto been found more uniform."—(*Mill's System of Logic*, vol. i. p. 330.)

" In some cases of apparently marvellous occurrences, after due allowance for possible misapprehension or exaggeration in the statements, it might be conceded that the event, though of a very singular kind, was yet not such as to involve anything absolutely at variance even with the known laws of nature :—very remarkable coincidences of events ;—very unusual appearances ;—very extraordinary affections of the human body ;—such especially as those astonishing but well-ascertained cases of catalepsy, trance, or suspended animation ;—very marvellous and sudden cures of diseases ;—the phenomena of double consciousness, visions, somnambulism, and spectral impressions ;—might perhaps be included in this class, and, subject to such natural interpretation, be entirely admissible. *Other instances might, however, be recounted more absolutely at variance with natural order*, such, e. g. as implied a subversion of gravitation, or of the constitution of matter; *descriptions inconceivable* to those impressed with the truth of the great first principle of all induction—the invariable constancy of the order of nature.

" In such cases we might imagine a misapprehension or exaggeration of some real event, or possibly some kind of ocular illusion, mental hallucination, or the like."—(*Powell's Order of Nature,* p. 270.)

It must however be considered that in the case of a miracle the fact which has to be brought within the order of nature is, not only the physical occurrence which takes place in the miracle, but that occurrence as coinciding with a positive announcement. This prophetical element in a miracle, it must be observed, enters not only into those miracles in which the physical occurrence is of itself reducible to the order of nature[n], but in those grander miracles as well, in which the physical occurrence is itself a violation of the order of nature. Should the question be raised, e. g. whether the miracle of our Lord's Resurrection was or was not a fact ultimately referrible to natural law; the fact, about which the question would lie, and about which we should have to inquire, whether it might be ultimately natural or not, would be, not the simple resurrection of a man from the dead, but that resurrection as coinciding with previous announcements of it, and with the whole character, life, and professed mission and office of Jesus Christ. And it is impossible not to

[n] " The simoon, or whatever it was, which swept off in one night the army of Sennacherib, and which was adopted as the instrument for effecting the *predicted* deliverance of Jerusalem, may have taken place in its appointed order of nature. Nay, there is nothing repugnant to the soundest faith or the deepest reverence in the supposition that the physical instruments employed for accomplishing the deluge, which are represented under the image of the 'fountains of the great deep being broken up, and the windows of heaven opened,' took place in their appointed order in the cycle of nature's operations ; and that their foreseen synchronism with the time appointed for 'the end of all flesh' was made subservient to the Divine counsels. The miracle is none the less for being transferred from the fact itself to its prediction and adaptation." (*Essays and Reviews considered, by Rev. H. A. Woodgate,* p. 93.)

see, even where the occurrence itself is of the most marvellous kind, how immensely this consideration of its correspondence to a notification, and adaptation to a whole set of circumstances, adds to the supernaturalness of the miracle, to its inexplicableness upon natural grounds. Because all this points, upon the argument of design or coincidence, to a special interposition of God, as distinguished from unknown physical causation. Those circumstances of a miracle which distinguish it from an isolated marvel, are also the great evidences of its supernatural character. No physical explanation of it *as* a marvel goes a step toward the explanation of those circumstances which distinguish it *from* a marvel.

Mr. Mansel makes some able and acute remarks upon the characteristic of personal agency, in the case of miracles, with reference to the question of their referribleness to natural causes :—

" The fact of a work being done by human agency places it, as regards the future progress of science, in a totally different class from mere physical phenomena. The appearance of a comet, or the fall of an aerolite, may be reduced by the advance of science from a supposed supernatural to a natural occurrence; and this reduction furnishes a reasonable presumption that other phenomena *of a like character* will in time meet with a like explanation. But the reverse is the case with respect to those phenomena which are narrated as having been produced by *personal agency.* In proportion as the science of to-day surpasses that of former generations, so is the improbability that any man could have done in past times, by natural means, works which no skill of the present age is able to imitate. The two classes of phenomena rest in fact on exactly opposite foundations. In order that natural occurrences, taking place without human agency, may wear the appearance of prodigies, it is necessary that the cause and manner of their production should be *unknown;* and every advance of science from the unknown to the known tends to lessen the number of such prodigies by referring them to natural causes, and *increases* the probability of a similar explanation of the remainder. But on the other hand, in order that a man may perform marvellous acts by natural means, it is necessary that the cause and manner of their production should be *known* by the performer; and in this case every fresh advance of science from the unknown to the known diminishes the probability that what is unknown now could have been known in a former age.

"The effect, therefore, of scientific progress, as regards the Scriptural miracles, is gradually to eliminate the hypothesis which refers them to unknown natural causes."—(*Aids to Faith*, p. 14.)

NOTE 2, p. 151.

"Particular theories as to the manner in which miracles have been wrought are matters rather curious than practically useful. In all such cases we must bear in mind the great maxim—*Subtilitas naturæ longe superat subtilitatem mentis humanæ.* . . . . Some find it easier to conceive of miracles as not really taking place in the external order of nature, but in the impressions made by it upon our minds. . . . . It is plain that these various hypotheses are merely ways in which different minds find it more or less easy to conceive the mode in which miracles may have been wrought."— (*Bishop Fitzgerald's Article on Miracles: Dictionary of the Bible*, p. 382.)

NOTE 3, p. 157.

Archbishop Trench adopts the ordinary distinction between the direct action of the Deity and His action by means of general laws; His action in the order of nature and His action in special interpositions. "An extraordinary Divine causality, and not that ordinary which we acknowledge everywhere and in everything, belongs to the essence of the miracle; powers of God other than those which have been always working." The writer, however, does not suppose that the difference lies in the Divine action itself so much as in the revelation of it. "The unresting activity of God, which at other times hides and conceals itself behind the veil of what we term natural laws, does in the miracle unveil itself; it steps out from its concealment, and the hand which works it is laid bare." (*Preliminary Essay*, chap. ii.) The writer of the article on "The Immutability of Nature," in the Quarterly Review, No. 220, speaking only of the philosophical question, denies the philosophical ground of the common distinction just referred to. "It is only an arbitrary unproved hypothesis, that in the ordinary operations of nature the Divine will acts only indirectly and not directly, precisely as in the case of miracles. How can you draw a distinction between the ordinary operations of the Divine will in the daily course of things and its extraordinary in the miracles of Christianity? . . . . . If a sovereign, directing the movements of a mighty host by secret telegrams every minute, or concealed under a disguise,. should on occasions for some wise consistent object appear at the head of his troops and give the word of command himself, would this startle the soldier? Would he call it an anomaly?" (p. 376.)

The author of "Dialogues on Divine Providence" rejects the distinction :—

"What do we know of the laws of nature more than you began by saying? They express a certain uniformity in nature; they assure us that the same cause will be followed by the same effect. But *why* this uniformity exists, *why* there is this connection between cause and effect, neither they can tell us nor can anyone tell us of them. . . . .

"*Ph.* I am disposed to think you are right. If so, what follows?

"*H.* Only this: it is a mere figure of speech to say that God acts *through* laws. The expression conveys to the mind an idea of a medium interposed between the Worker and His work. But the nature of general laws, if we have taken a just view of them, justifies no such idea. If we explain the expression, it comes simply to this—there is an uniformity in God's works. On the same occasions He acts in the same way." (*Dialogues on Divine Providence,* p. 17.)

"Providence and Law are both words by which we express, or endeavour to express, certain truths about the manner in which God works. Providence implies that in all the dealings of God with His creatures, He acts consciously, voluntarily, and knowingly, as an omniscient and omnipotent agent. Law implies, that in His works and dealings we can trace a certain amount of uniformity and resemblance, which the structure of our minds leads us to believe to. exist in a

still greater degree than we can trace it. In God, as a Being
of perfect knowledge and perfect power, there is no opposition
between the *greatest uniformity* of action and the most particular regard for the *issue of each action*, in all its multiform
consequences. He sees all things from the first, effects all
that He wills in His own way, never makes a mistake, never
miscalculates a consequence, never overlooks an element or a
condition, is never deceived or overpowered by independent
and subordinate agents, never need suspend His steps to
watch an event, or retrace His course to rectify an error.
But the wisest of men must often do this : and so, misled by
a false analogy, we are apt to attribute to God the imperfection of our own works. We form our calculations; and
they prove erroneous because the immutable laws around us
interfere with our plans in some unforeseen way. And this
makes us sometimes speak and think as if the events which
depend on the laws which God has made were in some way
independent of Him, and out of the reach of His power. The
most profound and thoughtful among us can never lay down
universal rules of conduct with such absolute accuracy that
considerations of justice, equity, or expediency will not sometimes lead him to make exceptions to his rule ; and we transfer
too readily this consequence of human imperfection to the
Supreme and Perfect Lawgiver. . . . . . . But do the limits
thus placed to *our* faculties afford us the least justification for
assigning any similar bounds to His? *Dare we assert that
His intuition of universal laws does not comprehend every actual
and possible particular instance?* Is it not to attribute human
fallibility to Him, to think that the uniformity of action which
He is pleased to observe cannot coexist with the most perfect
and delicate regard to the tendencies and consequences of all
His actions? We make a great assumption if we regard
general laws as *instruments and mediums* of Divine operations."
(*Dialogues on Divine Providence,* p. 70.)

   " Suppose then (I need not say that it is no merely
imaginary case) a person choked by a fish-bone, and so
killed. Life and death, we all allow, are in the hands of
God. A believer would not doubt that one who dies by
an accident of this kind, dies at the time and in the manner
which God, in His Providence, thinks best. The fish-bone
is the instrument of His Will. It has fixed itself in the
sufferer's throat by no miraculous agency, but in the ordinary
course of cause and effect. But only consider for a moment
the complication of causes which placed it there. The toil
of the crew of a fishing-boat some two nights before, the

conditions of wind and wave which caused a fish with a bone of this particular shape to be caught, the demand and consequent supply which brought it to a town some hundred miles from the sea, the little circumstances which led to the purchase in the town of this individual fish, and a hundred other points of detail ; such as the light by which the dinner was eaten, the exact degree of hardness or softness of the fish, as dependent on the precise manner of cooking, even the power of contractility in the eater's throat, which may again have depended on his general health, or on the bracing or relaxing state of the atmosphere. Vary but one of these conditions, and the same result would probably not have happened. And perhaps a medical man could not be found till too late; and his absence was caused by the illness of another patient, itself dependent on causes equally remote and obscure. Could you blame any one who, having first accepted the truth, that death in this case happened according to the Providence of God, saw His finger also in every circumstance which had led to it, and attributed them all to His Will." (*Dialogues on Divine Providence*, p. 111.)

NOTE 4, p. 160.

NATURALIZING rationales of miracles which assume the truth of the miracles themselves, as Divine interpositions, must plainly be distinguished from, because they are different in their whole ground and purpose from, those naturalizing rationales which aim at depriving the miracles of their miraculous character, and reducing them to natural law in the popular sense. The hints, somewhat scattered and obscure, which Bishop Butler has thrown out, of a naturalizing hypothesis of miracles, i.e. of the possibility that although exceptions to law they are at the same time consistent with and instances of law in some wider sense, have been interpreted in some quarters in a sense very different from that designed by the suggester himself. It is no physical explanation of a miracle which Butler has in view. He assumes the truth of the Scripture miracles in the ordinary sense as Divine interpositions, the question which is raised

by him being whether these very instances of Divine interposition, suspending the laws of nature, do not themselves
follow general laws.

What he means indeed by "general laws," when he makes
the supposition "that God's miraculous interpositions may
have been all along by *general* laws of wisdom," is not very
clear. He appears first to have in his mind certain general
rules laid down by Providence—so to speak—for its own
guidance on this subject, according to which "miraculous
powers are exerted at such times, upon such occasions, in such
degrees and manners," &c., (part ii. chap. iv.); which general
rules Providence observes, although on particular occasions
certain apparent advantages might follow from the infraction
of them; that such rules should issue in partial disadvantage
—that they should not provide for "every exigence," being the
very condition of their general benefit. And thus understood
the supposition that "God's miraculous interpositions may
have been by general laws of wisdom," would substantially
mean that there was an inherent limit in the nature of things
to the utility of miracles, beyond which they would produce
injury and disadvantage; the general bad result of the excess
being greater than the particular benefit of it; and that this
intrinsic limit was necessarily observed by the Author of
Nature. But if this be Butler's meaning, such a supposition
as this is not about the miracles themselves that they are
part of an order of nature, but to the manner of conducting
them that it is referrible to a plan or system in the Divine
mind.

° He appears to refer in the next place to an imaginary

° "But the only distinct meaning of that word [natural] is *stated, fixed,*
or *settled:* since what is natural as much requires and presupposes an intelligent agent to render it so, i. e. to effect it continually at stated times,
as what is supernatural or miraculous does to effect it for once. And from
hence it must follow that persons' notions of what is natural will be enlarged
in proportion to their greater knowledge of the works of God, and the dispensations of His Providence. Nor is there any absurdity in supposing that
there may be beings in the universe whose capacities, and knowledge, and
views may be so extensive as that the whole Christian dispensation may to
them appear natural, i. e. analogous or conformable to God's dealings with

supposition he has made of "similar" or "analogous" Divine
dealings to that of the miraculous dispensation of Christianity
going on *in other worlds;* upon which supposition, such a
miraculous dispensation would be *natural,* because " natural "
means " similar, stated, or uniform," and this miraculous dispensation would then be *similar* to and *uniform* with other
miraculous dispensations in other parts of the universe.　Such
a supposition then as this has the effect of creating an order
of nature to which the miraculous dispensation of the Gospel
belongs, because it takes the latter out of its isolation and
attaches it to a vast class of similar Divine dealings going
on in other worlds.　But were this supposition true in fact,
it would not be a physical explanation of miracles; for the
order to which they are attached is not an order of material
nature, but an order of *similar suspensions* of material nature
in other worlds; and the naturalness is gained not by altering
the miraculous character of the facts, but by the addition
of other sets of the same kind of facts, by the existence
of a class of facts in other parts of the universe upon the
same miraculous level as those here.　The supposition, however, is wholly imaginary : we do not know that other worlds
besides our own are inhabited, still less that they are inhabited by reasonable creatures, and still less that the intelligent beings in them have revelations made to them.
The consideration indeed that we do *not know* that there is
not an order of nature of this level to which miracles belong,
is a consideration of some weight, but it has not anything
to do with a physical theory of miracles.

　　In one passage, indeed, Butler throws out the idea of a
common ground for miracles and irregular physical phenomena, " storms and tempests, earthquakes, famine, pesti-
lence." (pt. ii. ch. iv.)　But with respect to the physical
analogies suggested there, it must be remarked, that the
strict sense of " law," as applied to physical facts, had not

---

other parts of His creation ; as natural as the visible known course of things
appears to us.　For there seems scarce any other possible sense to be put
upon the word, but that only in which it is here used ; similar, stated, or
uniform." (*Analogy,* pt. i. ch. ii.)

then been defined in philosophy; which accounts for some confusion in this part of Butler's language. He does not appear to be aware that general laws, in the physical world, are simply recurrent antecedent facts; and that therefore miracles, did they come under a common head with such physical phenomena as he mentions, would follow recurrent physical antecedents. For this latter is an assertion to which his whole language elsewhere would be opposed. Mere marvellous occurrences might come in in such a train of physical causes, but miracles are understood by Butler in the religious sense, as Divine interpositions, special acts of the Divine will; in which sense they stand upon a different ground, with respect to law, from that of irregular physical phenomena.

We have, again, in Mr. Babbage's rationale of miracles, a naturalizing theory of them which leaves their miraculous character and their evidential use intact; and which therefore is not to be confounded with physical explanations of miracles :—

" Let the reader imagine himself sitting before the calculating engine, and let him again observe and ascertain, by lengthened induction, the nature of the law it is computing. Let him imagine that he has seen the changes wrought on its face by the lapse of thousands of years, and that, without one solitary exception, he has found the engine register the series of square numbers. Suppose, now, the maker of that machine to say to the observer, ' I will, by moving a certain mechanism, which is invisible to you, cause the engine to make a cube number instead of a square one, and then to revert to its former course of square numbers;' the observer would be inclined to attribute to him a degree of power but little superior to that which was necessary to form the original engine.

" But, let the same observer, after the same lapse of time, the same amount of uninterrupted experience of the uniformity of the law of square numbers, hear the maker of that engine say to him, ' The next number which shall appear on those wheels, and which you expect to find a square number, shall not be such. When the machine was originally ordered to make these calculations, I impressed on it a law, which should coincide with that of square numbers in every case *except* the one which is now about to appear, after which no future exception can ever occur; but the unvarying law of squares shall be pursued until the machine itself perishes from decay.

" Undoubtedly the observer would ascribe a greater degree of power to the artist who thus willed that event at the distance of ages before its arrival.

" If the contriver of the engine then explain to him, that, by the very structure of it, he has power to order any number of such apparent deviations from its laws to occur at any future periods, however remote, and that each of these may be of a different kind; and if he also inform him, that he gave it that structure in order to meet events which he foresaw must happen at those respective periods, there can be no doubt that the observer would ascribe to the inventor far higher knowledge than if, when those events severally occurred, he were to intervene, and temporarily alter the calculations of the machine.

" If, besides this, he were so far to explain the structure of the engine, that the observer could himself, by some simple process, such as the mere moving of a bolt, call into action those apparent deviations whenever certain combinations were presented to his eye; if he were thus to impart a power of predicting such excepted cases, dependent on the will, although otherwise beyond the limits of the observer's power and knowledge, such a structure would be admitted as evidence of a still more skilful contrivance."—(*Ninth Bridgwater Treatise*, ch. viii.)

This rationale then of a miracle, it must be observed, supposing we adopt it as the account of the extraordinary physical occurrence, does not account for the part which the human agent takes in the announcement of that occurrence; —which latter is the distinguishing characteristic of a miracle, without which it would be a mere marvel. For the law which would produce the exceptional physical occurrence would not suffice to explain the act of the individual and personal agent in the matter: the act of the human will not coming under the same head as a subject of law with the material event. And therefore the personal agency in a miracle, which corresponds with the outward occurrence, is still left unaccounted for in this rationale, or is thrown

back upon a Divine impulse at the moment. The analogy
of the machine here fails. But, besides this, the operation of
this law is perfectly secret; it is in a state of invisible existence up to the particular moment at which the miracle on
each occasion takes place, when the cause originally implanted
in nature comes on a sudden into action. But such a law
is not a law of nature in the physical sense, which is in its
very essence a law in action, consisting of recurrent physical
antecedents; it is only, as some may consider, a more
philosophical conception of Divine action. It may be added,
that however convenient an *illustration* the action of the
arithmetical machine may be of this conception of Divine
action, it does not explain such action really, or make it any
the more comprehensible to us.

The case of a secret law of miracles, impressed originally
upon creation, would be somewhat analogous to the supposition of a creational law in force for the production of successive species, which law did not shew or substantiate itself
by uniform operation, but left enormous chasms and gaps
between the different animal formations which started whole
into sudden existence. A creational law which does not shew
itself by facts, i. e. by uniformity of operation, is not a law
of nature, but only a mode of conceiving Divine action, viz.
as a causing from the first, instead of being action at the time.
Such a distinction is simply speculative. For secondary causes,
to constitute an order of nature, must be visible; in the
absence of which visibility, either a miracle or a new species
is a change upon the order of nature in the midst of which it
appears, whatever be the mode of its causation.

NOTE 5, p. 165.

NEANDER contemplates a miracle in this light, as *assuming* this highest and supreme region of free-will :—

" Many will admit certain facts to be inexplicable by any known laws, and at the same time refuse to grant them a miraculous or supernatural character. Some are led by an unprejudiced admission of the facts to acknowledge, without any regard whatever to religion, that they transcend the limits of existing science, and content themselves with that acknowledgment, leaving to the progress of natural philosophy or psychology to discover the laws, as yet unknown, that will explain the mysterious phenomena. . . . . It is not upon this road that we can lead men to recognize the supernatural and the divine; to admit the powers of heaven as manifesting themselves upon earth. *Miracles belong to a region of holiness and freedom*, to which neither experience, nor observation, nor scientific discovery can lead. There is no bridge between this domain and that of natural phenomena. Only by means of our inward affinity for this spiritual kingdom, only by hearing and obeying, in the stillness of the soul, the voice of God within us, can we reach those lofty regions." (*Life of Christ*, bk. iv. ch. 5.)

Archbishop Trench dwells on the same point of view :—

" If in one sense the orderly workings of nature reveal the glory of God, in another they hide that glory from our eyes ; if they ought to make us continually remember Him, yet there is danger that they will lead us to forget Him, until this world around us shall prove not a translucent medium, through which we behold Him, but a thick impenetrable veil, concealing Him wholly from our sight. Were there no other purpose in the miracles than this, namely, *to testify the liberty of God*, and to affirm the will of God, which, however it habitually shews itself in nature, is yet more than and above nature ; were it only to break a link in that chain of cause and effect, which else we should come to regard as itself God, as the iron chain of an inexorable necessity, binding heaven no less than earth, they would serve a great purpose, they would not have been wrought in vain." (*Notes on the Miracles: Preliminary Essay*, ch. ii.)

A miracle is popularly called "a *violation* of the laws of nature." This phrase is objected to by some writers, upon the ground that the laws of nature which are spoken of as violated in a miracle, are not really violated but *continue in force* all the time, that force being not *annihilated* but only *counteracted* by a force or law above them.

"We should term the miracle," says Archbishop Trench, "not the infraction of a law, but behold in it the lower law neutralized, and for the time put out of working order by a higher. . . . . Continually we behold in the world around us lower laws held in restraint by higher, mechanic by dynamic, chemical by vital, physical by moral; yet we say not, when the lower thus gives place in favour of the higher, that there was any violation of law, or that anything contrary to nature came to pass; rather we acknowledge the law of a greater freedom swallowing up the law of a lesser. Thus when I lift up my arm, the law of gravitation is not, as far as my arm is concerned, denied or annihilated; it exists as much as ever, but is held in suspense by the higher law of my will. The chemical laws which would bring about decay in animal substances still subsist, even when they are checked and hindered by the salt, which keeps those substances from corruption." (*Ibid.*)

Upon the same ground Mr. Llewellyn Davies objects to the description of a miracle as "a *suspension* of the laws of nature:"—

"We do not say that the knowledge and the will of man when they come into play *suspend* the laws of nature. If I hold a stone in my hand, or set a magnet so as to hold up a heavy piece of iron, the law of gravity acts as regularly as if the stone or the iron fell to the ground. If the skill of a physician cures a patient of a fever, no physiological law is suspended any more than if the patient were left alone to die. But the human knowledge and will do effect results. Suppose them withdrawn, and things would be very different from what they are. So with the Divine Will. We ought not to say that any operation of it, however miraculous, suspends the laws of nature." (*Signs of the Kingdom of Heaven*, p. 37.)

Dr. Heurtley objects to the term "violation," but not to the term "suspension:"—

"A miracle is a violation neither of the laws of matter nor

of any other laws of nature. It is simply the intervention of a Being possessing or endued with *superhuman* power,—an intervention which, though it temporarily modifies or *suspends* the operation of the laws ordinarily in operation in the world, is yet in itself exercised in strict accordance with the law of that Being's nature, or *superinduced* nature, by whom it is exercised." (*Replies to Essays and Reviews*, p. 148.)

The writer of an article in the Christian Remembrancer (October, 1863) objects to both terms, "suspension" and "contradiction :"—

"An important inquiry still remains, viz. whether our definition of a miracle as an event with a supernatural cause is a sufficient one? In later times, as we know, this definition has not been thought sufficient; but another idea has been added to it, viz. 'contrary to nature,' 'suspension of a natural law or cause.' The inquiry is a most important one; for, if we adopt this addition, we lay the miracle open, as we shall see, to very formidable objections. In addressing ourselves to the solution of this point, the first thing to be ascertained is, whether this idea necessarily enters into our conception of a miracle. A little consideration will shew that it does not. Any event clearly ascertained to have a supernatural cause would undoubtedly be regarded as miraculous, even though not contrary to nature. The stone, for instance, rolled away from the door of the sepulchre we regard as a miracle, on the simple ground that it was done by angels. Yet it cannot be alleged that that event was contrary to nature, or that it involved a suspension of a law of nature. The same act might have been performed by man or by mechanical power, and in that case it would have been perfectly natural. We thus see that the distinguishing mark of the miracle, to our mind, is, not contrary to nature, but having a supernatural cause. We see, too, that the supposition of the suspension of the law of nature does not apply to all miracles. It does not apply to a miracle considered as a miracle. Consequently, if it does apply to some miracles it must be accidental to them."

By what particular expression we denote the difference from the order of nature involved in a miracle, whether we do or do not call it a violation of natural law, a suspension, &c., is a question of language and no more, *so long as* we strictly understand that the natural laws to which these terms

"violation" and "suspension" are applied are one set of
laws only, viz. that which comes within the cognizance of
our experience. The *effect* of these laws is in the particular
instance of a miracle hindered or prevented; something takes
place which would not take place if these laws alone were in
operation. Whether this prevention of the *effect*, or this
other *effect*, be called a violation of the *law* or not, is
immaterial, as far as regards the particular law in question;
it makes no difference whether we say that that law is
suspended, or continues in force but is *counteracted*. The
phrase "violation or suspension of law" in its ordinary
signification, has reference only to the particular material
laws which are concerned in the case, and therefore, as
commonly used, it does not appear to be objectionable.
What *is* of importance is that, if a miracle *be* a violation or
suspension of *particular* laws, there are other higher laws of
which it is an *instance*, at the very time that it is a violation
or suspension of the lower ones: and that a miracle is thus
not against law upon the scale of the *whole* of the universe;
the giving way of lower law to higher being itself an instance of law, the violation of the particular being the
observance of the whole.

"What in each of these cases is wrought may be against
one particular law, that law being contemplated in its isolation, and rent away from the complex of laws, whereof
it forms only a part. But no law stands thus alone; and
it is not against but rather in harmony with the system
of laws; for the law of those laws is, that when powers come
into conflict, the weaker shall give way to the stronger, the
lower to the higher. In the miracle this world of ours is
drawn into and within a higher order of things; laws are
then at work in the world, which are not the laws of its
fallen condition, for they are laws of a mightier range and
higher perfection; and as such they claim to make themselves felt, and to have the preeminence and the predominance
which are rightly their own." (*Trench, Notes on the Miracles :
Preliminary Essay*, ch. iii.)

Bishop Fitzgerald expresses the same idea with some
philosophical additions :—

"Again, when miracles are described as 'interferences with

the laws of nature,' this description makes them appear improbable to many minds, from their not sufficiently considering that the laws of nature interfere with one another; and that we cannot get rid of 'interferences' upon any hypothesis consistent with experience.   When organization is superinduced upon inorganic matter, the laws of inorganic matter are interfered with and controlled; when animal life comes in there are new interferences; when reason and conscience are superadded to will, we have a new class of controlling and interfering powers, the *laws* of which are *moral* in their character.   Intelligences of pure speculation, who could do nothing but observe and reason, surveying a portion of the universe—such as the greater part of the material universe may be—wholly destitute of living inhabitants, might have reasoned that such powers as active beings possess were incredible, that it was incredible that the Great Creator would suffer the majestic uniformity of laws which He was constantly maintaining through boundless space and innumerable worlds, to be controlled and interfered with at the caprice of such a creature as man.   Yet we know by experience that God has enabled us to control and interfere with the laws of external nature for our own purposes; nor does this seem less improbable beforehand (but rather more), than that He should Himself interfere with those laws for our advantage." (*Article on Miracles: Dictionary of the Bible,* p. 376.)

LECTURE VII.

NOTE 1, p. 179.

THE proof of Mahomet's measure of mankind lies in the whole moral code of Mahometanism; less however in that code taken by itself, than in it as compared with the Gospel system of morals from which it was so conspicuous and ignominious a descent. Mahomet was perfectly acquainted with the Gospel and with the moral standard of the Gospel: he wrote the Koran with the Bible, both the Old and New Testament, before him; he knew that the spirit and practice of the later dispensation was an advance upon that of the earlier, and that the standard of morals had been a matter of growth and progress; yet in promulgating a new religion, with the higher standard before his eyes, he adopted the lower one, and retrograded not only from Christianity but from Judaism. Not only was he fully acquainted with the Gospel revelation, but even professed his own to carry out and to succeed it in the Divine counsels: yet in engrafting his own religion upon the Law and the Gospel, he wholly threw aside the moral development and progress which marked the succession of the two dispensations; and his own dispensation which was given out to be an advance even upon the Gospel, and the crown of the whole structure of revelation, went back for its moral standard to a stage prior to both. It is commonly stated that the Mahometan code, though far inferior to that of the Gospel, was still an improvement upon the moral standard of the Arabian tribes which Mahomet converted. But it is one thing to institute a carnal and lower moral system, as an adaptation to man's weakness, at an earlier and an infant stage in the progress of revelation, when no better system has come to light; another thing to institute the same in the maturity of revelation, when the legislator has a more perfect moral system before his eyes. The true principle of adaptation and accommodation has not respect to the inferior condition of the party which is the subject of it singly and solely; nor is that circumstance alone one to justify the application of the principle : were it so, Christianity could in no age of the world, not even in our own, be preached to the heathen without some intermediate religion being preached first as an *accommodation*. The principle of adaptation, as a legitimate rule and principle, has respect not only to the condition of the people to be converted, but also to the progress of revelation. The moral condition of the unconverted world may be bad, and of course is bad ; but nothing can justify the choice of a lower religion and moral code to which to convert them, when there exists before us a higher one. Yet this was Mahomet's course ;—a course which indicates his estimate of human nature.

Thus on the subject of polygamy, divorce, and concubinage, the Mahometan code was doubtless an accommodation to the moral standard of the Arabian tribes ; but it was an accommodation when the Gospel existed, and it was an accommodation much lower than that of the Mosaic law. Mr. Forster, who partly excuses Mahomet upon the ground of accommodation, says : " The same cause or causes which introduced into the Mosaic code the tacit admission of polygamy, and the more express toleration of divorce, would operate with equal force to extort from the legislator the recognition of the state of concubinage." " But," he adds, " the liberty of concubinage granted or rather preached by the pretended successor of Moses, widely separates the religions in their moral aspect—the studiously restricted latitude of the one, the unbridled and unbounded licentiousness of the other." (*Mahometanism Unveiled*, vol. i. p. 332.) Again : " The Mahometan law of divorce, as it stands in the Koran, like so many other parts of that pretended revelation, is a compound of the precepts of the Pentateuch and the traditional adulterations of the Rabbins." (p. 330.)

The same estimate of human nature moulds the legislator's directions on the subject of the property rights of wives and orphans. Here are cases in which the proverbial rapacity of the Oriental would be very difficult to deal with; and a stringent rule, which admitted of no escape, would provoke him, and only appear, in the eye of the accommodating lawgiver, certain to meet with violation, and, along with violation, contempt. The directions therefore in the Koran are constructed with evident loopholes : "And give women their dowry freely; *but if they voluntarily remit unto you any part of it, enjoy it with satisfaction and advantage.*" (*Koran*, ch. iv.) It is easy to see what the practical operation of such a clause as this would be,—that it would be no difficult matter for a man in many cases to extort or win a consent from a female under his power to a surrender of part of her property. A proviso respecting female orphans leaves a dangerous discretion to the guardian: "And give not unto those who are of *weak understanding* the substance which God hath appointed you to preserve for them" (*Ibid.*): a good rule if used fairly, but which is rather suggestive of an unfair use of it. It was not likely that an Arabian guardian would part with the legal possession of any property sooner than was necessary; nor was overhaste in surrendering an estate to a female orphan of weak mind a fault which he would be in the least likely to commit. He need hardly then have been cautioned against it. And on the other hand, he might and would not improbably extract from such a rule a permission to constitute himself an arbitrary judge of his ward's power to manage her own affairs, and to detain her property upon the slightest excuse on that head.

The promulgator of a new religion, who with a high and spiritual code before him adopts a lower and laxer one as that of his religion, not only adopts that lower code but implicitly pronounces judgment upon the higher one which he rejects. He says virtually that he considers such a code impracticable, that it may be put forth in a book, but that human nature cannot be brought to practise it, and that it is better to have far easier laws more obeyed, than more difficult ones less.

NOTE 2, p. 188.

" IF the special character of this deliverance be investigated, we find it summed up in the word *nirvána*, 'extinction,' 'blowing out.' Such was the supreme felicity of the Buddha: such the goal to which he ever pointed the aspirations of his followers. It was formerly disputed whether more is meant by the expression *nirvána* than ' eternal quietude,' ' unbroken sleep,' ' impenetrable apathy ;' but the oldest literature of Buddhism will scarcely suffer us to doubt that Gautama intended by it nothing short of absolute ' annihilation,' the destruction of all elements which constitute existence. . . . . But while we charge the creed of Gautama with atheism and nihilism, we must acknowledge that it rose in one respect superior to all other heathen systems,—in the loftier tone of its morality. . . . . . We must not overlook the emphasis which Buddhism uniformly placed upon a class of gentle and retiring virtues,—which were wellnigh banished from the rest of heathendom,—meekness, resignation, equanimity under suffering, forgiveness of injuries. Much as these are found to differ from the corresponding virtues of the Christian, and symptomatic as they often are of womanly, instead of manly and heroic qualities, they could scarcely fail to benefit a multitude of savage tribes to which they were propounded. For example, when the Buddhist finds himself assailed by calumny or open violence, he restrains his animosity by reflecting that the blow has been necessitated by misdemeanours committed in some previous existence. He is thankful that no heavier penance has fallen to his lot, and even at the last extremity, when death itself must be confronted, he can welcome it as the appointed means of liberation from this unclean body.

" Truth, however, calls for the addition, that fair and lovely as might be the outward forms of Buddhism, its inherent principles were such as made it wellnigh powerless in the training of society, and therefore it has left the countries which it overran the prey of superstition and of demon-worship, of political misrule, and spiritual lethargy. Confessing no supreme God, who is at once the Legislator and the Judge, its moral code was ultimately void of all authority. Denying also the true dignity and freedom of the human agent, it invested moral sentiments and relations with a kind of physical outsidedness ; they were all parts of a great system with which the fortunes of the Buddhist, why he knew not, were mechanically connected. He spoke, indeed, of ' laws,' but these were only common rules of action, according to which all things are found to happen: vice had no intrinsic hideousness, and virtue was another name for calculating prudence; while love itself was in the creed of Buddhism little more than animal sympathy, or the condolence of one sufferer with his fellow. Buddhism also could discourse of 'duty,' but such duty, as it had no object and no standard, was devoid of moral motive: it shrank into a lifeless acquiescence in some stern necessity, a blind submission to some iron law. The Buddhist's principle of action was 'I must;' he could not say 'I ought.' (*Hardwick's Christ and other Masters*, pt. ii. pp. 66-70.)

Dr. Rowland Williams's representation of the Buddhist doctrine of *nirvána* is a slight, but very slight, modification of Mr. Hardwick's statement. "It seems acknowledged that such a conception of passiveness in Deity affects your notions of the life to be expected hereafter: for it takes away all clear individuality, and leaves a breathless absorption." (*Christianity and Hinduism*, p. 528.) The Brahman doctrine of the final state professes some difference from the Buddhist; but both schools maintain in common the characteristic of impersonality as attaching to the final state. "When liberated from the body, the soul of one who has attained such blessedness of knowledge goes straight by the shortest way, whether it be, as some hold, through the solar rays and the realm of fire, to the abode of the gods, and from thence, being helped at each stage by the presiding deities who for that object chiefly dwell at convenient distances, it is conducted, like a faint person by a guide, until it enters the realm of Indra, and thence attains the very abode of Prajápati, who is no other than pure Brahm;—or even if the path of the spirit should be in any respect different from that which our sacred books have presented to the imagination in wise parables,— still in any case the soul which has never prostrated itself in worship to any meaner or more earthly being, but gazed steadfastly with the eye of devout knowledge upon That ineffable which is without stain as it is without duality, goes straight, whatever may be the shortest way, to reunion with the pure and divinest being of Brahm, and having been long ago freed from every trammel, or impression, or personality, is restored to Oneness, becoming therein not a thinker, but thought; not omniscient, but omniscience; not joyful, but very joy. Not indeed that I myself, my friend (would that it were so!), profess to have attained as yet the certainty of this blessedness, but rather shall count myself happy if I gain possession of the lower liberation which belongs to the humbler feelers after immortality. Yet the impediment alike to greater achievement by myself, and which prevents so many men from even thinking of these things, or suspecting their own glorious capacities, resides chiefly in that which we have already spoken of: for the human soul, being cased in a body, as in a succession of sheaths, the first of which is intellectual or apprehensive, and the second affectionate or capable of joy and grief, and the third merely psychic or vital, unites itself with these so as to form a *personality*, and thus individualises itself in isolation from the supreme soul : therefore also in its many passages from life to life the unhappy soul of man carries with it this subtle body above spoken of, and thereby is constituted what we call a person." (*Christianity and Hinduism*, p. 92.) This personality, however, vanishes in the final state, when the soul is restored to oneness. " You will not," continues the Brahman speaker in the dialogue, " accept the term *void* as an adequate description of the mysterious nature of the soul, but . . . . . you will clearly apprehend soul [in the final state] to be unseen and ungrasped being, thought, knowledge, and joy, no other than very God." (*Ibid.*)

NOTE 3, p. 189.

The elevating principle in patriarchal religious life Mr. Davison considers to have been *prophecy* :—

" I conclude by resuming the authentic testimonies of prophecy. The dispensation of it was not confined to Abraham. It reached through the Patriarchal age, and the whole body of predictions belonging to this age easily combine together. The oracles of God became to the Patriarchs a bond of personal religion. His name and His worship were

invested with authority and honour among them, whilst idolatry and corruption of life and practice polluted the nations
around them.   Their faith was directed by multiplied promises of His favour, but still involving the same specific
objects which were contained in the revelation to Abraham,
the blessing of mankind, and the possession of Canaan.   But
prophecy deigned to take these early disciples of it by the
hand.   We see their personal fortunes, and in many particulars their life and conduct, were guided by it: this was a
present pledge, a sensible evidence, of the faithfulness of God
in all His promises; and so the supports of their faith grew
with the enlarged duties of it: reserved and distant hopes
acquired a footing to rest upon, and drew strength from the
conviction which they had, not only of His revelation, but of
His experienced providential care and goodness.   'They drank
of the brook in the way.'   Immediate mercies guaranteed the
greater in prospect.   Such was the service rendered to religion by prophecy in the Patriarchal age, which was the first
æra of its more copious promulgation."   (*Davison on Prophecy,*
p. 93.)

Again, the institution of sacrifice, typical under the Mosaic
law, and before it, according to the general opinion of
divines, of the Great Atonement upon the Cross, educated the
devout Jew, and imparted to him ideas tending toward the
Gospel as their goal, so making his religious character an
anticipation of the Christian one.

" The action of the moral and ceremonial law combined,
I conclude therefore to have been such as would produce, in
reasonable and serious minds, that temper which is itself
eminently Christian in its principle; viz. a sense of demerit
in transgression; a willingness to accept a better atonement
adequate to the needs of the conscience, if God should provide it, and a desire after inward purity, which bodily lustra-
tion might represent, but could not supply; in short, that
temper which David has confessed and described, when he
rejects his reliance upon the legal rites: ' For thou desirest
no sacrifice, else would I give it thee; but thou delightest
not in burnt-offerings.—Wash me throughly from my wicked-
ness, and cleanse me from my sin.   Lo, thou requirest truth
in the inward parts, and shalt make me to understand wisdom secretly.'   In which state of mind, produced, as I understand it to have been, by the instruction of the law, there is
such a preparation made for a Christian faith, although it is

clear there was no distinct perception of the Christian *object* of faith, that we cannot reasonably doubt the penitent of the Law would have been the devout disciple of the Gospel, had God been pleased to reveal to him the real sacrifice of pro-pitiation which the Law did not provide, and thereby the pardon and acceptance which the penitent so earnestly de-sired." (*Davison on Prophecy*, p. 143.)

"With reference to the Patriarch and the Jew, those anti-cipations of Gospel truth had a twofold purpose, immediate and prospective: prospective in the gradual preparation of the world for Christianity; immediate in the infusion of Christian feelings, sentiments, and hopes into the bosoms of the faithful even in the earliest times. . . . . Such were the sentiments of Abraham, when at the successive resting-places in his pilgrimage ' he builded' an altar unto the Lord, and called on the name of the Lord.' And such no doubt were the sentiments of many a primitive worshipper, when he laid his hand and confessed his guilt upon the head of the victim." (*Dr. Hawkins's Discourses on the Historical Scrip-tures*, p. 154.)

"Imo vero, ut sic loquar, quemadmodum se veritas habet, non nominum consuetudo, Christianus etiam ille tunc populus fuit." (*Augustine, Serm.* 300.)

NOTE 4, p. 194.

"IL est dangereux de trop faire voir à l'homme combien il est égal aux bêtes, sans lui montrer sa grandeur. Il est encore dangereux de lui trop faire voir sa grandeur sans sa bassesse.

"Il est non seulement impossible mais inutile de connaître Dieu sans J.-C. Ils ne s'en sont pas eloignés, mais ap-prochés; Ils ne se sont pas abaissés mais. . . . *Quo quisquam optimus est, pessimus si hoc ipsum quod sit optimus ascribat sibi.*

"Aussi ceux qui ont connu Dieu sans connaître leur misère ne l'ont pas glorifié mais s'en sont glorifiés. *Quia non cognovit per sapientiam, placuit Deo per stultitiam prædicationis salvos facere.*

"Non seulement nous ne connaissons Dieu que par J.-C. mais nous ne nous connaissons nous mêmes que par J.-C." (*Pensées de Pascal*, pp. 85, 316, 317.)

"It was a beautiful and generous thought which Plato adopted, that all sin arises from ignorance; and that man

only needs to be enlightened as to the true good in order
to embrace and follow it. But *solvitur ambulando* is a good
rule. The world has had the advantage of some experience
since the days of Plato ; and that experience has not been
of a nature to establish beyond question the justice of his
view. The idea of Plato was tried for more than three
hundred years, and the result was that certain stern facts
were graven deep into the consciousness of mankind. Society under the discipline of philosophy had attained thus
far—to the absence of all faith and of every higher motive,
to universal selfishness and moral degradation—in a word,
to a state of things at which men like Plutarch were overcome with despair. Now facts such as these have hitherto
been supposed to prove that knowledge alone is not a re-
generator ; that σοφία does not always beget ἔρως, nor is
ἐπιστήμη always and necessarily the ἰσχυρὸν, the ἡγεμονικὸν,
and the ἀρχικόν. At any rate, one fact is abundantly
certain, that Christianity professedly and pointedly took its
stand on the opposite position, the insufficiency of knowledge, cultivation, and every natural means. Man could
only be raised through the introduction into the world of
a Divine power. How well is all this depicted by St. Paul,
not only in passages such as this, ' For after that in the
wisdom of God the world by wisdom knew not God, it
pleased God by the foolishness of preaching to save them
that believe,' but, more strikingly still, in the despairing
cry of the natural man, ' O wretched man that I am ! who
shall deliver me from the body of this death?' and then,
in the exulting thought that at length a Deliverer had been
found, ' I thank God through Jesus Christ our Lord.' "
(*Christian Remembrancer : Article on Miracles, October,* 1863.)

NOTE 5, p. 198.

" If at the present day any very extraordinary and unaccountable fact were exhibited before the eyes of an un-
biassed, educated, well-informed individual, and supposing
all suspicion of imposture put out of the question, his only
conclusion would be that it was something he was unable
at present to explain ; and if at all versed in physical studies,
he would not for an instant doubt either that it was really
due to some natural cause, or that if properly recorded and
examined, it would at some future time receive its explanation by the advance of discovery.

" It is thus the prevalent conviction that at the present
day miracles are not to be expected, and consequently alleged
marvels are commonly discredited." (*Powell's Study of the
Evidences of Christianity*, p. 107.)

LECTURE VIII.

NOTE 1, p. 208.

" THIS important circumstance," says Dr. Newman, " must
be considered, which is as clear as it is decisive, that the
Fathers speak of miracles as having in one sense ceased with
the Apostolic period ;—that is, (considering they elsewhere
speak of miracles as existing in their own times,) they say
that *Apostolic* miracles, or miracles *like* the Apostles', whether
in their object, cogency, impressiveness, or character, were no
longer of occurrence in the Church ; an interpretation which
they themselves in some passages give to their own words.
' Argue not,' says St. Chrysostom, ' because miracles do not
happen now, that they did not happen then. . . . . In those
times they were profitable, and now they are not.' He proceeds to say that in spite of this difference, the mode of conviction was substantially the same. ' We persuade not by
philosophical reasonings, but from Divine Scripture, and we
recommend what we say by the miracles then done. And
then they persuaded not by miracles only, but by discussion.'
And presently he adds, ' The more evident and constraining
are the things which happen, the less room there is for faith.'
(*Hom. in* 1 *Cor.* vi. 2, 3.) Again, in another part of his works :
' Why are there not those now who raise the dead and perform
cures ? I will not say why not; rather, why are there not
those now who despise the present life ? Why serve we God
for hire ? When however nature was weak, when faith had
to be planted, then there were many such ; but now He wills,
not that we should hang on these miracles, but be ready for
death.' (*Hom. VIII. in Col.* s. 5.)
" In like manner St. Augustine introduces his catalogue of
contemporary miracles by stating and allowing the objection that miracles were not then as they had been. ' Why,
say they, do not these miracles take place now, which, as
you preach to us, took place once ? I might answer that

they were necessary before the world believed, that it might believe.' (*De Civ. Dei*, xxii. 8.) He then goes on to say that miracles were wrought in his time, only they were not so public and well-attested as the miracles of the Gospel.

"St. Ambrose, on the discovery of the bodies of the two Martyrs, uses language of surprise which is quite in accordance with the feelings which the miracles of Antony and Hilarion seem to have roused in Alexandria and in Sicily. ' You know, you yourselves saw that many were cleansed from evil spirits, very many on touching with their hands the garment of the saints were delivered from the infirmities which oppressed them. The *miracles of the old time* are come *again*, when by the advent of the Lord Jesus a fuller grace was shed upon the earth.' Under a similar feeling he speaks of the two corpses, which happened to be of large size, as ' miræ magnitudinis, ut prisca ætas ferebat.'

"And Isidore of Pelusium, after observing that in the Apostles holiness of life and power of miracles went together, adds, ' Now, too, if the life of teachers rivalled the Apostolic bearing, perhaps miracles would take place ; though if they did not, such life would suffice for the enlightening of those who beheld it.' (*Ep.* iv. 80.)

"The doctrine thus witnessed by the great writers of the end of the fourth century is declared by as clear a testimony two centuries before and two centuries after. Pope Gregory at the end of the sixth in commenting on the text, ' And these signs shall follow those that believe,' says, ' Is it so, my brethren, that, because ye do not these signs, ye do not believe ? On the contrary they were necessary in the beginning of the Church : for, that faith might grow, it required miracles to cherish it withal ; just as when we plant shrubs, we water them till they seem to thrive in the ground, and as soon as they are well rooted, we cease our irrigation. This is what St. Paul teaches, ' Tongues are a sign not for those who believe, but for those who believe not ;' and there is something yet to be said of these signs and powers of a more recondite nature. For Holy Church doth spiritually every day, what she then did through the Apostles corporally. For when the Priests by the grace of exorcism lay hands on believers and forbid evil spirits to inhabit their minds, what do they but cast out devils ? And any believers soever who henceforth abandon the secular words of the old life, and utter holy mysteries, and rehearse as best they can the praise and power of their Maker, what do they but speak with new tongues ? Moreover, while by their good exhortations they remove evil from the heart of others, they are taking up serpents, &c. . . . . Which miracles are the greater, because they are the more spiritual ; the greater because they are the means of raising not bodies but souls ; these signs then, dearest brethren, by God's aid, ye do if ye will.' (*In Evang.* ii. 29.)   And St. Clement of Alexandria at the end of the second century: 'If it was imputed to Abraham for righteousness on his believing, and we are the seed of Abraham, we too must believe by hearing. For Israelites we are, who are obedient, not through signs, but through hearing.' (*Strom.* ii. 6. p. 444)."—*Essay on the Miracles of the Early Ages,* p. 39.

The confession of the Fathers that miracles had ceased in their days, while at the same time they allude to miracles going on in their day, has evidently reference to the *kind* of miracles which the current marvels of their own day were, as compared with the body of Gospel miracles.   In the body of Gospel miracles, the *greater* miracles, as they are called, miracles of a sublime and majestic type indicative of a supreme dominion over nature, occupy a prominent place; amid the current miracles of the Patristic age they appear so rarely, and, when they do appear, are mentioned with so little of that circumstance and particularity which constitute a condition of truth in facts, that they do not materially affect the character and rank of those miracles as a mass.   As a body they consist of exorcisms, visions, cures in answer to prayer; the latter in the fourth century becoming connected with the memories and relics of particular saints and martyrs. Irenæus, in a well-known passage (*Contra Hær.* ii. 31), alludes to some who had been raised to life again by the prayers of the Church—μετὰ νηστείας πολλῆς καὶ λιτανείας ἐπέστρεψε τὸ πνεῦμα τοῦ τετελευτηκότος. But the reference is so vague, that it possesses but little weight as testimony.   " Irenæus," observes Dr. Hey, " only affirms this in general without mentioning any particular instance, and it is somewhat strange that no instance was ever produced in the three first centuries. . . . . There is not however the same want of instances with regard to the other branches of miracles said to have been performed in the Church, namely, seeing visions, prophesying, healing diseases, curing demoniacs, and some others." (*Kay's Tertullian*, p. 168.) Neander doubts whether Irenæus is clear in his own mind as to what he intended to assert here, and supposes that he may not have meant by the death from which the persons had been raised real death, but only some form of apparent death (*Church History*, sect. i.), but at any rate the indefiniteness of the reference takes away all accuracy from the reported fact. Professor Blunt attaches somewhat more value to the statement of Irenæus than either Neander or Hey, but still comments on the obvious vagueness and indefiniteness of it :—

" Here we have another witness, he also a man of education and research, and though perhaps not a martyr to the death, a man who, for the sake of teaching the truth, was content to forego the charms of his native land, and migrate to a distant, a barbarous, and as it proved a dangerous station ; we have this man, I say, still testifying in another quarter of the world, too, in Gaul, to the existence of miraculous powers in the Church ; exorcism ; healing both of natural infirmities and sickness ; prophecy ; tongues ; discerning of spirits ; and even raising the dead : but perhaps expressing himself with different degrees of confidence whilst treating of these several gifts. Thus, with respect to exorcism, ' some really and truly eject evil spirits,' (οἱ μὲν γὰρ δαίμονας ἐλαύνουσι βεβαίως καὶ ἀληθῶς), is his language—' we have *heard* brethren speak with tongues, and detect spirits,' so I understand καθὼς καὶ πολλῶν ἀκούομεν ἀδελφῶν ἐν τῇ ἐκκλησίᾳ προφητικὰ χαρίσματα ἐχόντων, καὶ παντοδαπαῖς λαλούντων διὰ τοῦ Πνεύματος γλώσσαις, καὶ τὰ κρύφια τῶν ἀνθρώπων εἰς φανερὸν ἀγόντων ἐπὶ τῷ συμφέροντι. And in these instances, as well as in some others which I have named, he uses the present tense, δαίμονας ἐλαύνουσι, πρόγνωσιν ἔχουσι, τοὺς κάμνοντας ἰῶνται, χαρίσματα ἐχόντων, παντοδαπαῖς γλώσσαις λαλούντων, τὰ κρύφια τῶν ἀνθρώπων εἰς φανερὸν ἀγόντων. But when the miracle of raising the dead is touched on, the expressions are less definite, sæpe evenit fieri, πολλάκις, the phrase indefinite as to time—ὁ κύριος, οἱ ἀπόστολοι, ἡ πᾶσα ἐκκλησία, the language again indefinite as to agents—so the tense in these cases is no longer the present, but the aorist, τὸ πνεῦμα τοῦ τετελευτηκότος ἐπέστρεψε, the spirit of the dead returned—ἐχαρίσθη, he was granted to the prayers of the saints—νεκροὶ ἠγέρθησαν καὶ παρέμειναν σὺν ἡμῖν, the dead have been raised up, and have continued with us. There is something remarkable, at least, in the change of tense, something which, when coupled with the looser construction of the sentences, would lead us to think that though Irenæus had no doubt of the fact of the resurrection of the dead having been effected by the brethren, he had not witnessed a case with his own eyes." (*Blunt on the Early Fathers,* p. 387.)

Augustine again, long after, alludes in his list of miracles (*De Civ. Dei,* xxii. 8) to some cases in which persons had been raised to life again by prayer and the intercession of martyrs, whose relics were applied. But though Augustine relates with great particularity and length of detail some cases of recoveries from complaints in answer to prayer, his notices of the cases in which persons had been raised to life again are so short, bare, and summary, that they evidently represent no more than mere report, and report of a very vague kind. Indeed, with the preface which he prefixes to his list, he cannot be said even to profess to guarantee the truth or accuracy of the different instances contained in it. " Hæc autem, ubicunque fiunt, ibi sciuntur vix a tota ipsa civitate vel quocunque commanentium loco. Nam plerumque etiam ibi paucissimi sciunt, ignorantibus cæteris, maxime si magna sit civitas; et quando alibi aliisque narrantur, non tantum ea commendat auctoritas, ut sine difficultate vel dubitatione credantur, quamvis Christianis fidelibus a fidelibus indicentur." He puts down the cases as he received them then, without pledging himself to their authenticity. " Eucharius presbyter . . . . mortuus sic jacebat ut ei jam pollices ligarentur: opitulatione memorati martyris, cum de memoria ejus reportata fuisset et super jacentis corpus missa ipsius presbyteri tunica, suscitatus est. . . . . Audurus nomen est fundi, ubi ecclesia est et in ea memoria Stephani martyris. Puerum quendam parvulum, cum in area luderet, exorbitantes boves qui vehiculum trahebant, rota obtriverunt, et confestim palpitavit exspirans. Hunc mater arreptum ad eandem memoriam posuit; et non solum revixit, verum etiam illæsus apparuit." There are three other cases of the same kind, in which there is nothing to verify the death from which

the return to life is said to take place, as being more than
mere suspension of the vital powers ; but the writer does not
go into particulars of description or proof, but simply inserts
them in his list as they have been reported to him.

The comments of the heathen world upon the miracle of
our Lord's Resurrection, which are incidentally alluded to
in the Apologetic and other treatises of the Fathers, shew
how completely the heathen distinguished between their own
current miraculous pretensions and real and undoubted
miracles, where they had the opportunity of comparing the
two. They had their own popular and established supernaturalism, which they professedly respected and accepted ;
their exorcisms, their rites of augury, their oracles, their
miraculous cures, which were registered in temples ; but as
soon as a miraculous fact was presented to them, about which
there could be no doubt that it was miraculous, they exhibited
as much astonishment and incredulity as if they only pretended to believe in the powers of nature and the order of
nature. That a man should rise from the dead was treated
by them as an absolutely incredible fact. " The mystery of
the Resurrection," says Origen, who speaks of it as including
the miracle of Christ's Resurrection, which he has just mentioned, " is spoken of by the unbelieving with ridicule "—
Θρυλλεῖται γελώμενον ὑπὸ τῶν ἀπίστων. (*Contra Cels.* lib. i.
s. 7.) Celsus places the account of our Lord's Resurrection
in the same list with the legendary descents of Zamolxis,
Rhampsinitus, Orpheus, Protesilaus, Hercules, and Theseus
into the infernal regions, and their return thence. " Has
any one," he asks, " who has been really dead, ever risen
again ?" (lib. ii. s. 55.) Celsus, it is true, did not profess
much belief in current heathen supernaturalism ; he speaks
however of the art of magic not like one who wholly rejected
it, excepting philosophers from liability to the magician's
influence, just as Origen excepted devout Christians from the
same. (lib. vi. s. 41.) " Celsus," says Neander, " expresses
himself as though he considered magic to be an art possessed
of a certain power, though held by him in no great account."
(*Church History*, sect. 1.) Cæcilius, the representative of hea-

thenism in the "Octavius" of Minutius Felix, professes his
belief in the rites of augury, in heathen prophecy, and in
various heathen miracles ; but he declares that he cannot
believe that any one has ever risen again from the dead ;—
" Quis unus ullus ab inferis remeavit horarum saltem com-
meatu ?" (c. vii. xi.)   The heathen Autolycus challenges
Theophilus to produce an instance of a dead man rising to
life again.   Augustine, in the 22nd book of the "De Civitate
Dei," devotes himself to the defence of the doctrine of the
resurrection, against the notion of the philosophical heathens
that it was a simple impossibility ; and the particular resurrection of Christ is defended against the same charge.   " Sed
hoc incredibile fuit aliquando : ecce jam credidit mundus
sublatum Christi corpus in cœlum, resurrexionem carnis."
(c. v.)

NOTE 2, p. 224.

" *We lay out of the case such stories of supernatural events
as require on the part of the hearer nothing more than an* otiose
*assent ; stories upon which nothing depends, in which no interest
is involved, nothing is to be done or changed in consequence of
believing them.*   Such stories are credited, if the careless assent
that is given to them deserve that name, more by the indolence of the hearer, than by his judgment ; or, though not
much credited, are passed from one to another without inquiry or resistance.   To this case, and to this case alone,
belongs what is called the love of the marvellous.   I have
never known it carry men further.   Men do not suffer
persecution from the love of the marvellous.   Of the in-
different nature we are speaking of, are most vulgar errors
and popular superstitions : most, for instance, of the current
reports of apparitions.   Nothing depends upon their being
true or false.   But not, surely, of this kind were the alleged
miracles of Christ and His Apostles. . . . . . . They who
believed Christianity acted upon it.   Many made it the
express business of their lives to publish the intelligence.
It was required of those who admitted that intelligence,
to change forthwith their conduct and their principles, to
take up a different course of life, to part with their habits
and gratifications, and begin a new set of rules and system

of behaviour. The Apostles, at least, were interested not to
sacrifice their ease, their fortunes, and their lives, for an idle
tale; multitudes beside them were induced, by the same tale,
to encounter opposition, danger, and sufferings.

"We may add to what has been observed of the distinction
which we are considering, that, where miracles are alleged
merely in affirmance of a prior opinion, they who believe the
doctrine may sometimes propagate a belief of the miracles
which they do not themselves entertain. This is the case of
what are called *pious* frauds; but it is a case, I apprehend,
which takes place solely in support of a persuasion already
established. At least, it does not hold of the apostolical
history. If the Apostles did not believe the miracles, they
did not believe the religion; and, without this belief, where
was the *piety*, what place was there for anything which could
bear the name or colour of piety, in publishing and attesting
miracles in its behalf? If it be said that many promote the
belief of revelation, and of any accounts which favour that
belief, because they think them, whether well or ill founded,
of public and political utility; I answer, that if a character
exist, which can with less justice than another be ascribed to
the founders of the Christian religion, it is that of politicians,
or of men capable of entertaining political views. The truth
is, that there is no assignable character which will account
for the conduct of the Apostles, supposing their story to be
false." (*Paley's Evidences*, pp. 131, 133.)

NOTE 3, p. 227.

"One of the saddest portions of modern controversy," says
Dr. Pusey, "is the thought how much is owing to forged
writings; to what extent the prevailing system as to the
Blessed Virgin came in upon the authority of writings which
Roman Catholic critics now own to have been wrongly ascribed to the great Fathers whose names they bear; to what
extent the present relation of Rome to the Eastern Church
and to ourselves is owing to the forged Decretals. . . . . The
forgery of the Decretals after they had 'passed for true during
eight centuries' was owned by all, even by the Church of
Rome. But the system built upon that forgery abides
still." (*An Eirenicon*, pp. 236, 255.)

"Up to this period the Decretals, the letters or edicts of

the Bishops of Rome, according to the authorized or common
collection of Dionysius, commenced with Pope Siricius, towards the close of the fourth century.   To the collection of
Dionysius was added that of the authentic councils, which
bore the name of Isidore of Seville.   On a sudden was promulgated, unannounced, without preparation, not absolutely
unquestioned, but apparently overawing at once all doubt,
a new code, which to the former authentic documents added
fifty-nine letters and decrees of the twenty oldest Popes from
Clement to Melchiades, and the donation of Constantine;
and in the third part, among the decrees of the Popes and
of the councils from Silvester to Gregory II., thirty-nine false
decrees, and the acts of several unauthentic councils.   In
this vast manual of sacerdotal Christianity the Popes appear
from the first the parents, guardians, legislators of the faith
throughout the whole world. . . . . The author or authors
of this most audacious and elaborate of pious frauds are unknown; the date and place of its compilation are driven into
such narrow limits that they may be determined within a few
years, and within a very circumscribed region.   The false Decretals came not from Rome; the time of their arrival at Rome,
after they were known beyond the Alps, appears almost certain.   In one year Nicholas I. is apparently ignorant of their
existence, the next he speaks of them with full knowledge."
—(*Milman's Latin Christianity*, pp. 303, 305.)

A writer in the Christian Remembrancer, April 1854, has
investigated with the most elaborate care and most penetrating research the miracle of the " House of Loretto."   He
concludes :—

" It is a fiction that has exercised and is still exercising
enormous practical influence throughout Western Christendom. . . . . It has amassed treasures that would have fed
almost the entire poor of Europe for their lives.   It has
extorted homage from Erasmus, from Descartes.   Into it
has been introduced the purest of virgins and holiest of
mothers, for the purpose of stamping with her authority the
clumsiest as well as the falsest of all legends.   It forms,
finally, the sixth Lection of a special office set forth by Papal
infallibility, and by no means obsolete, in which Almighty
God is venerated for a miraculous exercise of His power,
which, according to the framers of the story, clearly ought
to have been exerted, but never was!   While the seventh
Lection consists of a portion of the first chapter of St. Luke's

Gospel, in the preceding one—as it were to illustrate the
contrast between light and darkness—what follows is assumed to be no less trustworthy !

" 'The house in which this Virgin was born, hallowed by
the divine mysteries, and snatched by the ministry of angels
out of the hand of the infidel, was translated first into Dal-
matia, and afterwards into the territory of Loretto, in the
province of Picenum, during the Pontificate of the holy
Celestine V.   And it is proved to be the very one in which
the Word was made Flesh and dwelt amongst us, as well
by papal diplomas and the abundant veneration of the whole
world, as also by the constant power of miracles and the
grace of heavenly benefits. Whereupon Innocent XII., moved
by these things, in order that the faithful might be more
effectually stirred up, and put in mind of the worship of our
most beloved mother, gave directions to celebrate with mass
and office appropriate, the translation of the said holy house,
which is observed throughout the whole province of Picenum
with anniversary solemnity.'

" What a train of melancholy reflections is thus afforded
by December 10th !   The largest portion of Christendom by
far insisting upon Papal infallibility as a vital principle ;
Papal infallibility thus solemnly pledged to an untruth !"

NOTE 4, p. 228.

" Solas pro sanctitate virtutes exposcere videtur S. Joannes
Chrysostomus *in inscript. actorum* (*pag.* 64, *Oper. tom.* 3) *:
Actio quidem bona etiam sine signis eos, a quibus peracta fuerit,
introducit in cælum.   Miraculum autem et signum absque conver-
satione deducere ad vestibula illa non possunt :* quod ipsum
latius prosequitur Anastasius Episcopus Nicænus, qui vixit
post Concilium Trullanum (teste Cardinali Bellarmino *de
Scriptoribus Ecclesiasticis*) in opere cui titulus, *De quæstionibus
in sacram Scripturam, qu.* 23. *to.* 1. *Biblioth. Patrum,* ubi ait :
*Non oportet autem aut virum orthodoxum ex signis, aut Pro-
phetam dijudicare, quod sit sanctus ; sed ex eo quod vitam recte
instituit &c.   Quoniam ergo, ut ostensum est, a peccatoribus et
incredulis sæpe fiunt signa et prophetiæ per quamdam dispensa-
tionem, non oportet de cetero ex rebus ejusmodi dijudicare quem-
piam, ut sit sanctus ; sed ex eorum fructibus, ut dicit Dominus,*
cognoscetis eos, *Fructus veri et spiritalis viri ostendit etiam
Apostolus dicens ; Fructus autem spiritus est charitas, gaudium,
pax, Fides, Mansuetudo, continentia.*   Supra vidimus, B. Petrum

Damiani nulla in historia vitæ S. Dominici Loricati miracula
narrasse, et respondisse, id mirum esse non debere, cum nec
legatur, ullum factum fuisse miraculum a Beatissima Virgine
Maria, nec a S. Joanne Baptista. Callisto II. summo Pontifici
miracula requirenti pro Canonizatione S. Conradi Episcopi
Constantiensis Ulricus ejusdem Ecclesiæ Episcopus ita re-
spondit (*apud Pistorium Script. rer. Germ. tom.* 3. *p.* 638).
*Operam dedi, ex Patrum schedulis, hujus Viri dignissimam Deo
conversationem potius, quam miracula, quæ nonnumquam re-
probis cum Sanctis communia sunt, continentibus, sequens opus-
culum colligere, vestræque sublimitati examinandum dirigere.* . . .

　"At, his minime obstantibus, de necessitate tum virtutum,
aut martyrii, tum miraculorum in causis Beatificationis et
Canonizationis nulla rationabilis dubitatio esse potest, uti
sæpe in hujus operis decursu a nobis dictum est. Virtutes,
et miracula exposcit Honorius III. *in cap. Venerabili de testib.
et attestat.* ubi sic loquitur : *Super vita, et miraculis,&c.* Et Gre-
gorius IX. in bulla Canonizationis Sancti Antonii Patavini,
Ecclesiam triumphantem ab Ecclesia militante distinguit, et
pro sanctitate in Ecclesia triumphante solam ait sufficere
perseverantiam usque ad finem, pro Ecclesia vero militante
duo statui necessaria, virtutem videlicet morum, et veritatem
signorum, uti videri potest *lib.* 3. *hujus operis cap.* 42. *num.* 11.
Resumi quoque possunt, quæ in primo hujus ipsius operis
libro fuse a nobis adducta sunt de necessitate miraculorum
etiam in causis martyrum. Ad persuadendam miraculorum
necessitatem in causis Beatificationis et Canonizationis satis
superque esset asserere, inconcussam semper fuisse et esse
Apostolicæ sedis praxim miracula in his causis requirendi,
quam praxim exornant Contelorius *de Canoniz. SS. cap.* 19.
n. 2. Baldellus *Theolog. Moral. tom.* 2. *lib.* 3. *disp.* 14. *num.* 1.
Pater Mabillon *in epistola edita sub nomine* Eusebii Romani
ad Theophilum Gallum, num. 12. Rotæ Auditores in relatione
causarum S. Franciscæ Romanæ, *par.* 3. *art.* 1. de miraculis
in genere," &c. (*Benedict XIV, Opera, lib. iv. pars iii. c.* 5.
§§ 2, 4.)

NOTE 5, p. 230.

It is disputed when ecclesiastical miracles begin. Dr. Hey
denies that the Apostolical Fathers make any allusions to
themselves working miracles.

　"For fifty years after the ascension of Christ, none of the
Fathers made any pretensions to the possession of miraculous

powers. We have already spoken, in a former Lecture, of those Fathers who are called the Apostolic, of Ignatius, Poly-carp, Barnabas, Hermas; now it is an historical truth not to be omitted, that not one of those pious men, though they were the principal governors of the Church, and the imme-diate successors of the Apostles in that government (as well as their companions and friends), ever speaks of himself as capable of counteracting the ordinary powers of nature; they all endeavour to inculcate the morality and religion of the Gospel, but that merely as *men*, possessed indeed of the sense and meaning of the sacred writers, but entirely void of their extraordinary power. . . . . I only affirm, however, that none of the Apostolic Fathers speaks of *himself* as endued with a power of working miracles; we must not absolutely say that no miracles have ever been said to be wrought about the time they lived: because there is a very celebrated letter extant from the Church of Smyrna, giving an account of the mar-tyrdom of Polycarp, which is said to have been attended with circumstances sufficiently miraculous."—(*Kay's Tertullian*, p. 165.)

Professor Blunt decides that they allude to miracles as going on in the Church :—

" It has been disputed whether the Apostolical Fathers, properly so called, speak of contemporary miracles at all. Considering how short are their works, and the practical purpose for which most of them are written, the absence of all allusion to miracles in them would prove little or nothing, and might well be accidental. Such an expression, however, as that of Clemens Romanus, that there was in the Church of Corinth 'a plentiful outpouring of the Holy Ghost upon all,' (πλήρης Πνεύματος Ἁγίου ἔκχυσις ἐπὶ πάντας ἐγίνετο)—or that of Ignatius, addressed to the Church of Smyrna, ' that it was mercifully blessed with every good gift,' (ἐν παντὶ χαρίσματι,) ' that it was wanting in no good gift,' (ἀνυστέρητος οὖσα παντὸς χαρίσματος)—such phraseology, I say, being compared with that of times both before and after, when it undoubtedly had miraculous as well as other gifts in contemplation, would lead us to think, I agree with Dodwell, that Clemens and Ignatius did not exclude such gifts from their account."—(*Blunt on the Early Fathers*, lect. vi.)

Bishop Kay states his view of the early Church miracles in the following passage :—

" The supposition that miraculous powers were *gradually*

withdrawn from the Church, appears in a great measure to account for the uncertainty which has prevailed respecting the period of their cessation. To adopt the language of un-doubting confidence on such a subject would be a mark no less of folly than presumption; but I may be allowed to state the conclusion to which I have myself been led, by a com-parison of the statements in the Book of Acts with the writings of the Fathers of the second century. My con-clusion then is, that the power of working miracles was not extended beyond the disciples, upon whom the Apostles con-ferred it by the imposition of their hands. As the number of those disciples gradually diminished, the instances of the exercises of miraculous powers became continually less fre-quent, and ceased entirely at the death of the last individual on whom the hands of the Apostles had been laid. That event would, in the natural course of things, take place before the middle of the second century; at a time when, Chris-tianity having obtained a footing in all the provinces of the Roman Empire, the miraculous gifts conferred upon its first teachers had performed their appropriate office,—that of prov-ing to the world that a New Revelation had been given from heaven. What then would be the effect produced upon the minds of the great body of Christians by their gradual cessation? Many would not observe, none would be willing to observe it; for all must naturally feel a reluctance to believe that powers, which had contributed so essentially to the rapid diffusion of Christianity, were withdrawn. They who remarked the ces-sation of miracles would probably succeed in persuading them-selves that it was only temporary, and designed by an all-wise Providence to be the prelude to a more abundant effusion of supernatural gifts upon the Church. Or if doubts and mis-givings crossed their minds, they would still be unwilling openly to state a fact which might shake the steadfastness of their friends, and would certainly be urged by the enemies of the Gospel as an argument against its Divine origin. They would pursue the plan which has been pursued by Justin Martyr, Theophilus, Irenæus, &c.; they would have recourse to general assertions of the existence of supernatural powers, without attempting to produce a specific instance of their exercise. . . . . . Let me repeat, that I offer these observa-tions with that diffidence in my own conclusions which ought to be the predominant feeling in the mind of every inquirer into the ways of Providence. I collect from passages already cited from the Book of Acts, that the power of working miracles was conferred by the hands of the Apostles only;

and consequently ceased with the last disciple on whom their hands were laid. I perceive in the language of the Fathers, who lived in the middle and end of the second century, when speaking on this subject, something which betrays, if not a conviction, at least a suspicion, that the power of working miracles was withdrawn, combined with an anxiety to keep up a belief of its continuance in the Church. They affirm in general terms that miracles were performed, but rarely venture to produce an instance of a particular miracle. Those who followed them were less scrupulous, and proceeded to invent miracles; very different indeed in circumstances and character from the miracles of the Gospel, yet readily believed by men who were not disposed nicely to examine into the evidence of facts which they wished to be true. The success of the first attempts naturally encouraged others to practise similar impositions upon the credulity of mankind. In every succeeding age miracles multiplied in number, and increased in extravagance; till at length, by their frequency, they lost all title to the name, since they could no longer be considered as deviations from the ordinary course of nature." (*Kay's Tertullian*, pp. 98 et seq.)

Upon the question of the continuance of miraculous powers in the Church our earlier divines decline to draw any precise line, and are favourable to an indefinite prolongation of their existence in the Church. Thus Jackson :—

" Generally, miracles were usual in the infancy of Christianity, as we read in ecclesiastical stories : nor can it be certainly gathered when they did certainly cease. To say they endured no longer than the primitive Church, can give no universal satisfaction, save only to such as think it enough for all the world to have the light of the Gospel locked up in the chancel of some one glorious church : for some churches were but in the prime or change, when others were full of Christian knowledge. The use of miracles at the same instant was befitting the one, not the other. For God usually speaks to new-born children in Christ by miracles or sensible declarations of His power, mercy, or justice : as parents deter their children from evil in tender years by the rod, or other sensible signs of their displeasure ; and allure them to goodness with apples, or other like visible pledges of their love : but when they come to riper years, and are capable of discourse, or apprehensive of wholesome admonitions, they seek to rule them by reason. Proportionably to this course of parents doth God speak to His Church: in her infancy (wheresoever planted), by sensible documents of His power; in her maturity, by the ordinary preaching of His word, which is more apt to ripen and confirm true Christian faith than any miracles are, so men would submit their reason unto the rules set down in Scripture, and unpartially examine all events of time by them, as elsewhere, God willing, we shall shew.

" These grounds, well considered, will move any sober spirit at the least to suspend his assent, and not suffer his mind to be hastily overswayed with absolute distrust of all such miracles, as either our writers report to have been wrought in this our land at the Saxons' first coming hither, or the French historiographers record in the first conversion of the Franks, or in the prime of that Church." (*Jackson's Comments on the Creed*, bk. i. ch. 13.)

Professor Blunt dissents from Bishop Kay's position respecting the early Church miracles :—

" Though the Bishop of Lincoln's theory is one which is well calculated to reconcile a sceptical age to the acceptance of ecclesiastical miracles in a degree, and though I have sometimes felt inclined to adopt it myself, yet on further reading and further examination of the subject, I am led to doubt if the testimony of the Fathers can be squared to it, if it can satisfy the conditions of the case." (*On the Early Fathers*, p. 406.)

Warburton admits some special miracles, rejects the great body, especially those of later times, and for the rest adopts the position of a suspense of judgment :—

" Not that it is my purpose positively to brand as false every pretended miracle recorded in ecclesiastical and civil history, which wants this favourable capacity of being reduced to one or other of the *species* explained above. All that I contend for is, that those miracles, still remaining unsupported by the nature of that evidence which I have shewn ought to force conviction from every reasonable mind, should be at present excluded from the privilege of that conviction.

" Indeed, the greater part may be safely given up. Of the rest, which yet stand undiscredited by any considerable marks of imposture, we may safely suspend our belief, till time hath afforded further lights to direct our judgment." (*Divine Legation*, bk. ix. ch. 5.)

An able and thoughtful writer on "Miracles," in the Christian Remembrancer, puts the necessity of miracles as evidence of our Lord's Divine Nature in the following point of view :—

"Truths, such as 'God is a Spirit,' or, 'Do unto others as you would they should do unto you,' are abstract truths, resting on fundamental principles in the human mind. They therefore appeal to the human mind for their evidence, and to nothing else. By a mental process they are transformed from the sphere of feeling or intuition into that of logic, and when we appeal to an innate sense for their truth we simply appeal to the consciousness of every man to say whether this process has not been rightly performed. But the proposition, God was incarnate in Jesus Christ for the deliverance of the world, is of a totally different nature. It is not an abstract truth, but a historical fact, and consequently by no power of intuition could we assure ourselves of its truth. However much the fact embodied in these words may answer to a want and longing in the heart, however much the thought of it may thrill our nature to its very depth, still this is no proof of its truth. This very want and longing has given rise to many pretensions, which, alas! we know to have been baseless. That God was Incarnate in Christ Jesus is a fact which must rest upon evidence just as any other historical fact. There is no power of clairvoyance in the human mind by which we can see its truth independent of evidence.

"But this writer not only fails to perceive that the Christianity he adopts is a historical fact resting upon evidence, but that it is a supernatural fact, and, consequently, that it needs evidence of a peculiar kind. It is evident that to prove that our Lord was Incarnate God we need not only evidence that He lived and died, that His life was blameless, and that He spake as never man spake,—all this would prove that He was wonderful among the sons of men,—but we need something more before we can acknowledge the justice of His claim to be the Son of God. That He was God Incarnate was a fact above nature; it could, therefore, only be proved by a manifestation above nature, that is by miracle.

"This is so important that it merits further consideration. We say that the fact that Christ was God being a supernatural fact could only be proved by a supernatural manifestation. Now this assertion rests upon a fundamental principle of all our knowledge. We cannot know things according to that which they are in themselves, but only in and through the phenomena they manifest; and hence our judgment as to what anything is, is entirely dependent on the manifestations connected with it. How, for instance, do we satisfy ourselves as to the nature and identity of anything? Supposing a substance is presented to a chemist, and he is asked to determine of what nature it is, how does he proceed? He begins by carefully observing all its qualities, and noting the phenomena to which it gives rise, in any circumstances in which it may be placed. He places it in every possible relation, and notes the signs and tokens which are manifested. If it should happen that these phenomena are identical with those of any previously known substance, the identity of the substance inquired about with that substance is determined. But should the phenomena manifested be altogether unknown and strange, it is immediately set down as a new substance, and the idea we have of that substance is constructed out of the phenomena it manifests. In the same way the naturalist proceeds in determining the various species of plants and animals. He observes not only physical characteristics and relations, but, in the case of animals, actions and habits; and from these he is enabled to conclude as to the presence or absence of mind and intelligence, and generally as to the inner nature. In the same way, by a process of induction, we judge of the characters and mental capacities of those among whom we mix. We are in no doubt when we are in the presence of a fellow-being with human nature and sympathies like ourselves. We see his inmost nature manifested in a thousand outward tokens, from which we draw an almost instantaneous and infallible conclusion.

" It is in precisely the same way that we are to judge of the nature of Christ. If He exhibited in His words and actions only what was human, our unavoidable conclusion must be that He was nothing more. Whatever reason we may have for putting faith in His truth and goodness, still had He claimed to be the Son of God and exhibited no sign, we must have supposed that He was under a delusion. On the other hand, if in His words and deeds He exhibited tokens above man, we might not be able from these tokens, taken by themselves, to conclude that He was God, but we could certainly conclude that in Him was more than man.

" But the matter may be put in even a stronger light. As we cannot know things in themselves, but only in and through their outward manifestations, so we cannot think the existence of any being in relation with the things of this world without supposing the outward tokens under which it is revealed to us. According to this principle, miracles are the natural and necessary consequence of the Godhead in Christ, so much so that we cannot think Him truly God and imagine them absent.

" Let us realize to ourselves the circumstances.

" Supposing the question had been, not whether He transcended, but whether He fell short of, what is human; every one coming into His presence and conversing with Him could easily satisfy himself. A hundred outward tokens would reveal the presence of a living human soul. But just in the same way would it be evident to those around Him that His nature transcended that of man. If He were really more than man, there would be some outward token to manifest that higher nature. It is utterly impossible that it could be otherwise. However much He might hide His glory, still a thousand tokens, each transcending what belongs to man, would be visible. His very look, His air, the tone of His voice, His wisdom and goodness, His more than human knowledge, feeling, and sympathy, all these superadded to the visible assertion of His authority over nature, would combine to point Him out as one more than human. We do not know that due weight, in an evidential point of view, has ever been given to the astonishing fact that the unanimous verdict of every one privileged to come near our Blessed Lord has been that He was more than man. In this, friend and enemy, Jew, Ebionite, Christian, Gnostic, alike agree. Amid the innumerable theories that for 1800 years have been devised to explain the nature of that manifestation that took place in Christ, all agree in this, that He was more than man.

" Miracles are thus the natural and necessary consequence of the Godhead in Christ; so necessary indeed that it is impossible to think Him truly God and imagine them absent: just as we cannot think man existing without a certain conformation of body, and certain acts which are the appropriate expression of humanity, so no more can we think the Godhead in Christ without imagining those manifestations which are the tokens of God." (*Christian Remembrancer, October,* 1863.)

The New Testament of our Lord and Saviour Jesus

Christ, in the original Greek. With Notes, Introductions, and Indices. By CHR. WORDSWORTH, D.D., Archdeacon of Westminster. *New Edition.* In Two Vols., imperial 8vo. 4*l.*

The Greek Testament; with a critically revised Text:

A Digest of Various Readings: Marginal References to Verbal and Idiomatic Usage: Prolegomena: and a copious Critical and Exegetical Commentary in English. By HENRY ALFORD, D.D., Dean of Canterbury. *New Edition.* In Four Vols., 8vo. 5*l.* 2*s.*

Syntax and Synonyms of the Greek Testament. By

the Rev. W. WEBSTER, M.A. 8vo. 9*s.*

> The Syntax is based upon Donaldson's, with extracts from the writings of eminent English Theologians of the present day. The Chapter on Synonyms treats of many words which have not been noticed by other writers. In another Chapter attention is drawn to some passages in which the Authorized Version is incorrect, inexact, insufficient, or obscure. Copious Indices are added.

Directorium Pastorale: the Principles and Practice

of Pastoral Work in the Church of England. By the Rev. JOHN HENRY BLUNT. *Second Edition.* Crown 8vo. 9*s.*

> This Work has been written with the object of providing for Theological Students and the younger Clergy a Practical Manual on the subject of which it treats.
>
> Contents :—Chap. I. The nature of the Pastoral Office.—Chap. II. The relation of the Pastor to God.—Chap. III. The relation of the Pastor to his flock.—Chap. IV. The ministry of God's Word.—Chap. V. The ministry of the Sacraments, etc.—Chap. VI. The Visitation of the Sick.—Chap. VII. Pastoral Converse.—Chap. VIII. Private Instruction.—Chap. IX. Schools.—Chap. X. Parochial lay co-operation.—Chap. XI. Auxiliary Parochial Institutions.—Chap. XII. Parish Festivals.—Chap. XIII. Miscellaneous Responsibilities.

A Commentary on the Minor Prophets: with Intro-

ductions to the several Books. By EDWARD BOUVERIE PUSEY, D.D., Regius Professor of Hebrew, and Canon of Christ Church, Oxford. In 4to. Parts I, II, III, price 5*s.* each, are already published.

Libri Precum Publicarum Ecclesiæ Anglicanæ versio

latina, à GULIELMO BRIGHT, A.M., et PETRO GOLDSMITH MEDD, A.M., Presbyteris, Collegii Universitatis in Acad. Oxon. Sociis, facta. In an elegant pocket volume. *5s.*

A Commentary, Practical and Exegetical, on the

Lord's Prayer. By the Rev. W. DENTON, M.A. Small 8vo. *5s.*

The Age and the Gospel; Four Sermons preached

before the University of Cambridge, at the Hulsean Lecture, 1864; with a Discourse on Final Retribution. By DANIEL MOORE, M.A., Incumbent of Camden Church, Camberwell. Crown 8vo. *5s.*

The Inspiration of Holy Scripture, its Nature and

Proof; Eight Discourses, preached before the University of Dublin. By WILLIAM LEE, D.D., Archdeacon of Dublin, and Examining Chaplain to his Grace the Archbishop. Fourth edition. 8vo. *15s.*

The Public Schools Calendar; Edited by a Graduate

of the University of Oxford. Small 8vo. *6s.* (*Published annually.*)

In the Press.

The Annotated Book of Common Prayer; con-

taining the Text of the Sealed Book, with the Originals of all translated portions; Marginal References; Historical, Ritual, and Expository Notes; and short Illustrative Essays. By several writers. Edited by the Rev. JOHN HENRY BLUNT, Author of "Directorium Pastorale." In one volume of about 600 pages, imperial 8vo.

*** *This work is far advanced at press, and may be expected early in 1866. A Prospectus, with specimen page, may be had of the publishers.*

RIVINGTONS:

LONDON, OXFORD, AND CAMBRIDGE.